D1164221

Actual Reviews from Readers on previous books by Phyllis K. Walters

". . . I highly recommend this book. "

-From Goodreads- by Linda Keenan, President, The Writers League of The Villages

". . . The reader is allowed into her casework and her romance with the handsome Bucky Walker. The romance on the side helps soften the reality of these cases.

- From Amazon- by J.J. Clarke, award-winning author of Dared to Run, a suspense thriller.

". . . This well-written novel brings to light the very real and complex world of personal relationships where abusive partners or parents inflict damage upon those who they should be protecting. I look forward to reading Dr. Walters' next book."

- From Amazon- by Mel Harrison, author of three suspense novels inspired by his experience in the foreign service of the United State of America.

" Phyllis K. Walters skillfully helps the reader understand what makes . . . perpetrators do what they do with a mix of compassion, while she blends in some underlying humor to break up the seriousness of the subject.

-From Sally Galliers, beta reader

1

Editing/Design by: Paula F. Howard, Paula@aHowardActivity.com
Cover Design by: Robert Hurley at
ImpressionsBookDesignServices.com
ISBN: Softcover 979-8-9852263-7-9
PRINTED IN THE UNITED STATES OF AMERICA
AHA! A HOWARD ACTIVITY PRESS

More copies may be ordered online at Amazon.com
or through https://www.TheWritersMall.com

Husbands

Who

Kill

By

Phyllis K. Walters

Based on True Crime Stories

DEDICATIONS

I dedicate this novel to the memory of my parents, George and Katherine Kangas who inspired me to exceed, by far, the level of their educations.

George was the oldest of three children. His mother died of a broken heart following the accidental death of his baby sister. His father placed George in a local orphanage until he could remarry. After that, George and his younger sister, Eldora, were raised by their father, Steve Kangas, and stepmother, Emma. George quit school after the eighth grade to become a shoeshine boy in downtown Toledo and work beside his father. After marrying my mother, George served in the United States Army during World War II.

Katherine "Katie" Gaitanes Kangas was the only child of Liberty and James Gaitanes, who was a shepherd boy on the Greek Island of Tenedos before immigrating to the United States. Once established in Toledo, Ohio, he met and married my Yaya Liberty. My mother, Katherine, loved school despite her parents' limited knowledge of the English language and even skipped fifth grade altogether. Her parents, however, betrothed her to an older family friend after which she was compelled to quit high school. She and her husband had one son. But it was not enough to save the marriage. Several years after becoming divorced, Katie married her childhood friend, George Kangas. They had one daughter, me, then known as Phyllis Kangas.

Katherine lived long enough to see me bestow two precious grandsons upon her and earn a Ph.D. from the University of Toledo. Katherine later enjoyed a relationship with my first husband until his death, then with Dan Walters, my husband today.

-Dr. Phyllis Kuehnl-Walters

ACKNOWLEDGMENTS

I thank my husband, Daniel Walters, for his unconditional love, encouragement, and prayers and wish to also acknowledge my extended family, long-term friends from Ohio, and Villages friends to whom I rely upon for companionship, support, and laughter.

My current Beta readers who kindly sacrificed their time, provided valuable feedback, and shared their ideas have my complete gratitude. They assisted me in moving the plots and back stories along smoothly. Much appreciation to: Sally Galliers, Paulette Holbert, Penny Hyott, Ron Thompson, and Carol Wren.

A huge thank you to my editor and good friend, Paula Howard, who encouraged me to write this third book of my true crime series featuring Dr. Rosie Klein. Through collaboration, Paula helped me improve my writing skills with each revision.

Another thanks to my Life Group, pastors, and friends from Fairway Christian Church of The Villages, Florida. Their friendship and prayers lifted me up when my confidence and stamina waned.

Lastly, I acknowledge that without my faith and hope in Jesus Christ, I would not have remained motivated or had the discipline or focus required to bring to light these stories of broken people in a broken world. Those who are still alive and incarcerated, despite their circumstances, need our prayers.

PART ONE
CAST OF CHARACTERS
THE RANDY EVANS CASE

Dr. Sherri Bernhart..........Psychiatrist

Shannon Conrad..............Friend of Joanie Evans

Jackie Evans.......................Mother of defendant

Joanie Evans.......................Wife of Randy Evans

Randy Evans......................Defendant

Roger Evans.......................Sibling of defendant

Susie Evans.........................Sibling of defendant

Devon Gump.....................Defense Attorney

Stella Gump.......................College Roommate

Travis Gump.....................Defense Attorney

Gretchen Gunderson........Detective

Butch Harris......................Detective

Dr. Rosie Klein..................Forensic Psychologist

Esther Klein......................Mother of Rosie

Doris Mello.......................Pre-school Director

Bucky Walker....................Husband of Rosie

PART TWO
CAST OF CHARACTERS
THE SCOTT LARSON CASE

Reverend Samuel Christoff.....Hospital Chaplain

Mc Kenna Day...........................Assistant Prosecutor

Alexis Jackson............................First Wife/Professor

Olivia Larson.............................Wife and victim

Scott Larson..............................Defendant

Dr. Rosie Klein..........................Forensic Psychologis

Bart Meyer...............................Lucas County Prosecutor

Jake Morgan............................Defense Attorney

Renee Rapton............................Friend of Olivia

Dr. Robert Seifer......................Psychiatrist / landlord

Bucky Walker...........................Husband of Rosie Klein

Ruth Wayne..............................Office Mgr. of Dr. Klein

Part One

1

Roger's Memories

I remember the first time he struck her hard with the back of his hand. She had my baby brother, Randy, cradled against her chest with his little face nestled into her bosom. It was Randy he intended to hit. She was protecting him, and I wanted to be big and strong so I could protect her. But I was only five years old. He was a monster with no feelings but his angry, self-righteous ones, even if he was my dad.

Randy often cried from stomach aches. Mom called it "colic," and when he started crying, nothing would soothe him, or stop his loud, high-pitched wailing. Our mom had the patience of a saint. She would sing to him and rock or sway with him as she sang softly whenever it happened.

But he didn't care. All he cared about was his power, his big position as a lieutenant colonel in the U. S. Air Force, and his pension. Mom always tried to calm me down after his rages that sometimes left her injured. One time she told the ambulance guy that she fell off her bike. That was an outright lie. He had punched her in the stomach so hard, it ruptured her spleen. The monster had convinced her not to tell because he could lose his pension if she told on him. He made her think she would be in the poor house with no way to support us three kids if she left him.

Through the years, I heard them fighting. Our bedrooms were upstairs over the living room and they usually fought after my brother and I went to bed. Not only did I hear his loud, deep voice, but I could hear glass smashing and my mother's trembling words. "Stop! Please stop." Then there would be a smacking sound and a thud as her small body hit the floor. She always had bruises, so she wore pants with tops that had high collars and long sleeves, or full-length dresses. No one thought Colonel Evans was a brutal wife-beater. His colleagues and friends viewed him as an honorable, respectful man. They didn't see him behind closed doors. But I did.

Our bedroom was painted light blue, and our bunk bed was along the wall. Since I was in the top bunk, I could make marks on the wall, and he would never see them. Each time he hit her I used my fingernail to put a small mark on the wall beside my pillow. I don't know why it was important for me to keep track like that. Maybe I could pay him back someday when I grew up.

Time passed and I planned to escape on my eighteenth birthday. On that day, I hugged my mother, and brother, and left with my Marine recruiter.

As I walked down the sidewalk for the last time, I remember Mom with tears in her eyes. My brother was sitting alone in his room. My little sister, Susie, wasn't home for me to say goodbye. My father, on the other hand, never came out of his home office to wish me well. He couldn't understand why I wouldn't go to college and become a second lieutenant in the United States Air Force as he did. He told me that enlisting as I did, brought shame to him. It was always about him.

He tried to make me feel guilty when he found out about my decision, but I was firm about it. I didn't want to be anything like him.

2

Thoughts and Actions

The car with Roger and his recruiter pulled away from the curb. He didn't look back at the house. That life was over. But his thoughts weren't. He was lost in them.

Roger's Thoughts:

Am I being selfish leaving Mom, Randy, and Susie, to deal with Dad? I don't want to do anything I'll regret. But I just can't take it anymore. For now, I'm gonna think about myself for once. My recruiter, Sergeant John, said I should do well in the Marines. I can swim and shoot really well; I do have to thank my old man for that - but I'm also a quick learner. Maybe I could have learned on my own.

12

Still, already knowing how to shoot gives me an edge. I can run long distances and being tall certainly doesn't work against me. I've even heard the Marines have a basketball team. Maybe I can try out later. I know basic training will be tough. Still, it's what I want to do.

I hear the Carolinas are beautiful this time of year. I'll just need to get through basic training at Parris Island in South Carolina, then move on to a specialty area like being a heavy machinery operator. The sergeant was honest with me; he told me I don't qualify for the intelligence division because I don't have a year of college. Eventually, I want to go to college, and even join the FBI. since I don't plan to make the military a career. One day, I want my wife and kids to have roots and not be moving every couple of years like we had to. I want a home life like the one I never got - and I'll make it happen. Just watch me.

Randy's Thoughts:

Roger's leaving us. But why wouldn't he? If I was eighteen, I'd hit the road, too. But Mom, Susie and I are still home with the monster. What can I do? He's so strong and stands six foot two! I'm five-two and weigh a hundred pounds less than him . . . geez, I can't believe Roger's leaving. Mom won't have a chance of surviving the monster's wrath with her oldest son gone. That's what Roger's called our father for as long as I can remember- the monster. Not to his face, of course. Most people refer to him as 'Colonel' with respect. Even our neighbors and people at church call him 'Colonel.' If only they knew what he was really like!

Randy looked at the windowsill where his father kept a three-foot rod. *It's supposed to prevent intruders from sliding open the patio door. But he uses it for other things.*

The curtain hung in front of it, so it was out of sight for those who stepped through the front door. But Randy remembered the time he hit Roger across the back and butt with it. The memory brought tears.

I remember, Roger never flinched when Dad used it on him, never called out, never shed a tear. But I saw his hands balled into tight fists. I could see nails marks in his palms.

Mom never interfered, just stood with her head hanging down, hands clasped in front of her as though seeing her son struck was too much to bear. But she didn't stop it, either.

I knew what my big brother was thinking. He was saying to himself: 'When I turn eighteen, I'm out of here.' I bet he was wishing the monster was dead, too. Mom taught us God expects us to repent and forgive. Repent for what? Our hateful thoughts, or our neglect of chores? Mom told us it was in our best interest to study, too. She kept saying that getting good grades, would open doors for us. I know my mom wants the best for us kids, but the monster doesn't repent, he's never sorry for anything. His rage just gets worse. I'm beginning to question her judgment. Maybe Mom doesn't know best.

Randy's Strategy:

Roger came and hugged me goodbye before he and his Marine recruiter pulled out of the driveway. Dad's downstairs going nuts now that he realizes Roger is gone! He sees it as disrespect. He thought Roger would go to college and become a second lieutenant in the Air Force like he did. But Roger said he didn't have the grades to go to the Air Force Academy. Dad said that was an excuse. Roger's school counselor even told him he'd do fine at a community college. But that wasn't good enough for the monster. He wanted us to study hard and get good grades so we could do what he wanted us to do. Mom's downstairs crying at the kitchen table because her favorite, oldest son is leaving.

Geez, with all the chaos in this house all the time, who could concentrate on schoolwork?

Chaos. I just learned that word in my eighth-grade English class. It's a good word, but the spelling is tough. It says exactly what we've gone through every day. Mom walks on 'eggshells.' I even remember her saying that when I was little, I didn't know what she meant then. I never saw eggshells on the floor since she kept the kitchen clean. But now I understand. She had to be careful what she said around the old man. Listen to him downstairs now, yelling like a crazy man.

Right now, I'm staying up here in my bedroom. Once the yelling downstairs stops, Dad will call for me. He'll be angry . . . even though he says I'm his favorite. But I won't be for long. I've faked being his "little buddy" as long as I can remember. I've lied for him to protect his reputation even when he ruptured Mom's spleen with a solid punch to her gut. I remember the hospital social worker coming to the house. He took me aside, and asked me what I saw. I said Mom fell off her bike just like the monster wanted me to say. Even Mom told the nurses that story. Everybody lied for Dad.

He always threatened us that if she told anybody about his abusive rages, it would cost him his career, and she would be penniless without a nickel to raise us. She knuckled under that threat. I don't see why she believed him. She has an education and taught school since I entered kindergarten. I think she makes enough money to support us. Maybe we'd have to get a smaller house or go to another school, but so what?

We've moved a lot with Dad's military career. We're used to it. I once heard him tell her that if she didn't do exactly as he said that she would never see me again, that he would take me with him. Maybe, but she wouldn't lose all three of us. They always knew Roger would stay with Mom, and Susie, too. Dad is such a phony, like when he brought her flowers the day after he hit her and told her how sorry he was. I doubt he felt sorry at all. But she believed him. . . until it happened again.

I think I hear him yelling at her downstairs. Once he smacks her around, he'll yell for me to come down to him This time I won't go down. The monster will thunder upstairs, and I'll be ready for him. I know what I have to do. The only good thing I learned from him is how to shoot this gun.

My rifle will take the place of the muscles I don't

have to do the job. Now that Roger has basically run away, I'm ready to do whatever it takes to protect my mom and sister. I don't care about the consequences. My mom will be fine . . . and free.

***

Randy positioned himself between the bed and the wall, then shouldered the rifle against his right arm. The room was dark. He took aim at the doorway and waited for his father to come into his room. It didn't take long.

As Randy's dad opened the bedroom door and peered into the dark, he couldn't see Randy or the gun. But as he moved menacingly into the room, he heard the loud report of the gun going off. It was the last sound Colonel Roger Evans ever heard.

3

Mom Remembers

I remember the day Roger was born. It was at a hospital in San Antonio, Texas. The maternity and delivery rooms were so modern. Roger weighed eight pounds, six ounces, and had all that curly, dark hair.

Big Roger couldn't help not being there. He was assigned temporary overseas duty and missed everything. . . missed the birth of our first son. The Evans family was there for me, though, as well as my Parrish side of the family. That's back when Life was good.

Two years later, it was a miscarriage that devastated us. I told them at the emergency room that I tripped on a rug in the kitchen. I know Big Roger didn't mean for us to lose the baby. Even though he shoved me hard in the back, I was the clumsy one who fell. We were quarreling because little Roger still wasn't potty-trained and this new little one was on the way.

Big Roger didn't believe me when I told him the pediatrician said it was normal for boys to take longer to learn bathroom habits. I don't remember falling, but I do remember feeling his hands between my shoulder blades before I blacked out. I'm sure it was all my fault.

Later, when a truly kind doctor told me there was no damage to my uterus, I was happy, but he cautioned us to wait a while before getting pregnant again. Then, still groggy after the D&C following the loss of the baby, I clearly remember him telling me to follow up with him at his office in six weeks. His private doctor's office was near our home.

Then, I remember a nurse pushing me in a wheelchair out to the curb where Big Roger waited. He brought a gorgeous bouquet of flowers and helped me into the passenger seat. When I told him what the doctor had said, he seemed happy that we could have more children. But that's when he told me we were being transferred to Wright Patterson Air Force Base just outside Dayton, Ohio, and no follow-up appointment could happen. That made me sad.

He said he was shipping out the following Monday. I would have three weeks to pack up the house. The Air Force would send a crew to load and ship everything, but little Roger and I were to drive ourselves to Ohio. The thought of driving across the country with a two-year-old, especially so close following the loss of the little one, sent chills down my spine. I felt numb. At least the education degree I was working on could be completed online; I could begin teaching again, once Roger was in school.

Sure enough, time passed, and we had another son, Randy. He weighed six pounds, ten ounces with blonde hair and blue eyes. They say an infant's eyes change color over time and Randy's eyes became hazel just like mine. People would comment: "Jackie, that little guy looks just like you."

Little Roger was a great big brother. He helped feed Randy and sat on the floor beside him watching cartoons. Roger always tried to amuse the baby in so many ways. He knew how much Randy's crying irritated their father.

Big Roger always worked hard and came home grumpy and tired. I suppose I would be that way, too, if my job were as demanding. He always said he just wasn't into babies, but he was glad to have sons. It took a long while for him to take an interest in the boys, As little Roger grew older, his father finally did take an interest in him. Big Roger began trying everything to make little Roger be just like him.

He seemed to enjoy taking Roger fishing in the pond at the end of our cul-de-sac. He just got so annoyed, though, when Roger preferred chasing ducks instead of sitting still on the bank to fish. I tried telling him that's what little boys do.

Other than that, we did nothing together as a family. I stayed at home with Randy and three and a half years later, our precious baby girl, Susie, came along.

By the time little Susie was potty-trained and attending pre-school, Randy was in school all day. That's when I could go back to teaching and began with fifth grade at their elementary school. By then, Roger was in middle school and rode a school bus. We all ended up coming home at about the same time. Just in case little Roger beat us home, though, a spare key was hidden under a rock beside the front door.

One day, Big Roger came home early with a migraine headache. He was furious to see Roger coming through the front door without me. When Randy, Susie, and I arrived, Roger grabbed me by the arm, pushed me into the den, and slammed the door. He pointed his finger in my face and threatened to knock my head off if I ever allowed our son to be at home alone again. I tried to explain that thirteen-year-old kids were babysitting our neighbors' children. Boy, did *that* set him off.

That's the time he punched me full in the stomach with his fist. It knocked me backward over a coffee table and I fell between the table and loveseat. I was dazed. It was a good thing my head snapped back against the cushion of the loveseat, or I could have broken my neck. I remember just lying there. He just left the room.

My head was still spinning when he came back. He told the kids he was taking me to the emergency room and told Roger to call his grandmother to come over. That's when I told the nurses I fell off my bike and stumbled into the house with the help of my son. That was the beginning of all the lies.

The surgical nurse informed me the accident ruptured my spleen and would require emergency surgery. She had an inquisitive look on her face as if she wanted me to respond with more details. But, for obvious reasons, I couldn't do it.

My mother stayed with the boys, and little Susie, until I was released and gained my strength. That time, Roger didn't bring flowers, and he sent my mother to pick me up. His excuse was that he had to attend a meeting in Cleveland. She stayed and tried to pry the truth out of me, but I refused to admit the nightmare I was living.

Meanwhile, I never told my mother that I had found a tube of very red lipstick between the front passenger seat and the door of his truck. I knew better than to confront him about whatever he was doing when he wasn't home. I simply chose to let whatever relationship he might be having, run its course. And, I began thinking about a divorce, but once, in an angry fit, he had yelled that I shouldn't even think of it because it would ruin his military career.

I consoled myself by thinking that whoever she was, maybe she was reducing his stress somehow, and helping him not respond so impulsively any time my behavior or attitude annoyed him. If only she knew she could have him all to herself, at any time.

Upon returning home from his so-called meeting in Cleveland, Roger announced he was being deployed to the Middle East as part of Operation Desert Shield. I hoped he didn't see my sigh of relief. I was very glad we weren't expected to move with him. He said we would remain in base housing until he was reassigned back to the United States. That was just fine with me.

4

Susie's View

This is the saddest day for me. I came home early from my overnight at Diane's house just to hug my big brother goodbye. Roger is going off to join the Marines. Sure, he says he'll write me and call as soon as basic training is over. I sure hope he does, but, tonight, I missed him! Now he's gone, and I can't find my other brother, Randy, anywhere. I can't believe they won't let me go upstairs. An ambulance just pulled away from our house with something in a big, black bag on a stretcher. There's yellow tape at the bottom of the steps. What's going on?

Who's that sitting with Mom in the family room a policewoman? Where's dad? He's been so hateful to Roger since he realized Roger enlisted in the Marines. No eighteenth birthday party, either. Yesterday, Roger was stuck in his room since Dad came home from work. When he saw Roger packing a duffel bag, he asked 'Just where do you think you're going?' Roger said he had joined the Marines, and his recruiter would be picking

PHYLLIS K. WALTERS

him up today, Saturday.

Boy, was that the wrong thing to say. He was instantly grounded without dinner. Dad started screaming at Mom. . . said it was all her fault. Mom was afraid to tell him the truth. But we all know it: Roger is leaving to escape Dad's horrible, angry temper. Lucky him! I wish I could leave, too. But, oh, how I will miss my big brother.

Roger and his girlfriend used to take me to Baskin-Robbins for ice cream sometimes. Being here with Randy won't be the same; he can't drive yet, since he's only fourteen.

Now it's just him and me against Dad. Maybe we can still have fun, though, like barricading ourselves in his room and listening to music. Sometimes, we turn the music up, so we don't hear the screaming downstairs.

Why is Mom crying? I can tell by the tears running down her face that it must be awfully bad news.

Susie listened closely to what her mother was saying, then came to full attention. *What? What's that? Dad is in the body bag? What's happened? Where's Randy? What? He shot Dad?!*

There was silence.

I wonder if Dad was going to hit Randy, or maybe he already hit Mom. What if he punched Roger? I better listen some more.

Susie turned her attention to her mother's conversation with the officer.

"Ma'am, do you have a pastor or priest you can

24

call?" Mom shook her head.

"Yes, we do," Susie interrupted. "Call Pastor Kimble. He's the youth pastor at Faircreek Christian Church. I've been going there with my friend, Diane, on Friday nights. I have Diane's number. She can get in touch with the church."

The policewoman took down the information and said in a kind voice, "My name is Detective Dana Reagan. You may also want to contact a lawyer, a good one."

"We don't have one," Mom said, shaking her head.

"I'm going to give you the name of someone to call. His name is Travis Gump. Here's his card." She handed it to Mom. "You can always call me if you need anything."

Then, Randy appeared in the doorway with his hands behind his back and head slumped forward. He was in handcuffs with the other detective holding him by one arm.

"I'm so sorry, Mom," Randy said, "I'm so sorry."

Mom and I both jumped up and went over to him. The detective let us put our arms around him.

"I couldn't let him hurt you anymore," Randy said, crying now. He kissed me on the top of my head. I wrapped my arms around his waist. The moment didn't last nearly long enough. I lost two brothers on the same day.

5

What Grandma Noni Saw

What in the world is happening? It looks like police cars with twirling lights are in front of my daughter's house. Here comes my little granddaughter, Susie, and she looks extremely upset.

"Susie, Susie, take a deep breath!" I said as Susie walked up to me. "Tell me what's going on."

"Grandma, he's dead! He's *dead*! Randy shot Dad with a rifle. They took him away in handcuffs. Mom and I just said goodbye to him. Grandma, he's only fourteen! Come in and talk to Mom away from the cameras."

"I will, sweetheart. Calm down. Randy will be okay. He's just a kid trying to protect his mother and you. Nothing bad will happen to him."

"I'm praying, Grandma. But I'm so scared for him. Pastor Kimble is coming over any minute. He's the youth pastor at Faircreek Christian Church. Dad never knew I was going over there with my best friend, Diane, on Friday nights. I'll feel better when Pastor

Kimble gets here."

Soon, we watched as Randy was led down the sidewalk to the police car. The neighbors were standing around and television cameras were filming everything.

Then, Jackie came out of the small first-floor guest bathroom with a washcloth to her face, wiping away black mascara that had run down both cheeks. She approached me, and I held out my arms.

"Susie just told me what happened. Is it true that Randy shot Big Roger?"

"Yes, I'm afraid it's true. They don't seem to be calling it self-defense since Roger never got close to Randy to hit him. But Randy shot him as he came through the bedroom door. He dropped on the spot. We've hidden our history of domestic abuse for so long, we've denied and disguised it so everyone thinks we're the perfect family. How will an attorney ever get him off, Mom?"

"Let's call an attorney now. The sooner his lawyer gets to him down at the Juvenile Detention Center in Xenia, the better off Randy will be. He should not be answering questions or offering explanations."

"Detective Dana Reagan referred this lawyer to me. Please, call him for me. I don't think I can talk to anyone just yet," Jackie said, handing me a card. "But it's the weekend. Probably no one will answer." I looked at the number and dialed it. Surprisingly, the phone was answered on the second ring, and I heard a voice.

"Attorney Travis Gump speaking. Who's calling, please?"

"Yes, this is Noni Parrish. My fourteen-year-old grandson was just arrested for shooting his father. Detective Reagan gave my daughter your card. Her name is Jackie Evans. We need representation badly, Mr. Gump, will you help us?"

"Of course. Let me go down to the detention center, but I'll need verbal consent from your daughter. She's Randy's mother, right? Is she there?"

As I handed the phone to Jackie, I mouthed the words: "He needs your permission."

Jackie took the phone and cleared her throat. "Hello? Mr. Gump, thank you so much for answering the phone on a weekend. Yes, of course, you have my permission. We will retain you immediately, just please help my son. Randy Evans is his name. He shot his father to protect me. My husband has been abusing me . . . us . . . for a long time. Randy was just protecting his little sister from my husband's anger today." The words tumbled out of Jackie's mouth; she couldn't tell the story fast enough.

Poor Mr. Gump, I thought, *Hope he can make sense of all her words.*

"Our oldest son just joined the Marines against my husband's wishes," Jackie continued. "But he turned eighteen today and couldn't leave fast enough. He was picked up by his Marine recruiter just before my husband came home. Big Roger was a lieutenant colonel in the Air Force and our son, Roger, has tried to keep him from seriously hurting us for a long time. Today, he couldn't wait to leave this house fast enough and Randy was out of his mind with fear for our lives with Roger leaving."

"Let me get back to you after I've spoken to Randy," Attorney Gump said. "Meanwhile, I will call the correction officers at the Greene County Juvenile Detention Center and advise them *not* to talk to Randy before I get there. Don't worry, Mrs. Evans. Try to collect your thoughts because I will need to see you on Monday in my Kettering Office."

Jackie hung up and looked at me. "He sounds very caring, Mom. Will you go with me on Monday? He wants to see me in his office. You might have a more objective view of how our lives have been. I've even forgotten some details too horrible to remember, and I don't want to drag Susie into this mess."

"Of course, I'll go," I said, mentally rearranging my day's schedule. "There is no way you can recall a lot of details when you were so often unconscious or sedated at the hospital. I've seen for years how badly big Roger was treating you. But I was trying to stay out of your life that way. Now, I would love to call young Roger before he sets out for basic training. Or would you prefer I don't interrupt him just yet?"

"What good would it do? He would just want to come back to help Randy. And we won't be having a funeral at this point. Maybe a memorial next spring. What do you think, Mom?"

"I agree. No funeral at this point. We have enough to deal with now. Besides, aren't big Roger's Air Force buddies about to ship out? They won't be here anyway."

"I think so. They were the only ones who saw him in a positive light. Anyone else would want to support us, and I can't face up to that with Randy in trouble. And then there is the woman with the red lipstick."

"What? Jackie, was he seeing another woman?"

"Let me put it this way: Someone was in his vehicle and conveniently left her lipstick. I figured she wanted to let me know she was special to Roger. I'm not as naïve as everyone thinks."

6

Attorney Travis Gump

"Well, that was an interesting call," Travis said to his wife, Stella. "Look what happens when you stop in the office on a Saturday. I was just coming in to pick up paperwork for another client's Monday arraignment and find out this young kid needs help now. In my mind, that is no coincidence. It's divine intervention."

"Uh, oh," Stella said. "So much for enjoying our leisurely afternoon by the pool. At least we were able to enjoy a ride together to your office."

"Yeah, this kid needs help and needs it immediately," Travis said. "I don't want them convincing him to write out a confession just because he was caught red-handed with the weapon in his hand. There is a back story to be told. I can sense there was good reason for his act."

"No doubt, and if anyone can do it, you can, Travis. We can skip lunch since we're going out for dinner. Why don't you just drop me off at home."

"Thank you for being so understanding, Stella. And since you're the director of the county Foster Care

Program, this kid – Randy – could actually end up in your hands. His mother may not be in the best mental shape to properly take care of him. He could be placed with you temporarily. Who knows?"

"I understand the possibility completely," Stella said. "Without a caring father and loving grandparents, I could have been like Randy, too. But, honestly, hon, from my experience, I doubt the boy will see the light of day before he ages out of Juvenile"

The couple returned to their shiny black sports car parked behind the back entrance to the office building. Stella whipped out her Dayton Dragons baseball cap from the console. She loved riding in their vintage, 1966, Corvette Stingray convertible, and Travis enjoyed cruising the back roads instead of the interstate. His mind, however, was not on the moment, but on the afternoon ahead. He would switch vehicles after he took Stella home, and drive to the county parking lot across the street from the Juvenile Detention Center. No charge on Saturdays.

As they turned into their driveway, Stella said, "Oh, and don't forget tonight we're going out with Rosie and will finally meeting Bucky. They're in town for her mother's wedding. It will be a relatively private event and their small reception should be over by late afternoon . That will give us time to be ready to meet them by five at our house. You should beat them home by that time, don't you think?"

"Yes, I'm sure that'll work. My initial interview with Randy Evans won't take long."

"Great. By the way, do you remember how Rosie helped me with my American History course at Adrian? She was the best roommate a girl could have. I hated losing her when she went back to Toledo to live at home and finish school there to become a forensic psychologist. But at least we kept in touch."

"Yeah, I do remember," Travis said. "I also think about the time we went sledding in the Irish Hills on the cafeteria trays. Our rear-ends got soaked. Or should I say mine did? That was fun. Didn't Rosie also transfer to Toledo University? She wanted to become a half-time dancer for the university basketball team, is what I remember."

"Yup, that's Rosie. The professors loved her because they could talk with her about the game on Monday morning. Those friendships opened doors to grad school for her and built her confidence for sure. Who would ever imagine she would marry a college athletic director? I think they honeymooned at Saint Martin and married on the beach. If it hadn't been out-of-town, I'm sure she would have asked me to be her maid of honor. I'm really looking forward to meeting Bucky at dinner."

"Me, too. Let's take them someplace nice like the Oakdale Club. We can get a round table in the back where it's quiet, and we can hear one another speak. Did you tell me they're bringing a dog?"

"Well, Jocko is not just *any* old dog, Travis. His pictures are amazing. Large, big brown eyes, and as dedicated to Rosie, as she is to him. He'll be fine at our house," Stella said.

"Do you think Rosie would consider evaluating Randy on Monday? I'm thinking it could be extremely useful in my defense. And she can identify what assistance he will need during his incarceration. I agree with you that he will be in Juvenile until he ages out."

"Let's ask them to stay overnight and possibly Monday night as well. If Bucky needs to get back to Toledo earlier, I can drive Rosie home on Tuesday. Will that help?"

"Absolutely. She can interview Randy's other family members on the phone and read the discovery material when she gets back to Toledo. That could work out just fine."

"Sounds like a plan," Stella said as they pulled into their driveway. She gave Travis a peck on the cheek and got out of the car.

I really love this man, Stella thought as she headed inside. Thoughts about their relationship flooded into her mind.

Travis Gump had grown up in Adrian, Michigan, where he had been recruited to play football for Adrian College. They met on the first day of freshman week. She was from Centerville, Ohio, and not the least bit impressed with Travis. He was tall, handsome, and full of confidence, attracting pretty co-eds by the dozens. She was warned about guys like him from her protective father. Her mind was set on attending Adrian on an academic scholarship and becoming a psychiatrist. Men were not on her radar.

Her mother had struggled with mental illness for years and ended up losing her life in a tragic accident. Stella's brother was a third-year resident doctor at an osteopathic teaching hospital in West Virginia. When their mom had gone to visit him, somehow, she had ridden her bicycle off a cliff. No one could know her state of mind when that happened. Was it really an accident – or intentional? Stella's Dad was left to finish raising her, only in eighth grade at the time. Her brother, Jason, was left with feelings of guilt and regret for having invited their mother for the fateful visit.

Travis and Stella had ended up in several classes together. He pledged Alpha Tau Omega fraternity and she pledged Tri Sigma. They were thrown together at "Greek" events. He didn't attend tailgate parties because he was in the locker room preparing for football games. But afterward, they would sometimes sit around a bonfire and drink rum and cokes, strictly forbidden by this conservative, Methodist college.

At the end of the football season, Stella had agreed to attend the homecoming dance with Travis. That year, she was voted freshman attendant to the homecoming queen, without knowing Travis had been the anonymous student who nominated her for the honor.

During the summers, Stella stayed at Adrian and attended summer school. She had a part-time job in the library which she absolutely loved. Solitude and wages! What could be better? Travis attended summer football camps and was a counselor at a local YMCA day camp.

At least once a week, they were able to get together, and Stella grew to know his family. She adored his pretty mother and felt the love of an older woman for the first time having lost her own mother so young. Thinking back to the time her mother had been there, she realized she had lost her own mother to schizophrenia long before she actually died. Her mother had simply not been capable of guiding and loving a daughter or son, or husband, for that matter.

During their senior year, at the homecoming game, Stella and Travis were crowned King and Queen which came as no surprise to the students or faculty. They appeared to be the couple most likely to succeed in both their personal and professional lives. On Christmas Eve of that year, they became engaged and married the week after graduation. Stella's father gave her away, and Travis' mother assisted her in dressing for the lovely occasion.

Together, the newlyweds attended the University of Dayton graduate school and lived in married student housing, also known as The Ghetto. Stella pursued a master's degree in social work, thinking it could prepare her for private practice without a medical degree. Besides, she figured, psychiatrists dispensed drugs and she wanted to counsel clients with depression or anxiety, and not simply medicate their symptoms.

She had seen a wonderful counselor following the untimely death of her mother and grew to know how valuable such support could be. At the same time, Travis began his trek through law school. He always felt compassion for the underdog and believed he could become a competent defense attorney. So, he did.

Now, they were still happily together, satisfied with their professional paths and personal relationship, and looked forward to helping others.

7

The First Interview

Travis walked up the steps to the juvenile detention center, sometimes called the JDC, and met Officer Billy Lee at the door.

"What brings you to this fine institution on a beautiful, warm Saturday afternoon?" Lee greeted him.

"I'm here to see Randy Evans. He was probably just processed."

"Right, but you know the drill. I haven't seen you in juvie lately, so you have to sign in at the window, Travis."

Travis nodded and walked over to the window. He grabbed the visitors' log clipboard and entered the required information. Date, name of the inmate, visitor's name, title, and time of visit.

"You're the first visitor, so far, Mr. Gump." Officer Lee said.

Travis recognized her comment with a smile and slight wink, friendly-like not flirtatious. The Gumps sometimes had dinner with Officer Lee and her husband. Once, the two couples had bid on the same paintings, and each couple ended up going home with an RG Gorman. Well, not exactly.

The Gumps' corvette could not hold the 36x48-inch portrait of a Navaho woman filling a decorative bowl with corn husks. So, the Lees obliged them and drove the large painting home in their large van. That's when the friendly relationship began.

Travis placed his weathered, brown briefcase and keys on the conveyer belt and walked through the metal detector. Instantly, a buzz sounded.

"Shoot, Billy," he said to the corrections officer. "I forgot to remove my knock-off Rolex." They both laughed.

"Not the first time, Travis," Billy said, "and likely it won't be the last. Take care of yourself."

"Will do. Have a nice shift."

A stern-faced officer, unknown to Travis, brought Randy to the visitation room reserved for professionals such as lawyers, and their clients. Randy was dressed in a one-piece, orange jumpsuit with a white tee shirt visible at the neckline. He wore thin, jail, open-toed slippers with white socks to protect his feet. The attending officer removed his handcuffs, left the room without a word, and locked the door behind him. He would likely stand nearby at an intake station and watch when Travis requested the young inmate be taken back to his fourth-floor pod.

Randy sat down with his back to the glass door across from Travis. Attorney Gump introduced himself. "Don't be nervous, Randy. Your mother and grandmother asked me to represent you. From now on, don't talk to anyone about your case or circumstances without me in the room or my permission. This is extremely important in order to help you. Do you understand?"

"Yes," Randy said softly without looking up. He rubbed his wrists to relieve the discomfort from the handcuffs. "Is my mother, okay? She can take care of my little sister now. My grandma will be there to help, too. No matter how bad it looks, I'm glad he's gone. My mom will be okay now. She's always been there for us. I had to help her."

"Randy, in your own words, tell me what happened this morning. It is strictly confidential. I am not employed by the court."

"I knew when my brother left for the Marines that Dad would be extra mad. I knew he would take it out on Mom like so many times before. But, this time, I wasn't going to let it happen. Under Roger's bed, there's always been a rifle, a fishing rod or two, and a tackle box. When I opened the tackle box, I expected to see hooks, fish lures, and wire. But when I lifted the shelf in the box, there was ammunition.

"As Roger walked down the sidewalk with his recruiter, I loaded the gun, went to my bedroom, and shut the door so I couldn't hear the yelling."

"What happened next?"

"I heard him come up the stairs yelling like usual. Then, he stood in the doorway pounding his fists on the door frame and glaring at me. I was done with him. He wasn't gonna hurt us anymore. So, I pulled the trigger and closed my eyes so I couldn't see the expression on his face, or any blood I knew would spurt out of his chest. I pulled the trigger three times, thinking one of them would stop him." Then, Randy put his head down on his arms on the table and sobbed. Travis reached across the space and touched his hand, then stood and patted his head.

"Randy, I can see it would be difficult for you to answer any more questions today. I'll speak to your mother on Monday and see that you have clothes to wear to the arraignment. You'll likely be charged with premeditated murder because you had loaded a weapon with the intent to do bodily harm to your father. My job is to get you a reduced sentence, if possible, and see that you are assigned to a juvenile facility nearby. One that has the least restrictive environment. It will have pods, not cells during the day, and indoor and outdoor exercise areas. Do you understand?"

"Yes. Thank you, Mr. Gump."

"One last thing. Were you interviewed prior to my arrival today, and if so, were you read your rights?"

"I wasn't interviewed here, but the lady detective talked with me in the squad car on the way. We didn't discuss the case or anything. She was kind and tried to calm me down. She told me what to expect and that you would probably come to see me this afternoon. She told me your name and said

I could trust you. I do, Mr. Gump."

Travis walked over to the door and tapped on the glass with his keys. The officer on duty had changed but the new man quickly unlocked the door. Randy stood and the officer cuffed him. Travis nodded at both, took his briefcase, and walked swiftly out of the secured area. Signing out on the visitation form, he headed to his car. A breath of fresh air was always appreciated after seeing his clients behind bars, especially one so young.

8

The Trip

Rosie attached Jocko's red leash and lured him outside to the car with a piece of cookie. He jumped into the back seat and sprawled on his blanket, getting comfortable. Jocko was used to the pleasure of two human parents now: Rosie and Bucky, having been Rosie's tried and true companion for the past few years.

At first, the dog had been standoffish with Bucky when they returned from their two-week honeymoon on St. Martin, the beautiful Caribbean Island where she and Bucky had married. But now he seemed to understand that Bucky was a permanent part of the household.

The honeymoon period was the first time he and Rosie had ever been apart for two weeks; even though he enjoyed his stay with the Lober family, he hadn't understood that Rosie would be returning for him. Now, after six months, he was used to sharing Rosie's bed with another large human being.

Rosie's had first met the Lober family after investigating a sex trafficking ring involving the Lober Stables and the disappearance of two young girls while attending a hayride there a while ago. After the Lobers were absolved of any wrongdoing, Rosie began an enjoyable relationship with them. That's where she had taken Jocko to stay while she and Bucky were honeymooning.

Bucky closed the condo door behind him and got in the car. Turning to his new bride he asked, "Have everything? Your dress for your mom's wedding? Our wedding pictures on the beach to show the Gumps . . . oh, and I hope you didn't forget your Adrian yearbook. I can't wait to hear about your year at college with them."

"That's what I love about you, Bucky," Rosie chuckled, ruffling his hair affectionately. "You really care about me." She secured her seatbelt. "You and Travis have a lot in common, you know. He's a jock, too, and I think they may be taking us to a Dayton Dragons baseball game tomorrow."

"That'll be fun. Okay, we're all set," he said buckling up. He looked at Jocko in the backseat who had just pricked up his ears. "No, we aren't taking you back to the stable. This time, you're going with us, buddy." Jocko relaxed on his blanket. "How do you think he'll do alone at your mother's while we are at the wedding?"

"He'll be fine if you don't mind walking him around the block to stretch before we leave for church.

44

Or just walk him while I help my mother get dressed."

"Sounds like a plan. Jocko and I are becoming fast friends. Now, Rosie, would you please find some Southern gospel music? If you can't, I have several concert CDs; besides, I'm tired of talk radio, aren't you?" Bucky said jovially.

"Yes, but what I'm not tired of is the sound of the surf and tropical breezes we enjoyed on St. Martin. Now that we've bought a time-share villa there, we can return again soon. What a surprise wedding gift that was. Thank you, again, sweetie."

***

Travis!" Stella called out to her husband relaxing with a beer in his favorite lounge chair on the pool deck.

"What, hon?" he responded in a relaxed tone.

"Rosie and Bucky are on the way here from her mother's wedding," Stella called from the doorway. "You might want to get some ice out of the fridge. I'm bringing out more beer, some shiraz, vodka, cranberry juice, and limes."

The doorbell rang just as she stepped back into the house. Opening the front door, she smiled and grabbed Rosie by the shoulders, planting a kiss on each cheek, European style.

"Rosie! How wonderful you look! And you must be Bucky. Congratulations to both of you." She extended a hand. "It's such a pleasure to finally meet you."

"Stella, the pleasure is all mine," he said.

"So, this is Jocko." Stella leaned down and patted the friendly gray dog on top of his curly head. "Until now, I thought Jocko was the man of the house, Rosie. How's he taking his demotion?" They all shared a laugh.

"How was your drive down, and how was your mother's wedding?"

"The drive was fine, and the wedding was beautiful! I'm really glad to see mom so happy."

"Come out to the pool and see Travis. He's waiting to meet you, Bucky, and he'll think Rosie looks amazing because you do. Travis can help Bucky unload your stuff and whatever you've brought for Jocko.

"Sounds great, Stella," Bucky said, feeling comfortable in the surroundings.

Stella slid open the patio door and all three of them with Jocko, stepped into the pool area. Rosie was stunned by the beauty of the ceramic pots of all sizes, containing multi-colored flowers. Purple and white blooms were obviously Stella's favorite, their sorority colors, Rosie noted. Travis stood from his chair and approached Rosie, wrapping her in a friendly bear hug. Rosie reciprocated before standing back to introduce Bucky. She knew Travis would be sizing him up as he had done with everyone she had ever brought around as a freshman in college.

Like a big brother, she thought.

Travis offered Bucky a beer and Rosie accepted a glass of shiraz. "I swear, Stella, you have the memory of an elephant. You remembered I was not a Merlot or Cabernet girl, didn't you?"

"Learning more and more already," Bucky piped in to more laughter.

"Rosie," Stella said, "how about we relax with a drink, and you tell me all about the wedding while the guys get acquainted. I'll bet she made a beautiful bride. What was she wearing?" Stella asked.

"Well, I've never seen her look more beautiful. Her dress was avocado green, a two-piece crepe sheath, knee-length, with a matching jacket that had satin tuxedo lapels and cuffs. It had one button at her slim waistline, and a brocade bodice. She wore beige pumps and carried yellow roses with satin streamers."

"Sounds stunning. Did you walk down the aisle with her?"

"I actually walked behind her. The minister asked who was giving her away, and I said that I was. Then she handed me her bouquet and Caleb took both her hands in his.

"How sweet. So, what did you wear?"

"I wore a yellow linen dress with a jeweled neckline and a flared knee-length skirt. Sleeves were three-quarter length. I opted for a wrist corsage to keep my hands free to receive my mom's bouquet. I wore a pearl necklace and earrings that my mother gave me for being her matron of honor," Rosie pointed to them now.

"They're lovely! I take it the guest list was small." Stella said.

"Yes, otherwise, you and Travis would have been invited. The reception just included a sit-down luncheon with four round tables of eight people each. Basically, two tables of the bride's friends and two tables of the groom's friends, plus the head table with Bucky, me, Caleb's daughter and son-in-law, and the bride and groom. Simple but sweet. I feel privileged to be related to my new step-father and so happy for my mother."

"Oh, look, Travis is waving us over. They must be done with their sports talk. Shall we join them?" Stella asked with a laugh.

"Great idea," Rosie said with a little sigh of relief that Bucky and Travis had apparently hit it off.

"Is it okay to share the itinerary with you guys, now?" Stella asked.

"Absolutely," Bucky and Rosie said in unison.

"We thought we'd go to dinner first, then take you for a drive through the university housing where Travis and I lived in grad school. We can show Bucky the university baseball diamonds which we think he'll enjoy. Now, our choice of restaurants includes Dominic's Italian, Marion's Pizza, or someplace quieter and nicer like The Oakdale Club. We want you to pick.

"Any preference, Bucky?" Rosie asked.

"Not really. If you let me treat, I say we go to the Oakdale Club."

"I like the idea of the Oakdale Club, too, but no way are you treating," Travis said. "This'll be our wedding gift to you; you can tell us all about St. Martin. Then tomorrow, we have tickets to the Dayton Dragons home game, then we plan to cookout here at home. We assume you won't be seeing your mother anymore this trip since they'll be on a honeymoon, right?"

"Exactly. They drove right on to Cincinnati after

the reception. In the morning, they're flying to Vienna for a Viking Riverboat Cruise," Rosie said.

"So, why don't the two of you get settled in the guestroom," Stella said. "Travis has a business question which can probably wait until after dinner? Is that okay with everyone?"

"My thinking, exactly," Travis said. "Bucky and I will unpack the car, and you girls can sit here and start catching up. How long has it been since you've seen one another?"

"The last time I saw Rosie, was at her father's funeral in Toledo. When was that? Five years ago?" Stella asked.

"Yup. I think you're right. We tried to plan a girls' weekend once before, but our lives became too busy and complicated," Rosie said. "And it took a wedding to get us all together again."

9

Making Plans

Between Saturday dinner at the Oakdale Club and now Sunday dinner at the Walnut Creek Country Club, Rosie figured Bucky and Travis had established the beginning of a meaningful friendship. They had a lot in common with their love of sports.

"This has been one great weekend, Stella. We loved the Dragons game. Fine, talented young men, right, Bucky?" Rosie laughed. "So, when can we expect you and Travis to visit us? No excuses accepted."

"Well, Bucky, Travis, and I have all talked and agree it should be sometime soon. You know how short life can be. You can show us your favorite restaurants and stomping grounds. In the fall, let's go up to Adrian for a football game or a homecoming reunion. Maybe in the spring, we can catch a University of Toledo baseball game." Stella sounded cheerful.

"We were just talking about that while you girls were in the powder room," Travis said.

"At least Bucky was able to cancel his Monday appointments so we could stay until after Randy's hearing tomorrow. After I talk with him early in the morning, we'll need to be home by late tomorrow evening. On Tuesday, I have clients in my Springhill office that Ruth can't reschedule. We don't want to overstay our welcome with you either. What are your plans, Stella?"

"After you meet with the family tomorrow morning, Rosie, I thought you and I could take Bucky to Doubleday's for a late lunch. They have avgolemono, Greek chicken soup, gyros, and spanakopita with Greek salad. Or, you can have a big Pappas' Greek salad with a large scoop of potato salad buried in the middle of the greens."

Just then, Dr. Steve Cunningham and his beautiful wife, Sarah walked in the country club. "Hello, Travis. How's your golf been lately?"

"Why, Steve and Sarah, hello!" Travis said, "Let me introduce you to our dear friends, Dr. Rosie Klein and Bucky Walker, recent newlyweds. Oh, by the way, I forgot to ask, Rosie, have you taken the name of Walker?"

"I think, for the time being, I'll be keeping the name 'Klein.' Once I retire, I plan to use Walker," Rosie said, turning to smile at the Cunninghams. "But it's so nice to meet you both."

"Rosie is the forensic psychologist I've appointed to the Randy Evans case. I'm sure you've both heard about it. But she lives in Toledo, and they are heading back later tomorrow afternoon," Travis said.

"I'd be glad to welcome your visit to our group psych practice, Rosie. We have three locations. Sarah manages the North office, I manage downtown, and our third partner, manages the South office," Steve said.

"Gee, thanks Steve. I would love to visit your practice sometime in the future. We'll be coming back to visit my mother soon. She lives here in Oakdale, but is on her honeymoon right now," Rosie replied. "How wonderful! Sure, having you visit at a later time sounds like a plan. Next time you're in town, stop by one of our offices."

"Make it mine, Rosie, and we can have lunch in Centerville," Sarah said. "I see our table is ready. Let's talk again soon. So glad you stopped to say hello."
"What lovely people," Rosie said as the Cunninghams left the table. "I really like it here."

10

Rosie Interviews Randy

Early Monday morning, Rosie stepped in front of the Juvenile Detention Center's visitation window and identified herself to Deputy Maxwell who was seated behind the desk. He had watched her enter and walk toward the window. "Photo ID and identification," he said somewhat brusquely, "and proof of occupation." She greeted Officer Maxwell with a smile and addressed him by the name on his badge.

"Of course, Deputy Maxwell. I'm here to see Randy Evans, please." In each jurisdiction, the routine was the same, but in Toledo, she usually was easily recognized as an established, professional visitor, and well-known. Now, however, she quietly provided her credentials and signed the logbook.

Deputy Maxwell called upstairs to clear the visit, and then looked again at Rosie. "Please place your personal articles on the conveyer belt and step through security," his voice was flat and matter of fact. Rosie tossed her briefcase and large, black suede purse on the conveyer belt to be scanned and stepped through the metal detector. Once on the other side, she removed her jewelry from her purse, put on her watch, bracelet, and stud pearl earrings.

Usually, for professional visits such as this one, she always wore a dark suit, long sleeve blouse, and closed-toed pumps to portray a polished, professional appearance. But since she hadn't expected to be doing a professional visit following her mother's wedding, she wore clothes she had packed for the visit. She had long ago stopped wearing dangling gold earrings ever since an uncooperative inmate had reached across the metal table and ripped one out of her ear. Doubtful such a thing would happen with a juvenile offender, she still didn't want to take a chance.

By the time Rosie got off the elevator on the third floor, Randy Evans was seated in the visitation room with a correction officer standing in the hall just outside the door. Rosie introduced herself to the guard who acknowledged her, quickly unlocked the door, and stepped aside. She entered the room, smiled at the young boy, and spoke to him.

"Good morning, Randy. I'm Dr. Klein. Your attorney, Mr. Gump, asked me to come and speak with you today. How are you feeling?" Rosie spoke in a soft, quiet tone.

Randy looked up and responded, "I guess I am okay. I am just so confused. I don't know what's going to happen next. Mr. Gump said there would be a meeting this afternoon with the prosecutor and a judge."

"I can understand your confusion. You will know more about what to expect after that meeting. It's an informal hearing. You're fourteen years old, with no prior record, right?"

"Yeah. I've never been in trouble before. Some friends of mine were caught shoplifting two liters of Coke at a convenience store once, but I wasn't with them that day. They ended up paying a fine and doing community service all summer."

"I am afraid your charges will be more serious, Randy. If the judge appoints me to evaluate you, we won't have a confidential agreement. Do you understand what that means?" He shook his head. "It means that whatever I learn about you today, I can report about in your hearing. However, it could help you, too. Are you still willing to talk about what happened?"

"I don't care who knows about it, Dr. Klein. I don't have anything to hide." Randy's voice quivered and he clasped his hands together to keep them still.   "Okay, that's fine, Randy. I have a form for you to sign before we talk that says you understand what I've just told you and that you are giving up your rights to confidentiality so you can tell me your story. A second form outlines your history for me and when you sign it, you are saying that what is written is what happened. I will go through it with you today. Then, if I am assigned to your case, I'll use the information to speak to teachers, coaches, neighbors, and friends who will share their feelings about you."

"Okay. The judge needs to know what kind of kid I am. I know what they will say about me, and most people won't believe what I did. But a few of my friends and their parents know how really mean my dad was to me. Don't forget to talk to my mom and sister, Susie, too. How are they?"

"From what I've heard, they're doing okay and are staying at your grandmother Noni's house. Your house is still closed off to everyone."

"When can they visit me? Is there any chance I can get out on bail?" Randy's eyes moistened with tears. He looked so young to Rosie. She watched him use the back of his hand to wipe the tears across his cheeks.

"I can't answer the question about bail, Randy. Mr. Gump will discuss your options this afternoon." She hesitated only a minute after he had signed the two papers.

Tell me about school. What are you taking and what is your favorite subject?"

"Two weeks ago, I graduated from eighth grade. My dad came but sat the whole time with his arms crossed like usual. He never clapped or even smiled like the other kids' parents. It's like he doesn't even like me. . . or didn't, I mean." He briefly sat in silence remembering his father was dead . . . by Randy's own hand. Perhaps, he was reliving it. Then, he seemed to come back to the moment.

"In school, my favorite subject is history. My favorite teacher is Mr.Serago. He is the best, funniest, history teacher and keeps encouraging me to go to law school. Mr. Serago told me he has regrets about not going, himself. He even tried convincing my dad to let me go to Europe later this summer with other students. I think I *want* to be a lawyer."

Rosie looked at him. She wasn't sure this could happen with what he had done. Maybe his record could be expunged. Time would tell.

"In fourth grade," Randy continued "I started in this program called EDGE for gifted kids. Anyway, that's what they called it. That's where I met my girlfriend, Joanie. She was in the EDGE program, and we would meet at the library on Saturdays and make up the work we missed in class on Friday afternoon when we went to EDGE classes."

"Your girlfriend?"

"Yeah. In fourth grade, we were only friends. But now, she is my girlfriend. She has a great family, too, and they love me. You can talk to Joanie's parents, Bev, and Stan Martin. They'll give you the scoop on my dad. They saw what I went through and have always been kind and helpful to me."

"What about high school? Do you plan to take advanced subjects?"

"Yes. Biology, Honors Geometry, Honors English, Second year Spanish, and World History. I don't think my dad was ever proud of me no matter what grades I brought home. Of course, that's not why I killed him," Randy's voice wavered. "I had to stop him from hurting my mom."

"I'm sure that's how you feel. Tell me what led up

to shooting your dad."

"Like I told Mr. Gump, my brother was leaving for the Marines. It was his eighteenth birthday and dad was really mad Roger had enlisted. He thought Roger should go to college and become an Air Force officer like him. But Roger isn't like me. He *hated* school and would have skipped out most classes if his football coach would have allowed it. You couldn't go to practice if you were absent from school, and you couldn't play on Friday nights if you missed practice. So, Roger tolerated high school. He had more friends than me. They were the jocks, and I was Roger's nerdy little brother."

"I see. Did you play sports at all? What do you do in your spare time?"

"When I was little, I played baseball in the spring and soccer in fall. My dad coached my little league team. To say I disappointed him is an understatement. He would scream 'hit the ball' when I would swing and miss. He would take off his baseball cap and throw it on the ground. Other parents disliked him and groaned when they heard their kids were going to be on my dad's team.

"As far as soccer, he saw it as a sissy sport and didn't watch me play. I was a decent player. I'm taller than some guys, and I could even jump up and head the ball. Sometimes, I played goalie which is a tough position. My arms reached higher and wider than most kids. I play saxophone, too, and my long arms help with that. My mom plays the piano and she made us take two years of piano before we could pick a horn.

"Roger never did play an instrument after the mandatory two years of piano. If I had my way, I would play in the high school marching band, but Dad wouldn't sign the permission slip for summer band camp. You can't be in the band in the fall if you don't go to summer camp."

"Tell me about the morning Roger left."

"I was upstairs in my room listening to music. I didn't want to go down and say goodbye to Roger because, honestly, I would've cried. Then Dad would've made fun of me, and Roger would've felt more guilty about leaving than he already did."

"Why did he feel guilty?"

"He knew he was leaving mom without his protection. He couldn't always protect her, but he ran interference sort of like in football. He would step between them and act as a distraction, then Dad would get mad and hit *him* which was better than hitting Mom. Susie was terrified of our dad, too, and she adores Roger. According to Dad, Mom couldn't do *anything* right. According to us three kids, she is a saint. She did our laundry, shopped, cooked, cleaned, and drove us wherever we had to be. He never said 'thank you' to her and never, ever took her any place nice. He would make her go to Air Force things, but never anywhere she wanted to go. He knew right where to hit her, too, where it didn't show or leave any bruises that military people could see."

"Did he ever seriously injure her, Randy?"

"Yup. Once, he punched her in the gut and

ruptured her spleen. We all lied and told everyone she hit the handlebars when she fell off her bike. He made us lie about it."

"Now, on the day it all happened, you said you were up in your room, and Roger was ready to leave. What happened next?"

"I knew Dad would be angry, so I went into Roger room and removed a rifle from under his bed. I didn't *plan* to shoot it. I just planned to use it for protection, maybe to threaten Dad with it. It wasn't loaded, but then I spotted the old, green, tackle box. I opened it and saw fish lures, hooks, and wire. I don't know why I lifted the little shelf, but I did, and there was the ammo. I don't know what came over me but I loaded the rifle, closed the tackle box, and shoved it back under the bed. Then I went into my room and sat on the carpet between the bed and the nightstand. Just sitting and thinking . . . and waiting."

"Then, what?"

"I heard the screen door slam and him yelling for me to come down. I didn't budge. He stomped up the steps, opened the door, and stood with his fists clenched against the molding of the doorframe. He had fire in his eyes. Glaring at me. I had the gun pointed at the doorway the whole time . . . and . . . I just pulled the trigger, three times. I didn't see his face 'cause my eyes were closed. After that, I couldn't move, I couldn't think. Dr. Klein, I was numb."

Rosie looked at Randy's face. He was staring straight ahead.

"Is that when you were arrested?"

"Yeah. Mom ran upstairs and saw dad's body sprawled in the doorway. She told me to sit and not move, then ran downstairs to call 911. I didn't see her again until they took me downstairs in handcuffs. The lady detective, Dana Reagan, was nice to me. Her partner, Detective Winslow, wasn't mean or anything either. He wanted me to tell him the whole story. He reached down, put on gloves, took the rifle, and pulled me up. We sat on the edge of my bed for a while. He probably thinks I was lying because it took me so long to speak out loud, but I just couldn't believe what I had done. I finally did tell him what I just told you and Mr. Gump. Mr. Gump told me not to talk to anyone else about my case. The whole weekend I've been here and no one else has asked."

"Randy, I live quite a distance away from Dayton. I will need you to look over this personal information form, see if anything is missing, and give it to Mr. Gump. It has medical, school, and other things on it. He'll mail it to me. At the end of the form are some incomplete sentences. I would appreciate it if you would finish each one with the first thought that comes to mind. Okay?"

"Okay. I'm kind of bored here anyway. I'll do it as soon as you leave. That way I'll give it to Mr. Gump this afternoon."

"I also brought you a journal, Randy. Write your thoughts down all this week and don't share them with anyone. Mr. Gump will send me what you write. You can draw pictures or write songs or anything that comes to your mind. Also write specific times you remember anyone in your family being abused by your father. If you remember dreams or events, write them down too. I have to leave now. But it was nice of you to be so open and honest with me. I know this is extremely difficult.

"Remember, second best to talking to someone is writing down your feelings. It keeps your thoughts from going round and round in your head and can help you sleep better at night. Do you understand?"

"Yes," Randy nodded. "Oh, I forgot one thing. A chaplain stopped to see me earlier and prayed with me. He left a Bible and I spent the last two days reading and praying. Is it okay to talk to him?"

"Yes, Randy. What you say to a chaplain is confidential. Do you remember his name?"

"Pastor Kimble. He volunteers here. I knew him from being a youth pastor at Faircreek Christian Church. I'm sure he'd like to talk to you, Dr. Klein. I signed a release for him to talk to any professional on my case. I hope he doesn't tell me I might go to hell."

"I don't think he'll do that, Randy. By the way, I brought you some peanut butter crackers and a couple of nutrition bars. I know the meals are slim here. So, use them as evening snacks." Rosie and Randy both stood up. She slipped the food into his hands.

"Don't worry; you have a terrific lawyer. I'll provide him with all the background information I can gather. If you have phone numbers of people who would support you, write them down. That can be useful at the final hearing before the judge."

"Thank you, Dr. Klein,"

The door opened and a uniformed officer nodded at Rosie before cuffing Randy's hands in front of him.

"Thanks, sir. That's much more comfortable than behind my back," Randy said in a voice much too grownup for a boy of fourteen."

"You're welcome, son."

11

Interview with Randy's Family

After leaving the juvenile detention center, Rosie drove directly to Travis' office at Lincoln Park Center where he had arranged for Randy's mother, Jackie Evans, and her mother, Noni Parrish, to meet them. The ladies would talk with Rosie while Travis attended the arraignment hearing. Jackie brought a set of clothes for Randy to wear which Travis would deliver to the visitation officer before they met in front of the judge. He also had a brief meeting scheduled with the prosecuting attorney, Brooks Wright.

"I think Brooks will show compassion once he hears the true character of Lieutenant Colonel Roger Evans," Travis told Rosie that morning before they left the house in separate cars. "I know a few things about Brooks' own family circumstances. He lost a young teenage son to an overdose of cocaine. Apparently, the young man had also struggled with severe bouts of depression which he hid from the family. So, he self-medicated as many addicts do, and soon it was too late.

Brooks has been through a lot himself." After parking, Rosie entered the well-appointed building and arrived at the front reception desk.

"Good morning. I'm Dr. Klein. Attorney Gump is expecting me. Has he arrived yet?"

"Yes, Dr. Klein. He's in the conference room with Mrs. Evans and Mrs. Parrish. Would you care for something to drink?"

"Thank you. A cup of coffee would be great if it isn't too much trouble, Janet." Rosie had noticed the receptionist's nameplate.

"No trouble at all. Cream or sugar?"

"Just black, please."

Janet escorted Rosie to the conference room and returned quickly with her coffee. The logo of Gump & Gump was on the mug. Travis' father had founded the firm and still kept a small, discreet office in the back, overlooking a duck pond and sparkling fountain. An exit door allowed the elderly gentleman the freedom to sit outside at one of the staff picnic tables, take in the view, and breathe fresh air once in a while. After years of smoking Cuban cigars, his lungs were said to be less than fifty percent functional. Most weekday mornings, during seasons of mild temperatures and bright, blue skies, the elderly attorney could often be seen out there enjoying the Dayton Daily News sports section with a cup of coffee.

"Welcome, Dr. Klein. Please have a seat. I'd like you to meet Randy's mother, Jackie Evans, and his grandmother, Noni Parrish," Travis said.

"Thank you. I've just met your son earlier this morning and found him to be an exceptional young man despite the current circumstances." Rosie scooted her chair in and took a sip of coffee. Then she took out a small tape recorder. "Do you mind if I tape our meeting? I'll be leaving town this afternoon and would like to record your thoughts and version of the events to review later."

"That's fine with us, Dr. Klein," Randy's mother, Jackie, said.

"Ladies, if you will excuse me, I'm going to leave the three of you and head downtown with Randy's clothes," Travis said. "Feel free to stay and talk as long as you like. Later today, Dr. Klein and I will compare notes and get back to you. This afternoon, I'll be able to let you know what the judge and prosecutor decide. Judge Clark has been a juvenile court judge for many years. You can be sure he has seen similar cases over time and has a lot to say about end results and the release of young people 'back to the streets,' as we say.

"Whatever sentence he imposes will focus on rehabilitation primarily directed at education and training. It's less likely for a young man like Randy to commit future crimes as an adult if he enters society with an education and work skills. The other aspect of rehab is to ensure his attitudes, beliefs, and abilities will abide by society's rules."

"Thank you, Mr. Gump. I can't tell you how much we appreciate what you just described. If I understand you then, they won't be locking Randy up and just throwing away the key, right?" Mrs. Evans asked with some hope in her eyes.

"That's correct. However, his background will likely determine the degree of security he will require. They will assign him a location as close by as possible for visitation purposes, but they will also consider how restrictive his environment needs to be. That's where Dr. Klein's evaluation and recommendations will factor into the judge's determination. You do know, he won't be out on bond, nor released on probation with community service."

"Yes, we do," Mrs. Evans said. "We realize he's committed a terrible crime even though he did it for my protection, and his sister's. He wasn't thinking of himself or his future. I only wish I could have stopped him. I had no idea the rifle was under Roger's bed and truly no idea Randy could resort to such an act. He has never been aggressive or mean. He was the kid who always stood up to bullies.

Mrs. Evans covered her face with her hands and attempted to maintain control. Her breathing was rapid but irregular, and her skin appeared pale and clammy. Her mother, Mrs. Parrish, removed the cap from a bottle of water and passed it over to her daughter with a tissue .

"Okay, then. Thank you for sharing that information, Mrs. Evans. I'm heading to my meeting with Attorney Wright." As Travis was leaving, Janet entered with a fresh pot of coffee.

"Can I top off your coffee, Dr. Klein and ladies?"

Janet asked. "Is there anything else I can get you?"

"Thank you. I believe we're fine. We appreciate your kindness," Rosie said as Janet poured fresh, hot coffee into Rosie's Gump & Gump mug. Then she left and quietly closed the door on her way out.

"My questions to you both will be relatively brief. I would also like to stop by and see Susie on my way out of town. Is that possible?" Rosie asked.

"Absolutely. We left her with her best friend's mother so we could attend this meeting. She won't be returning to school for the time being. She may also want to add a few things about Randy that we aren't privy to. You know how kids are. They have their little secrets," Mrs. Evans said.

"Randy told me that he's been in the EDGE program. What does that consist of Mrs. Evans?"

"It's for exceptional students who have IQ's above 130. The school psychologist recommended Randy after testing him in the third grade. He has an IQ of 144. Though he's not gifted in athleticism, he is in all other areas, including music. We were supposed to go to Europe with a group of twenty-five seventh and eighth graders this July. Each year, four teachers plan a whistle stop tour of four countries in ten days. Twelve adults are allowed to accompany the group. I was to be one of the twelve. We're not the chaperones, though. The teachers do the wake-up calls and supervision. We just show up on the bus.

"The planning has been going on all year. I hated the idea of leaving Susie behind with her father, but she is too young to participate. I thought it was important for Randy to have this opportunity, and surprisingly, his father agreed. I guess he wanted free time away from me. He never needed me other than for appearance-sake anyway. I think he only married me because he believed it would take him further in the military, you know, if he was a married man. In his opinion, this has proven to be true," Jackie explained in a bitter tone.

"I've been wanting a divorce and was prepared to keep Susie, if her nasty father agreed. So far, he was non-committal. It's not as if he would take her places and enjoy her company one-on-one. He was being arrogant," Jackie Evens said.

"There was no love lost for our side of the family," Grandma Parrish said.

"Mrs. Evans, how did Randy handle his emotions in the past. Did he show anger inappropriately? Did he get into trouble at school? Did he use words or action mostly to show his feelings or attitudes?"

"Randy never acted up at school and certainly never acted out at home. His father would not tolerate any backtalk. He demanded respect. Lots of it. That meant you had to jump when he requested something of you. Randy never showed anger other than if his dad wasn't home and I reminded him of a chore his dad had requested. He shared his feelings openly when we were together. He knew he could say what wanted with me. His brother teased him unmercifully about it, and if their dad wasn't around, they would wrestle even though Roger tried not to hurt Randy. And the only laughter in our home occurred when their father was away." Mrs. Evans showed a small smile for the first time in the interview.

"I remember something sweet, Dr. Klein," said Mrs. Parrish. "The boys taught Susie how to roller skate. On Saturday afternoons there was an open skate at the Kettering rink. They put a pillow in her elastic waist jeans to keep her from hurting herself if she fell. Each one took a hand and lifted her arms. She loved it. She still talks about it when I take her skating with her little friend, Diane. Susie loves those brothers. You'll hear about them when you talk to her this afternoon."

"I think Randy kept a journal under his mattress. I don't know how up to date it is, but I noticed it once when I was changing the sheets. He might have expressed his feelings there. I'll look for it and give it to you if you think it might help," Mrs. Evans said. "That would help, Mrs. Evans. One last topic before we adjourn. Tell me about church activities or affiliations. Randy mentioned Pastor Kimble and Faircreek Christian Church.

"I'm ashamed to say I've not involved the kids or myself in church. We were transferred here, and I should have insisted, but I knew what my husband, Big Roger, would say. He often intimidated me with what he might do. Going to church was not one of his activities. Then, when my parents moved closer to us, it was the only issue I wanted to confront. "Basically, he didn't want us having personal gatherings with my parents. So, I met with my mom for coffee at a Starbucks near the school where I taught. My dad is self-employed so he would come over on days Big Roger was working. He would repair a faucet or patch drywall damaged by Big Roger's fist. It was assumed that I had hired someone to do it. Roger never knew it was my dad who did the work."

Mrs. Parrish had remained quiet, until now, but spoke next. "I knew the kids were involved with a youth group at Faircreek. Usually, Diane's father brought Randy and Susie home. On rare occasions, Susie spent the night with me, and I heard all about the exciting times she was enjoying at the church. It was sad they could never actually attend Sunday school or church on weekends. But I understand why my daughter wouldn't risk broaching that subject. I believe he wouldn't let her go places because he was afraid people would notice the bruises he left on Jackie and there might be questions. We've asked her to leave him for a long time now."

"Did Randy ever talk about his beliefs, Mrs. Evans?"

"No. But I did wonder where he developed an interest in southern gospel music. I would hear him listening to it on his radio in his room and even singing along. He taught himself to strum a guitar. That made four instruments Randy played, the piano or keyboard, tenor sax, and guitar."

"Where did you think he was on Friday nights?"
"I thought he was studying with Diane Chandler's brother, Charlie. They were both in EDGE and had to make up work they missed from Friday classes."

Rosie clicked off the tape recorder and said, "Well, ladies, I assume I will see you both at your house, Mrs. Evans. Does three-thirty work for you? Do you have art supplies? I would like to meet privately with Susie and have her draw something for me."

"Yes, we'll pick her up now. We do have art supplies. Susie can show you where they are. Thank you so much, Dr. Klein, for your interest in Randy's case."

Mrs. Parrish nodded in agreement and Rosie stood to shake both their hands.

***

Rosie rang the bell and was greeted by a cute, little girl, "Hi, there. I'm Dr. Rosie. You must be Susie," Rosie said.

"Yes, I'm Susie and my mom told me you were coming. Come in and I can show you my room," said Susie enthusiastically.

Rosie followed Susie upstairs and into a bedroom with stuffed animals and dolls on the canopy bed, and on the top of her dresser. Susie sat in a chair at a small, round table. Rosie took a seat in another little chair across from her,

"Do you like to draw with colored pencils? It looks like you have a lot of them."

"I do and I am pretty good at it," Susie said. "What do you want me to draw?"

"I would like you to fold the paper so there are six little squares. Then draw me a picture of six people you love, doing something they love to do," Rosie said.

"Okay. One person in each square. Can I have more than one person?" Susie asked.

"I'd rather you just draw one person for each square," Rosie answered.

"The first one is my mom. She's fixing supper. She wears an apron when she cooks." In the top row, Susie drew a small stick figure with long hair facing a stove."Great," Rosie said. "Who will be next?"

"My grandmother Noni is next. She likes to read to me. Can we both be in the picture?" asked Susie.

"Okay, since it's you," Rosie said.

"Now I'm going to draw Roger. He's my bigger brother and he is going to wear a football jersey with number nine on it and be holding a ball. I used to go to his football games, but he's joined the Marines, you know. I'm going to miss him." Susie's voice wavered.

"You do very nice work," Rosie said and patted Susie's hand to encourage her.

"Can I draw an animal? Randy loves dogs and he'll be next," Susie explained.

"Sure. I love animals too. I have a big, black dog named Jocko." "Can I include my friends?" Susie asked.

"Anyone you love is fine," Rosie said.

"Well, then, I'm drawing Diane and me roller skating. We love skating."

"Once space left," Rosie reminded her.

"I'm drawing myself praying. Jesus loves me and I'm praying for Randy. He did a bad thing, but he did it for a good reason," Susie explained.

"Can you tell me about it? Rosie asked.

"He shot our dad to protect my mom and me. Dad was very mean to Mom and sort of mean to me. He tried to make me think he was only spanking me for my own good, but I could never understand how it would help me." A tear trickled down Susie's cheek. She put the red pencil in the box and began gathering all the others. Then she said, "I'm not crying over my dad. I am crying over my brother, Randy. I already miss him." Susie rubbed both her eyes.

"I'm sorry, Susie. Is there anything else you want to tell me?"

"Just that I hope you can help the judge understand that Randy would never hurt anyone who didn't have it coming. I really need him at home to help me with my homework and play with me. He taught me to skate and ride a two-wheel bike and I figure when I grow up, he'll teach me to drive." Susie jumped up and gave Rosie a hug.

"Let's go down and see your mom, okay?" Rosie said."Can we show her my picture?"

"Of course," Rosie answered as she stood and took Susie's hand.

12

The Hearing

Travis looked at his watch as he approached the attorneys' conference room where he was meeting Brooks Wright to get his point of view on the Evans case. No sooner had he sat down than Brooks entered, apologizing for being late.

"No problem, Brooks. I just got here myself. I dropped clothes off to Randy Evans for the hearing," Travis said. He didn't mention that Randy had completed the homework for Rosie and given it to Douglas Bannister, the visitation officer. Officer Bannister had handed it to Travis so he could return it to Rosie. Now, he was eager to give Rosie the completed materials and hear her assessment.

"Before you ask," Brooks said, "I'm willing to stipulate that Randy Evans be tried as a juvenile, even though he premeditated the murder of his father."

"Thanks, Brooks. He has no prior history of violence or record of any kind. I think he acted as the lethal weapon of his mother. What are you recommending to Judge Clark?"

"I'll recommend he serve time until he ages out of juvie at age twenty-one. He needs to get an education to make it in society."

"I agree. I would also suggest he be placed where there is an opportunity to enroll in high school. He's a bright kid and doesn't need to settle for a GED. Some classes in his junior and senior years can be applied toward a college degree. That way he'll have an associate degree by the time he leaves the system. He's got the smarts to do it. Does that sit okay with you, Brooks?"

"Yes. Do you have documentation of his school performance and behavior, Travis?"

"Dr. Klein met with him this morning and she's investigating as we speak. He provided teachers' names and other adults who will support him. She'll submit a report to us. We can review it, make sure Judge Clark has read it, and discuss the findings at the sentencing hearing."

"Sounds good. Would you be willing to have me meet your client, with you present, of course?" Brooks asked.

"Absolutely. Just name a time and I'll make it happen," Travis said, shutting his briefcase and opening the conference room door.

A short time later, both men waited quietly in Judge Clark's chambers. They were seated in front of his desk with their own copies of the case file on their laps. Judge Clark entered and motioned for them to stay seated. This was to be a very informal meeting. For now, a brief discussion about the defendant's case would take place with the judge asking questions he needed to be answered before he set a sentencing date. Then they would adjourn to the courtroom and two deputies would bring Randy down to the front row where he would sit beside Travis. At that point, formality would be adhered to with the judge wearing his robe.

"Judge, I'm in agreement with Travis in regard to Randy Evans being tried as a juvenile with rehabilitation by means of education to be paramount."

"Yes, Judge, I am in the process of having a very competent, experienced psychologist evaluate Randy," responded Travis. "She's looking at his capabilities, emotional stability, and motivation. She'll submit a report to the three of us by next week. Her name is Dr. Rosie Klein."

"All right," the judge said. "Let's go to the courtroom so I can meet this young man. You'll make my job easier by cooperating with one another. My court reporter, Rylie Cooper, will make a formal record of the proceedings. You can request a transcript if you want. According to my docket, the sentencing can be held in three weeks."

"Thank you, Judge. I'll go meet my client. Also, I assume you won't permit bail, but I need to ask on his behalf."

"As much as I would like to do that, given the serious nature of his crime, I will decline a request for bail," Judge Clark answered.

As Travis entered the courtroom through the

judge's chamber doors, Randy was being escorted to his seat by Deputy Lee. Travis assumed his place as defense attorney beside Randy on the aisle to the left. Brooks Wright, as prosecuting attorney, stepped into the first row on the right across the aisle from Travis and Randy.

"All rise! The judge is in the courtroom," Bailiff Thomas Franklin intoned, and everyone stood.

"Would the attorney for the State of Ohio please address the Court?" the bailiff said in a deep, stern voice.

Attorney Wright stood and stepped to the podium directly in front of the judge's bench. "Your honor, the State is willing to stipulate that this defendant, Randy Evans, can be tried as a juvenile in the matter of The State of Ohio vs. Randy Evans."

"I assume the defense has no objection to that directive. Do you, Attorney Gump?" Judge Clark peered over the glasses perched upon his nose.

Travis stood and said, "No, your honor, the defense is in agreement with that decision."

"Mr. Randy Evans, do you know and understand the charges you are facing?" Judge Clark asked.

Randy stood as instructed by his lawyer. He cleared his throat, looked directly at the judge, and said, "Yes, Sir. I am being charged with premeditated murder of my father, sir."

"Are you satisfied with your legal representation?"

"Yes, your honor."

"Have you been apprised by your lawyer of the possible sentences for the crime for which you are charged?" Judge Clark asked. "If so, what are they?"

"Yes, sir, I have been told what sentences I face. If I'm tried as an adult, I could spend life in prison unless the charges are reduced, sir. If I am tried as a juvenile, I could be sentenced to Juvenile Detention until the age of twenty-one," Randy's voice remained firm.

The judge leaned toward Randy and asked, "Do you have anything else to say to the court at this time?"

"Actually, I do, sir." Randy looked at his attorney, seeking approval of his impulsive, unplanned decision to speak. "I am deeply sorry that I resorted to this terrible act and didn't come up with some other way to handle our family situation. I would never do it again. In a strange way, I miss my father." Randy's voice wavered and tears glistened in his eyes. It was a mature statement for such a young person, but, it was a serious crime he had committed which would affect the rest of his life.

"Thank you, Mr. Evans. Your candid response is noted and appreciated by the court. The deputies will return you to your pod. You will be notified as to the date of your sentencing, young man."

Randy turned away from the judge's bench and returned to his seat with his head down. Travis patted his knee as the bailiff said, "All rise."

Judge Clark left the courtroom and Officer Lee placed handcuffs on Randy's wrists, again.

"You did well, son, I'll be in touch with you soon," Travis said. Randy glanced back over his shoulder and nodded acknowledgment.

I should be pleased with the cooperation of Brooks Wright and Judge Clark, Travis thought. *But somehow, I can't shake the feelings of sadness and foreboding for Travis' future. Juvenile detention is a hard place to grow up.*

13

The Report and Findings

Arriving home later Monday evening, Rosie began reviewing Randy's paperwork in the quiet of their condo, with Jocko beneath her feet. His information sheet left no surprises, and basically agreed with information received from his mother and grandmother.

"Let's see, Jocko," Rosie rubbed her bare feet on Jocko's fluffy back as she flipped through Randy's materials. "Summer's coming, and I think I need to take you to the groomer for a trim. But, oh, how good your furry back feels on my tired tootsies."

Her phone rang. "Hi Rosie," Bucky said. "I checked my mail and am leaving my office now. Just called to see if you need anything at the grocery store. I know you have a busy day coming up, and I'm willing to make us a simple meal tonight with leftovers for tomorrow."

"How sweet of you. We don't need anything much. Surprise me. I'm propped up with Randy Evans' material and you're right, tomorrow will be a busy day. I thought I'd attack this material tonight. After my morning appointments, I plan to call Randy's favorite teacher, Mr. Serago, and his best friend, Charlie. If I'm lucky, I'll talk to his best friend's father, too. Those will be my character witnesses, I'm sure. What are your plans?"

"In the morning, I'm meeting with my realtor. She left a message saying she wants to show my place to a couple who has seen it once already. She's sure an offer will be made. I'm glad we decided to stay in your condo for now, aren't you, Rosie?"

"Absolutely. Moving my library and file cabinets to the Summerhill office was easy. That made it possible for both of us to use the third bedroom as an office. It's not like we're going to need it as a nursery," she laughed.

"Did I tell you that part of the reason I fell in love with you was because of your sense of humor?" Bucky reminded her.

After they hung up, Rosie began to look at the sentences Randy had completed. This exercise was a good look into a person's innermost thoughts and feelings.

- Today I feel…confused.
- I feel proud when…I do well in school.
- I could be perfectly happy if… I could be with my mother and grandma Noni, again.
- My dad gets mad when…I disagree with what he says about my mom.

- My mom gets mad when…I talk back to her.
- My idea of a perfect woman…is Joanie.
- Compared to most families, mine… is good but kind of crazy.
- I look forward to…going to college and being a lawyer.
- Most families I know…are happy but have their problems.
- I think that most mothers…don't get the love they deserve.
- It annoys me…to hear people who think they have problems.
- I sleep…very lightly at home.
- My chief worry…is dying in my sleep.
- I wish people…wouldn't hurt other people.
- My greatest ambition…is to achieve my goals.
- I am really afraid of …dying in my sleep.
- My mind…wanders from time to time.
- My looks…are fair enough for me.
- I feel proud of …how I was raised.
- I cannot understand what makes me…so angry at times.
- I regret….my childhood behavior.
- If I had my way…everything would be fine.
- My idea of a perfect man is …one who takes responsibility as a father.

- My favorite daydream is…talking to my mother and my girlfriend.
- If I could live my life over again I would…protect my family better.
- The thing I like to do best…is to protect and play my music.
- A lot of people have told me…I can make it if I want to.
- I hope…I never get divorced.
- I want to know…why my mom and dad can't be normal.
- People think…I am considerate and generous.
- People…need to be more patient.
- I get mad when…my big brother fights with me.
- Most brothers and sisters…argue a lot more than I do with mine.
- To me, homework …takes motivation and skill.

I'm kind of sorry I can't go over these answers with him, she thought. *I would like to explore his responses, such as why he would think his mother wasn't normal. Was it because she tolerated the abuse for so long or believed she somehow caused it?*

Rosie decided to ask Travis to discuss several of Randy's answers. *Along with why he didn't see his mother as normal, I want Travis to ask why Randy is afraid he might die in his sleep. Does he experience dreams to that effect? His regret was his childhood behavior. What does that entail? Doesn't he regret shooting his father? He makes no mention of that.*

Rosie's phone rang again just as Bucky came through the door. "Hi Ruth. Thank you for returning my call this evening. How was your day at the office? Anything I need to know before I get there in the morning?"

"Not really, Boss. It was a quiet day," Ruth said. "A fax came from Travis Gump with the witness statements, police reports, and paramedic reports. The only witness, Randy's mother, was present in the house but not in the room. She was sitting at the foot of the stairs and heard the shots as did a couple of neighbors sitting on their patio."

"Okay, thanks. I'll see you at nine. By the way, tomorrow, my client, Ashley likes cream for her coffee. Are we good on supplies?"

"Yes, boss lady. She also needs a ton of tissue which is sitting next to the loveseat," Ruthie added which brought a smile to Rosie as they said goodbye.

14

Checking References

Rosie waved at Ruth who was on the phone with the appointment book spread open. She effortlessly scheduled new group members, one of her many invaluable skills. Rosie poured herself a mug of steaming hot, black coffee, and opened the door to her inner office, balancing a full briefcase in one hand and coffee in the other.

Just then, her phone rang. Ruth would have answered if she hadn't already been engaged on another line. So, Rosie carefully placed the coffee on her desk and briefcase beside it, then picked up the phone.

"Good morning, Rosie Klein's office."

"Rosie! Good morning. No help today? It's Travis, and I'd recognize your voice anywhere. I have Randy's journal for you. His grandmother dropped it off earlier this morning."

"Hi Travis, that's great. My assistant is on the other line. But I'm glad you called.

"I haven't personally read any of his entries," Travis

said. "But I looked at his drawings and I must say, this young man communicated his feelings quite well in his pictures. Maybe he's as expressive in writing. You'll have to judge that. Oh, he also told me that he's writing a week's worth of thoughts for you. I'll overnight the journal to you, then fax his current writing later this week."

"That will be great, Travis. I'm looking forward to reviewing it. I've finished reading the material he filled out before the arraignment. The old journal and his seven-day journal should fill a lot more blanks than even finishing sentences did. Some of his answers left me with more questions."

"Well, that's all I have for you now. Hope your day goes well. When you return for the hearing, please feel free to stay with Stella and me. Bring Bucky and we'll enjoy a round of golf."

"Thank you. I'm not sure what my mother's plans are with her new husband. Staying with you will reduce any pressure she might feel to have us stay with them. You don't mind if we bring Jocko, do you? Mom doesn't have a fenced yard and he loved sprawling out on your pavement with the sun beaming down on him."

"It's fine to bring him. Our enclosed swimming pool is a great place for animals. We're keeping our son's golden retriever now while Devon is at law school. I'm pleased he's following in my footsteps."

His comment made Rosie think about Roger Evans who wanted his son to go into the Air Force the way he did. *Maybe fathers take great pride in being role models. But it certainly didn't work for the Evans family,* she thought.

"Thanks, Travis. Congratulations on your son's admittance to law school. On another note, you most likely aren't aware that Bucky isn't a serious golfer. He's only engaging in the sport because it's my passion. His background has always been team sports."

"Stella's a casual golfer too," Travis said. "The four of us should do simply fine. Besides, it's the nineteenth hole that lures us, right?" Travis laughed. Rosie hung up the phone with a more optimistic outlook on the day ahead. Between her morning clients and her afternoon clients, Ruth had scheduled several telephone conferences with her Randy Evans' references. It was going to be a full day.

The morning client visits went well. It was nearly noon when Rosie walked out to the reception area. "What should we do for lunch, Ruthie? Any thoughts?"

"Yes, boss lady. I thought I would call for a couple of chicken and cranberry salads from Bob Evans. I'll run over and pick them up. What dressing do you prefer today?"

"Hmm. I think I want the raspberry vinaigrette. Ask for a side order of blueberry muffins and I'll take them home for Bucky's breakfast tomorrow. Thanks, Ruth. I'm about to call Mr. Serago, Randy's favorite teacher. Just bring the salad to my office, okay?"

"Sure. By the way, what do you want to drink?" Ruth asked.

"A tall glass of ice water will hit the spot. I've had

enough coffee." Rosie returned to her office and shut the door. She sat in her leisure chair with a legal pad in her lap and dialed the number of Mr. Serago.

"Hello, Serago here."

"Mr. Serago? I'm Dr. Rosie Klein calling on behalf of my client Randy Evans. He was a student of yours. I'm sure you've heard about the trouble he's in, right?"

"Yes, of course, Dr. Klein. I'm more than happy to do what I can on behalf of that young man. He had such a bright future. His father was such an obstacle to Randy's hopes and dreams."

"Oh? In what way?"

"He limited Randy from participating in anything that didn't seem of value to Colonel Evans. He saw no value in the arts or field trips to historical sites. It stunned me that he was permitting Randy to go to Europe with us this summer. Mrs. Evans planned to accompany us if she could raise the funds as if the Colonel were hurting financially in any way. The kids had car washes and sold candy to pay for their airline tickets and hotels."

"Was Randy a good student, Mr. Serago?"

"Please call me 'Bob.' Yes, he was at the top of his class with two other classmates, both girls. You should have seen his father at Randy's eighth-grade graduation. He was like a bump on a log; showed very little support for Randy's accomplishments. At Randy's little league games, he stood and shouted, but it was ranting, not cheering. Do I sound disrespectful to the deceased?"

"I don't blame you for feeling the way you do. Any

other thoughts? Was he in clubs or the band?"

"He was in the EDGE program which functions much like a club. The kids are all good friends. His group started together in fourth grade. In middle school, they had an entire half-day together each Friday. I believe they did some community service work because I noticed a couple of small businesses donated to their travel expenses. The EDGE teacher, Mrs. Kern, would be more than happy to explain more to you as would the music teacher, Mrs. Hill. Randy's dad didn't know he was in the choir. Also, the middle school put on the play, "Annie" this year, and Randy played keyboard. He's a very talented young man. I think his grandmother bought the instruments he owned. I am almost positive that Randy didn't keep a keyboard at his house. He did manage to have a guitar. His saxophone was leased from Ace Music and again, his grandmother paid for that."

"Thank you very much, Bob. Do you have contact information for Mrs. Kern and Mrs. Hill?"

"Yes, I can fax them to your office along with a book report I think will interest you. I have kept it since Randy wrote it in the seventh grade. It really touched me, and I entered it in a contest for him. It ended up being posted in the Dayton Daily News. Oh, also, Randy was the editor of our middle school newsletter and wrote a column each month. What a great kid."

"Your input is extremely valuable. I look forward to your fax and will follow up with the teachers. If you have a chance, would you mind letting them know I'll be calling?"

"Certainly, Randy is fortunate to have your intervention in his case, Dr. Klein. Have a nice afternoon."

"Thank you for your time," Rosie said. "Enjoy your European trip."

By the time Rosie and Ruth finished lunch, a fax came through. "Sure enough," Rosie said, getting up from her chair. "Mr. Serago is sending the contact information for Randy Evans' teachers and a book report Randy wrote last year." She returned to the table with the faxed papers.

"I'd better call these teachers right away. School is already out for the summer, and I am guessing the teachers are only going to be there a few more days."

"Great idea," Ruth said. "It's likely they'll be cleaning out their rooms." Ruth picked up both plates and closed the door as she exited Rosie's office.

Rosie dialed Mrs. Kern's number but became confused when she heard: "Hello. This is Kaye Martin."

"Good afternoon. I may have the wrong number, I thought I was calling Mrs. Kern. My name is Rosie Klein."

"Oh, no, Dr. Klein, you have the correct number. I use 'Kern' at school, but over spring break I was married, and many staff members aren't aware of my new name," she explained. "I married Joanie Martin's uncle, John Martin."

"Well, congratulations, and just call me Rosie. I've recently married, too, six months ago, but haven't considered a name change yet. I was given your number by Mr. Serago and was hoping you would have a few minutes to discuss Randy Evans. I have been appointed by the court to evaluate him for sentencing."

"Yes, I've heard about his misfortune. I would be more than happy to talk with you Dr. Klein, I mean Rosie. Bob told me to expect your call. I am the director of EDGE here at the middle school. Randy has been with me since sixth grade. Our building serves sixth through eighth grade. I assume as a psychologist, you are aware that a child must score in the gifted range to qualify for an EDGE program.

"Randy qualified with an IQ of 144 when he was a little guy in the third grade. The program began in the fourth grade and included one period a day with the same teacher through fifth grade. Then they automatically entered the middle school program which involves a half-day on Friday. It's not a perfect set-up and kids complain about having to make up their Friday classwork before Monday. But they also love the program. And as I've just told you, the uncle of Randy's girlfriend, Joanie, is my new husband. We met at one of the car wash fundraisers. As for Randy, he's been such an asset to the program, always prepared and enthusiastic, always ready to assist other students, and has been completely involved in community volunteer work. He also volunteers to sing at the nursing home around holiday time. You are going to call Mrs. Hill, aren't you?"

"Yes, I'm contacting her as soon as we hang up. By the way, were you aware of the abusive environment in Randy's home?"

"Not really. But we did suspect something might be going on behind closed doors because his harsh military father was verbally abusive in public, and his body language projected hostility toward his son. There were times when I thought Mrs. Evans was dressed too conservatively. She wore turtlenecks and long-sleeved sweaters in warm weather and baseball caps that shielded her face. She never wore mid-length pants. It was as if she was hiding her body. Occasionally, we did see bruises on Randy's arms. If we asked him what happened, he always came up with an answer about a bike or skating accident. He and his little sister, Susie, went roller-skating with their older brother, Roger, occasionally. He was also protective of his mother to the extent that he would never talk about his father's abuse toward her."

"Well, that is all remarkably interesting.

Thank you for your input. I'll be preparing a report for the court. If anything, else comes to mind, please feel free to call me, or send me a fax. Randy had great things to say about his experience in EDGE."

"Everyone is so sad about this turn of events, Dr. Klein. If you want me to testify at his sentencing, let me know. Other teachers would be glad to write letters to the judge."

"Thank you. I'll pass along your information

to Randy's attorney, Mr. Gump. He'll contact you if he wants you at the sentencing hearing. And again, congratulations on your marriage." Rosie hung up with a smile.

Next, she dialed Mrs. Hill's number which was answered with a cheerful hello. "This is Rosie Klein, Mrs. Hill. Are you able to speak to me for a few minutes? I am evaluating Randy Evans. I assume you knew I would be in touch."

"Yes, Dr. Klein. I'm so glad you called. This is such a tragedy. Randy had a great summer planned and a wonderful future in whatever endeavor he selected."

"How do you know Randy?"

"He's in the school choir and participates in our semi-annual musicals. He could have had the male lead of Daddy Warbucks in "Annie," but we needed him on the keyboard. No other student could master the pieces, but he did. There were five performances. His mother was in the first row for every performance. She also helped with actors' make-up. They were both going to Europe with our group this summer until the tragedy happened. It's all so sad."

"Other than his talent, what else can you tell me about Randy?"

"He was very encouraging to other musicians who weren't as talented or experienced. He never was late or missed a practice unless his father prevented him from returning to school. When we neared the dates of performances, we used the stage later in the afternoon.

On Saturday mornings, we sponsored car washes to raise money for the European trip. Randy was a hard worker. If Colonel Evans were irritated with Randy or Mrs. Evans, he would manufacture excuses to keep him home. Chores, transportation, babysitting his sister, etcetera."

"Did Randy ever tell you that his mother was being abused or that his father doled out corporal punishment?"

"No. But we could see it for ourselves. Mrs. Evans would wear sunglasses indoors to camouflage black eyes. Randy would be quiet and not engage in humor with his classmates."

"Was he aggressive?"

"Absolutely not. You should have seen him wheeling little old people down to the dining room at nursing homes. They knew him by name. We sang three times a year. Christmas, Easter, and Mothers' Day."

"All of this is very helpful, Mrs. Hill. Thank you for your time. If Attorney Gump needs any more information, he'll be in touch."

"You are quite welcome, Dr. Klein. I hope Randy can continue his education and pursue his dreams when he gets out."

Rosie was suddenly tired. Sad for an otherwise outstanding young person who was caught in a legal bind. She put her notepad aside. The picture of this young man was clear. She picked up his journal and began to leaf through it. She knew what everyone thought of Randy and now needed to see what he thought of himself, and his circumstances.

Rosie's phone buzzed. "Rosie, there's a young lady on the phone who desperately wants to speak to you. Do you want to pick it up?" Ruth asked.

"Interesting. I'll take the call."

Rosie pushed line two. "Hello, this is Doctor Klein."

"Doctor Klein, this is Joanie Martin. I'm Randy's girlfriend. I need to tell you what a wonderful guy he is. He's smart, talented, and kind to everyone."

"Why, thank you for calling, Joanie. I've heard so much about you, too, from Randy. I guess the most helpful thing for us to talk about is what you knew about his father."

"His father was mean and spiteful. Randy and I met at the library on Saturday mornings to make up class assignments for Friday classes. You probably heard that we were in EDGE. Right?"

"Yes, Joanie. I did know that."

"Well, there were times Randy would be an hour late or not show up at all. His dad would come up with chores to deliberately interfere with our plans."

"Did you see bruises or other evidence that Randy was being beaten?"

"In the summer, when we went swimming, I could see bruises on his lower back and upper legs. He kept his tee-shirt on when we were with other kids. He didn't want to talk about it. He would get choked up if I asked what happened."

"All that's important information, Joanie. Is there more?"

"Just that I can understand about what happened. His father was a horrible man, Dr. Klein. Randy wouldn't have done this if he hadn't been driven to it by his father."

"I understand your feelings, Joanie, and want to thank you for calling. Once Randy is placed in a facility, you might be able to visit him. Would your family be opposed to that?"

"Oh, my gosh, no! They love Randy. Believe me, they will drive me. If they can't, my new Aunt Kaye will do it. Let him know, okay? Please tell him I'm thinking about him every day."

"I will do that. Feel free to call me at any time."

"Okay, Dr. Klein. Bye."

"Bye, Joanie." *No doubt about it, Randy was a good kid,* she thought. *Sometimes, life just gets in the way.*

More about Joanie's Counseling:

Joanie was a year ahead of Randy in high school and looking forward to them both attending college together once he graduated high school and became a freshman. When Randy was convicted of manslaughter and subsequent incarceration, she was devastated. It seemed too big a burden for a high schooler to carry, but she couldn't help her feelings for him.

After three agonizing months of no contact and severe depression, she began individual counseling with Dr. Sherri Bernhardt, a private psychiatrist referred by her high school counselor.

Joanie recognized that Randy was insecure and, through therapy, came to realize how controlling he was in their relationship even at his young age. Yet, she believed Randy loved her, and she loved him.

One incident that she remembered had left her feeling confused and extremely intimidated which she shared with Dr. Sherri. It happened when Joanie had knit Randy a blue and white striped, crew neck, sweater which he seemed to love. Although he was still in junior high then, they rode the same school bus together. On that particular day, after it was posted that she had made the freshman cheerleading team, she couldn't wait to share the news with him. As they were about to board the bus after school, she excitedly told him about making the team. He stopped and removed the sweater and threw it at her.

"Now that you have what you want, you don't need me," he had yelled and stomped away, not boarding the bus for home.

When Joanie told Dr. Sherri about the incident, she admitted to being speechless, not knowing what she had done wrong.

"When he went to juvie, I still loved him and hoped to visit him every other weekend," she said, perhaps more after getting her driver's license.

"Do you plan to wait seven years for him to get out of juvenile detention?" Dr. Sherri had asked her.

"I do," Joanie had replied. By then, she would

have a bachelor's degree and could support them until he could get on his feet. Dr. Sherri tried counseling her, but to no avail.

As Joanie continued in therapy, however, she became stronger, emotionally less fragile, yet kept to her promise of visiting Randy as often as she could. When she received her driver's license, her parents gave her a used Honda Accord. They thought it was big enough to protect her in the event of an unavoidable fender bender. However, they did not allow her to drive two hours by herself to visit Randy. This, along with school activities, created tension in their relationship and Joanie began writing more often to compensate for her absence.

As her therapy proceeded from weekly, during the first year, to every other week, she and Dr. Sherri agreed to go back to weekly sessions due to Joanie's feelings of guilt. She felt she was betraying Randy by going to homecomings and proms, even though she attended with friends rather than with dates. She even felt guilty missing a visitation because of having to take SAT tests, the driver's test, and even church camp where she felt most at peace. The first three years she had been a camper and the next two years she served as a cabin counselor.

As the years passed, Joanie felt committed to Randy and never wavered in proclaiming her love for him. Dr. Sherri could not completely understand this young girl's devotion.

15

Gathering Evidence

Rosie stepped out of her office and approached the reception area. She sat in a chair beside Ruth's desk positioned to help new clients with intake paperwork. Rosie had always insisted on a warm, encouraging environment to put new clients at ease.

"Boss lady, you must have a stiff neck from holding the phone to your ear so long. That young man has a lot of people supporting him, doesn't he?"

"Yes, he does."

"I know how thorough a job you do to evaluate a defendant and prepare your findings, Rosie. It must be difficult to be involved with a court case over 150 miles from home."

"Yes, it is," Rosie said quietly rubbing her forehead. She still held her coffee cup and looked at it, but her mind was miles away. "Travis Gump is overnighting Randy's journal to us. Next week he'll send the seven-day journal I asked Randy to keep for me."

"I'll watch for it," Ruthie said. "Are you done with your phone consults?"

"No. I have one more important call to make. I want to speak to Gary Chandler, the father of Randy's best friend. Maybe I'll talk to his friend, Charley, too. They both spent a lot of time with Randy and will definitely fill in some blanks." Rosie stood up, put her coffee cup down on the desk, stretched her arms above her head, and sighed. Then, she picked up her cup, nodded with a smile, and walked back to her office to dial Gary Chandler's number. An adult male voice answered the phone on the second ring.   "Hello?"

"Hi, this is Dr. Rosie Klein. Are you Mr. Chandler?"

"I am. How can I help you?"

"I'm the psychologist appointed by the court to evaluate Randy Evans. I understand your son is his best friend," she said over the phone.

"I'm extremely happy you called," he said. "We've been frantic over Randy's arrest. We cannot understand how this happened. He's such a good kid!"

"Well, I can tell you that he's being held in the Greene County Juvenile Detention Center and will likely be charged as a juvenile. The prosecutor agreed to that as did the judge. He has a fine attorney, not a public defender, and if you would like to speak to him, he would be glad to talk to you. I'm in Toledo now, but I met with Randy in detention, and am preparing a report with recommendations. My findings are a result of my interviews with Randy and the information gathered from people like yourself. I've spoken to his teachers and have been told that Randy is very bright and well-rounded."

"He's a fine young man," Chandler said. "He and my son have a close relationship. They were going to Europe with the teachers this summer. Now, my son, Charlie, has little interest in going. My wife is . . . or *was*, also going. Obviously, Mrs. Evans will not be participating now. How is she doing?"

"I don't know. She and her mother met with me in Attorney Gump's office before I left town. They had nothing but praise for you and Charlie."

"I can tell you this. Randy has never shown any violent outbursts or threats of violence to resolve conflict. The only time I ever saw evidence of any potential for aggression was when he stepped in to stop a bully from punching and shoving a younger, smaller kid. That was in the gym at church. He stepped between them, extended his arms with clenched fists, and told the bully he never wanted to see the kid within six feet of Sammy again.

Then Randy said: "For now, an apology is called for." The kid backed up, looked at Sammy, and told him: 'I didn't mean nothin'. Just kidding.' Randy told him: 'Apology accepted. Now get out of here.'"

"That was brave of him to intervene in front of everybody. Was Randy bigger than the bully?"

"About the same size, but I don't think it would have mattered how big the kid was, Dr. Klein," Mr. Chandler laughed.

"Did you know Colonel Evans, as he liked to be addressed?"

"No, I never met him. I can't understand how a father could not be proud of a son like Randy. He's talented, well-rounded, and a gentleman. Pastor Kimble and I have had many talks about how to approach Colonel Evans, but we never did it. Now we're left with regrets." Gary's voice trailed off.

"Would you like to talk to Charlie?" he asked. "He's very upset but wants to talk to you, Dr. Klein."

"Yes. I would like to do that."

"I'll put him on the phone." Within a minute, a younger voice came on the line.

"Hello, this is Charlie."

"Hello, Charlie. I'm Dr, Klein and I've met your friend, Randy. He said you're the best friend he could have and hopes you and your family are not disappointed in him."

"Disappointed! No way! I think his dad had it coming. Randy tried to be tough, but sometimes he broke down and cried at our house. It used to kill my mom that his mom would put up with so much abuse and wouldn't leave his father. Randy's mom and his sister are close to my family, but not with Colonel Evans. When I saw him at a game, he even wanted *me* to call him 'Colonel.' Randy and I had great plans to room together on our European trip. Now our summer is ruined, maybe even Randy's life. He never would have shot his dad if there had been another choice. His father must have really scared him for Randy to have pulled the trigger."

"Did Randy ever tell you he planned to shoot his father when his big brother left home?"

"No, not a word and we talked about everything, Dr. Klein. You probably know what fourteen-year-old boys talk about, right? Girls, sports, school, weekends, little sisters." Charlie mustered a laugh. "You might find out more about his dad from my mother. Women talk about different things."

"I think your mother wrote a statement for the arresting officers. She told them she knew Colonel Evans abused Mrs. Evans when he was frustrated or drinking heavily."

"I believe that. I've heard him in action. What a dirt-mouth. Once, we were upstairs in Randy's room and it sounded like he was swearing and smashing glasses in the kitchen below us."

"What did you do?"

"Randy turned the music louder. A couple of minutes later, we heard the door slam and the car engine start, so we thought he left."

"Did you and Randy talk about it?"

"No. Randy didn't like to get into it. About an hour later my dad picked me up. I didn't mention it because I didn't want my dad to stop me from going over to Randy's."

"Thank you, Charlie. Once Randy is settled, you'll be able to visit him. Okay?"

"Okay. Tell him I think he's a great friend." Charlie's voice sounded a little hoarse as he said goodbye and hung up.

Rosie headed for the coffee pot. Ruth had put on a fresh pot to help them through a busy afternoon. Rosie began settling down to read Randy's journal but decided to touch base with Bucky first. He answered on the second ring.

"Hi, husband. Just thought I'd call to tell you how much I appreciate your simple cooking. In my opinion, the way you season food is like a gourmet chef. But you cook like you're feeding an army."

"Yup," Bucky said. "That's how you get left-overs for lunch and dinner. I plan ahead."

"Well, Woman, it is my pleasure to serve you. My stressors haven't kicked in yet because my new position doesn't officially begin until August. Maybe once this case is behind you, we can spend a few days in Hilton Head. How do you feel about that?"

"Actually, I will have just a few days off. I am expecting a call from Attorney Singer. You remember him, right? He has a new case for me. Maybe I can review materials under a beach umbrella with you by my side."

"Sounds like a plan. You have friends on the Island to connect with, right?"

"I do, friends and family actually. And we can play a couple of my favorite golf courses, walk on the pier, watch the sunset, have lunch in Savannah on the way home."

"You can tell me about your new case tonight. I'm heading over to the fieldhouse to talk to some of the baseball players who are on campus for summer school. See ya about 6:00."

"I'll probably walk Jocko before you get home. I need some fresh air to clear my head. I'm about to read Randy's journal. Love ya."

"Love you too. Bye."

16

Follow-up with Randy

"Good morning, Randy." Rosie was already seated at the table. She glanced up as the officer released Randy's handcuffs and beckoned him to sit down across from her. "I'm so glad we're able to meet one more time prior to your hearing this afternoon."

"Me, too, Dr. Klein. It's been a long three weeks. I'm anxious to get this over," Randy said as he took a seat in the small visitation room.

"Attorney Gump asked me to help you prepare something to say to the judge before he announces your sentence. Do you want to say something?"

"Yes, definitely," Randy said. 'I've had all these weeks to think about it. So, I've written something and rehearsed it, too. Not like I've had much else to do. It's pretty boring around here. We go into the enclosed yard for thirty minutes in the morning and thirty minutes in the afternoon. They have basketball hoops, but I can't say I've joined in much. I just like being outside. I sure miss my friends, though, and wish I could see Joanie.

Wonder what she thinks of me, now. There are girls here, but they look and talk tough. None of them can compare with her. Joanie's really gentle. I appreciate everything so much more now."

"I understand the judge will bind you over to a facility not too far from here. It's likely that Joanie and your family will be able to visit once in a while."

"That would be amazing, Dr. Klein. If you want to hear my speech, I'd like to read it to you. It's kind of like what I said at the arraignment."

"I would love to hear it. Go ahead and read it to me, Randy. This may be the most valuable performance of your life."

"Okay, maybe, all those plays I've been in were meant to prepare me for this. I remember one Bible story about Esther. Her uncle told her that her life journey was meant to prepare her for all the troubles she faced, too. Of course, she was meant to save the lives of the Jewish people. Mine is just to save me," Randy said. "That's a big difference."

"But no less important, Randy. Every person is important in the eyes of God," Rosie said. "I take it you participated in more than sports at the church on Friday nights, right?"

"Before we played basketball, we gathered in a circle and Pastor Kimble opened with prayer. Then we sat and he told us short Bible stories to help guide our behavior and thoughts for the coming week."

"That sounds like a great opportunity for kids to learn the value of putting other people first and being resistant to the world's temptations. Go ahead and read to me."

He stood and cleared his throat: "Your Honor. I am Randy Evans and I appreciate the chance to speak to you this afternoon. I am not here to beg for leniency. Being tried as a juvenile is more than I deserve. For that, I thank you.

"What I would like to ask is that you, the court, consider placing me where I can be most useful to other inmates. Not to brag, sir, but I believe I have a lot to offer in the way of tutoring or teaching other kids. Although I've just graduated from eighth grade, my academic performance is equivalent to what most kids receive in their junior year. I want to give back, to offer a tangible way of expressing how sorry I am for what I have done.

"In the past, I've been involved in community service and, along with my school choir, have entertained residents of nursing homes and patients in hospitals. I've enjoyed being in those activities and want to offer my services in any way you see as helpful.

"I have no excuse for shooting my father. There is no sense in sharing our family secrets with you since you have received all the details from my teachers, pastor, family, and friends. I must admit that my emotional maturity is not equal to my academic accomplishments or musical ability. Otherwise, I would have taken a different path to somehow free my mother and sister from my father's wrath. Resources were available to me, but my mind could not grasp how to approach those who loved our family.

"I apologize to everyone I have hurt by my

impulsive decision and hope my story might help someone think ahead and prevent them from taking violent action as I did. Thank you."

Imagine, Rosie thought, *this kid is only fourteen years old.*

17

Eleven Years Later

An older, mature Randy Evans sat on a bench outside his high-rise office building eating lunch in the garden area. On this day, he was thinking about the seven years he'd spent in juvenile detention for shooting his father.

I won't say time went fast, he thought, *but who would believe it's been four years already since I got out. Geez, what a place that was. . . like doing hard time. Not everything was horrible, though, if you don't count the time the guards beat me for stealing a phone I didn't steal. But how could I admit to something I didn't do? I was set up by the older guys. Still, they threw me in solitary for three days with only water and a donut for breakfast and bologna sandwiches for dinner. No lunch. Speaking of inmates. The older guys made fun of me because I had no tattoos and wouldn't join a gang. But they didn't know my dad, the Colonel. They only respected the fact that I'd killed him. What screwed up thinking. Little did they know what he would have done if I'd come home with a tattoo. Whew. And I remember the bigger guys who made me get them candy and chips from the commissary. One thing my mother did, which helped a lot, was to keep an account for me there.*

On the positive side, I earned my high school diploma, and an associate degree in Graphic Arts. Joanie was always there for me. She really helped me get through it all, even if it was through snail mail. I looked forward to every letter from her and really couldn't wait for her visits every other weekend. She kept me up to speed on everything going on in town and with our friends as they all went through high school. Even though it was disappointing she couldn't visit more often. But, as she said, it was a long drive, and visitation periods were only two hours. Once a month, she could afford a motel and saw me two days in a row. When the weather was hazardous, she had to cancel, sometimes at the last minute, which was always disappointing. I even have to admit, those times made me angry.

Our wedding was pretty cool. Roger came home from Hilton Head to stand up for me, and my little sister, Susie, who isn't little anymore, was Joanie's maid of honor. Mom, Grandma Noni, and Grandpa Adam were there. Oh, yeah, Mom's new husband sat between them. I'm glad she has him, If he makes her happy, I guess that's what counts. I don't really resent all the traveling they did while I was locked up. It meant she couldn't come and see me, yeah, but, she deserved happiness after all the old colonel put her through.

I was always happy for the Christmas visits which included my whole family for two and a half happy hours. They were allowed to bring food into the visitation hall, and Grandma usually brought ham and scalloped potatoes, my favorites. I couldn't believe it when my new stepfather gave Joanie and me a late-model, red pick-up truck for our wedding. Of course, I'm the one who drives it since Joanie is mostly home with the kids. Besides, she doesn't need a car since she doesn't drive much. She pulls her little red Dayton Flyer wagon which is good enough for when she needs groceries or when she takes the kids to the park for play.

The kids love that wagon. It belonged to my grandpa and grandma. Noni saved it for my kids. It makes them feel like big shots, since it's the same color as my new truck. Otherwise, Joanie gets around just fine in our old, blue Volkswagen. Even though I don't like when she complains about it. She needs to learn how to make do.

Basically, life is good. It doesn't seem possible I just completed my internship at National Cash Register and am receiving a great salary with semi-annual bonuses. I love what I do. So, why do I get mad so easily? It's like a switch goes off in my head, and I can't control my words or actions.

I don't mean to take it out on Joanie. It's just that sometimes I have a tough day at work, and she doesn't seem to understand. Or when I lose at softball or at a basketball game. Those things are important! NCR's softball team relies on me; I'm their best pitcher. Our church's basketball team isn't bad either. When we play other churches, I have to remember not to lose my temper in the middle of the game. The pastor would bench me if he thought it could cost our team the game. He's a great mentor and role model. But sometimes, I just can't focus. It amazes me how easily the congregation welcomed me back after all those years locked up.

Later that afternoon, Randy arrived home to a house that was dark and locked.

Hmm, wonder where Joanie is? There was no note on the counter. Where could everybody be at six o'clock? There was no smell of a casserole or anything baking in the oven. Just then the phone in the dining room nook rang,

"Hello?" Randy answered. He assumed it was Joanie calling to tell him where she was, and what she was doing.

"Mr. Evans?" a strange voice asked. "This is Mrs. Mello, director of the preschool wondering when your wife is picking up Eric and Todd. You know there's a charge for every five minutes you're late after six o'clock, and we're getting ready to close."

"Mrs. Mello, I have no idea where Joanie is or why she didn't pick up the boys. She usually gets them after they play outside, no later than five-fifteen, right?"

"I agree with you. She didn't inform us this morning that she would be late, either. Can you get here as soon as possible? Everyone else is gone, and I need to lock up the facility."

"Of course, I'm only twelve minutes away. Be right there." Randy felt his heart rate increase and his feelings fluctuate between anger and worry. What in the world happened to prevent her from getting the kids? If she knew she couldn't get there, for whatever reason, she could have arranged for my grandma Noni to pick up the boys, or her best friend, Shannon.

Randy grabbed his keys and jogged out to the truck. There would be time later for him to figure out the 'why and what for' after he got his kids home and fed. But her excuse had better be good, he thought, feeling slow anger begin to simmer inside.

Once the kids were fed packaged mac n' cheese and hotdogs, he told them to watch cartoons. Then, he called his grandmother. "Hi, Grandma. Have you heard from Joanie today? She didn't pick the kids up. The school called and I just got them home."

"No, Randy. I haven't seen or heard from her since Bible study on Tuesday morning. When did you see her last?"

"She packed my lunch and kissed me good-bye this morning. Nothing was said about needing transportation for Eric and Todd."

"Do you need me to come over and watch them? That's very out of character for her not to be responsible like that. What do you plan to do?" Noni's voice had a caring tone.

"I'll call her friend, Shannon, and wait awhile. No need for you to come over now. If she had car trouble, I should hear from her soon. I can't imagine what else it could be." Randy said.

Later, Randy let Champ in the back door and

threw some dry dog food into his dish before refreshing his water. Then he popped open a beer and sat in his lounge chair. He left his shoes on in the event Joanie called needing assistance. The boys were on the floor engrossed in cartoons. Finished with dinner, Champ plopped down between them on the carpet. The clock showed seven p.m.

The boys will need a bath soon, he thought. On second thought, one night without a bath won't hurt. Nobody at school will notice in the morning. He recalled how Joanie always kept their hair clean and nails clipped. Their outfits for the entire week were already hanging in the closet. She's a good mom, Randy thought.

The boys shared a bedroom and used the third one as a playroom. Whenever they had a really big fight, the boys would beg to have the bunkbeds disassembled and put into their own separate bedrooms. Sometimes Randy worried about the aggression he saw in both boys. The older one, Eric, would pound on his little brother until he was physically stopped. If Toddy wanted a toy and his brother wouldn't share it, the little brother would throw objects at his big brother's head then run crying to his mother.

"Hello, Shannon. This is Randy. Have you seen Joanie today?"

"Hi, Randy. No. Why?"

"Well, she didn't pick the boys up from preschool today, and hasn't left a note to say where she's gone. I figured my grandmother, or you, would have been in contact with her or know what she had planned for today. The school called, and I picked Eric and Todd up after six. Now it's seven, and I still don't know what's going on."

"Well, I was at the park with them yesterday," Shannon said, "but, sorry, I don't know what to think. It's hard to believe she would not get the boys. You know how she structures her days around getting you off to work and transporting the kids. I'll come over and watch the boys. Maybe you could drive around your normal places looking for her. You could try the grocery, pharmacy, church, the gym, the playground at the park, the library, and the bookstore."

"I hate to bring you out so late, Shannon, but I guess I have no choice if you genuinely want to come over."

"Of course. Be there in twenty minutes. Don't worry. There must be an explanation."

Randy called the emergency rooms of three local hospitals while he waited for Shannon. "Have you had a patient today by the name of Joanie Evans? This is her husband, Randy, and I have permission to receive this information."

"One moment, sir. Please stay on the line and I'll check with admissions." The woman sounded compassionate and was back within a short time.

"Hello, sir? No, there's no record of a Joanie Evans being transported here or walking in on her own. Sorry."

The same message was repeated to Randy from all three major hospitals. He didn't know whether to think it was good news or bad. If she's had a medical emergency, or is seriously ill, she would have been treated or admitted by now, he thought. Now he really began to worry.

Shannon knocked on the door and Randy, phone in hand, waved her inside. He held his hand over the receiver. "I'm calling the police. She was not treated at any local hospital. I plan to explain that she's missing." Just then, a sheriff's deputy answered the call. "Sir, I need to report my wife missing." He asked for all the basic information, then said another deputy would be over right away.

"I don't know, Shannon. I just don't know." Randy said. "Maybe it's too soon to report Joanie missing. Don't they usually want you to wait twenty-four hours?" Randy asked, answering his own question. "But that seems like it would only make it more difficult to find her, don't you think?"

"You're right to do it now," Shannon said. "It's so unlike Joanie. I don't want to assume the worst but, the sooner they start looking, the more likely she'll be found. I don't mean to scare you, Randy, but I'm not saying anything you probably aren't already thinking." The doorbell rang followed by three quick, firm knocks. Randy opened it to a deputy and another man in plain clothes standing there.

"I'm Detective Harris. Are you Randy Evans, and did you call to report your wife missing?"

"Yes, sir. I'm Randy. I really appreciate your quick response. Care to sit down?"

Harris removed his hat, took a small notebook from his pocket and sat across from Randy. Shannon remained standing nearby as the deputy looked around. Detective Harris glanced at Shannon. She quickly explained who she was and what she was doing there. She also explained what Randy had done in calling the hospitals. Harris nodded his head and asked for Shannon's phone number. She recited it as he scribbled it down.

"When did you discover your wife missing, Mr. Evans?"

"Actually when the pre-school director called at six o'clock to say she had not picked the kids up; two boys, ages three and two. It's totally unlike Joanie to do something like that. She's very responsible and structures her days around the boys and me." Randy cleared his throat. Detective Harris did not make eye contact, just kept jotting down details. Shannon sat down on an ottoman in front of a wingback chair.

"I'll put out an all-points bulletin, Mr. Evans. Can you describe her car and the license plate number, please."

"It's a dark blue, two-door VW. The plate reads JE2000."

"I'll need to know the places your wife frequents and particularly what her Wednesday routine entails. Have you noticed if any of her belongings are missing or there is any sign of forced entry?"

"You know, I never had time to look. First, I fed the kids, then put them to bed. Nothing in the kitchen seems out of place and our dog, Champ, isn't acting strange in any way. He would bark loudly if an intruder attempted to break in. Actually, Joanie hates leaving the dog home alone, and even takes him with her on errands. So, the fact that he's here makes me wonder even more what's happened to her. I also just remembered that we might check at the preschool about the time she dropped them off this morning. There's a sign-in sheet we can check."

"Okay, Mr. Evans. I'd like you to come down to the station first thing in the morning, assuming your wife isn't located by then. You'll talk to my partner, Gretchen Gunderson. She may have information to share by then and more questions for you."

"Of course. I'm more than willing to do whatever it takes to bring Joanie safely back home." Detective Harris closed his notebook, grabbed his hat, and rose to leave. He handed Shannon a card.

"Detective Gunderson is really good with this kind of case. She'll most likely want to talk to you as well."

"I'll be there. I've been Joanie's best friend since grade school. Thought I knew her inside out, but this is definitely not like her to just disappear."

"Shannon, if you don't mind staying here with the boys, I'd like to drive around those stores we talked about. I won't be gone long. The parking lots are well-lit. Maybe I'll spot her car," Randy said.

"Sure. I'll check on the boys and stay by the phone. You go, Randy."

Randy walked out with the two men. Shannon glanced around to see if there was anything that might give a hint to whatever happened to her friend. She looked in the dishwasher and noted two coffee cups. One had lipstick around the edge.

That's Joanie. She has to look her best even when she's dropping the kids off at school. But it's unlike her to put a cup in the dishwasher without wiping off the remnants of her lipstick, she thought. The coffee pot on the counter beside the microwave had at least two cups of brewed, black coffee still in it. Almost as if Joanie planned to drink another cup after taking the boys to pre-school. Shannon glanced toward the utility room off the kitchen and noticed a laundry basket of light-colored clothes sitting on the floor in front of the washing machine. She opened the lid and saw a wet load of dark jeans in the bottom of the machine.

"Oh, my gosh," she said out loud. Joanie really did plan to return home. She would never have left wet clothes in the washer with another load ready to go. Besides, she wouldn't have left Champ in the yard all day. For the first time, Shannon became deeply worried about the well-being of her dear friend.

18

The Mystery Deepens

Shannon went upstairs and peeked into the boys' room. They were snuggled together on one bunk. *It's unlikely their father read to them or even kissed them good night with all that's going on,* she thought. *They look like they were trying to comfort one another without Mommy.* She quietly closed the door and turned on the light in the master bedroom. The bed was made, and the adjacent bathroom was in order with towels folded neatly on the racks.

Returning to the living room, Shannon plopped down in a chair beside the loveseat where her friend usually sat to read the newspaper or her Bible. The newspaper was still in its plastic wrap and the bookmark in her Bible was still on yesterday's proverb of the day. Shannon knew that Joanie read from her Bible as soon as she returned home from taking the kids to school. After that, the newspaper would wait until she finished her morning chores, which on this day, would have meant the laundry.

Whatever happened, it was early in the morning,

Shannon thought *before she really got a start on the day.*

Randy should be back any minute. She toyed with the idea of not mentioning the wet laundry. Otherwise, her inclination was to toss the clothes into the dryer. She stood up and walked into the laundry room. Opening the dryer door, she was shocked to find dry clothes inside. She knew in her heart that Joanie would not have allowed a load of dry clothes to sit and become wrinkled. Hangers were sitting on top of the dryer. Joanie had intended to hang the clothes and dry the load of darks. Something interrupted her after she dropped the boys off at school and before she read the paper or had a second cup of coffee. Or did she go somewhere after dropping off the boys instead of returning home? Would she have left the house after putting a load in the dryer and letting it run while she was gone? Not likely.

Shannon heard the garage door open. She quickly returned to her chair in the living room, hoping beyond hope that Randy would walk in with Joanie and her absence would be quickly explained. She made an instant decision to keep the details she had discovered to herself until she could meet with the police detective. What was her name? Oh, Gunderson. Gretchen Gunderson.

"Hi, Shannon. Nothing. Thanks so much for staying, but you should probably go home now. I'm sorry to have kept you this late. I looked everywhere but didn't find a thing. I can't believe this is happening."

Shannon saw Randy was close to tears.

"The police are on the case now, Randy, that's all you can do. Try to get some sleep. If they know anything, Officer Harris said they would call. Please call me if anything does happen, okay? Even if it's the middle of the night."

"I will. I called Grandma Noni while I was out; she'll help with the boys tomorrow. I'll get them to school, and she'll take it from there. They're given breakfast and lunch at school so all I have to do is get them dressed and drive them over to the school," Randy said.

"I knew Noni would help you. Since you lost your Grandpa Adam last year, helping with the boys has probably given her purpose. She must be worried sick about her grand-daughter-in-law."

Randy appeared exhausted and just nodded his head in agreement.

***

The following morning, Detective Gretchen Gunderson didn't recognize the caller ID and wondered why somebody was already calling at 7:30 a.m.

Ah, the day's gonna be busy, she thought while picking up the receiver.

"Good morning, Detective Gunderson."

"Good morning, Detective, this is Shannon Conrad. I met your partner at Randy Evans' house last night and he gave me your card."

"Yes, Shannon, how can I help?"

"I was told to call you if I had anything to talk

about. Well, I do. Can I come down to the precinct before Randy Evans gets there? I don't want him to know we've talked."

"How about if I swing by your place, Shannon. Are you available this morning?"

"Yes. My address is 667 Chipplegate Court. I'm on the corner of Marshall and Chipplegate."

"I know where that is and, actually, pass your corner on my way to work. I can be there in thirty minutes, if that works for you."

"That's wonderful. I'll have a pot of coffee on."

By the time Shannon took a quick shower and threw on a pair of jeans with a Wright State University tee shirt, the doorbell rang. Detective Gunderson stood on the front porch in street clothes. Shannon noticed she'd been driving an unmarked Honda Civic. This made Shannon feel comfortable in the event Randy might drive by her house. Not that she expected him to do so, but since he was searching for Joanie, anything was possible.

"Hi, Detective Gunderson. Come right in," Shannon said with a smile.

"Call me Gretchen. This morning I'm not on duty until eleven, but I'm glad to know you want to talk about your friend's disappearance."

"Would you like some coffee?"

"Just black, please." Gretchen took out her spiral notepad and sat on a stool at the kitchen bar.

"Well, last night, after Randy left to look in parking lots of stores that Joanie frequents, I began to look around the house. You have to know my friend to realize that what I saw was significant."

"That's interesting. Go on." Gretchen took a sip of her coffee and opened her notepad ready to write.

"Joanie is quite meticulous for a mother of two preschoolers and a rather sloppy husband, sorry to say. There were two coffee mugs in the dishwasher, but one had lipstick around the rim. Now, Gretchen, I've got to say that Joanie would *never* have put that mug in there without wiping the lipstick off. Then, I noticed wet coffee grounds in the coffee filter. Again, she would have dumped them if she was not planning to come back home after taking the kids to school."

"I see your point, Shannon," Gretchen said.

"That isn't all, by any means. I went up to check on the kids. They were sound asleep. Randy had put them to bed before he asked me to come over. But I saw their play clothes from yesterday still on the floor and in their bathroom, the toilet looked like it hadn't been flushed for a week. Not that Randy wasn't upset and all, but it looked like she hadn't been there for longer than a day. Nothing made sense.

"I've been friends with Joanie long before she had these kids and in all the times I have been there, clothes were always in the hamper and the toilet was flushed with the lid down. I honestly don't think Randy could have made all that mess in just a couple of hours."

"Uh-huh." Gretchen looked intrigued.

"Then, I went back downstairs and noticed a basket of dark clothes on the floor of the laundry room.

I opened the washing machine and saw another load of wet clothes. I opened the dryer and saw a load of dry clothes. If Joanie had just gone for a short trip and expected to be back home right away, she would have folded the dry clothes as soon as the dryer beeped, or not run it until she returned. She didn't ever want anything wrinkled. I think she intended to do the third load too, or it would have remained in the hamper upstairs." Shannon's voice was taking on a more concerned sound as she continued speaking.

"So, you're suspecting foul play at the house? Or, since you didn't want Randy to know what you saw, are you suspecting Randy?"

"Yes, I am suspecting Randy. I don't know that anything happened to her at the house, but I do wonder where her car is. Any luck with that, Gretchen?"

"I'm fairly confident her car has been found in the lot at a nearby park. It was locked and she wasn't inside, but her purse was there with no driver's license or identification in it."

"Are you sure it was hers?"

"By the description that Randy gave us, yes; but the real reason we know is that a bill with her name on it was found inside the purse."

"Oh, no, that's terrible! It means something horrible *has* happened to her. Why would her purse not have her driver's license unless someone was trying to cover up the facts? Joanie *never* drove without her license, trust me." Shannon put her head in her hands and began weeping.

Gretchen stood and put her arm around Shannon's shoulders to comfort her. "Think you can identify her purse? If so, I'd like you to come down to the precinct and look at it before it's sent to the evidence lab."

"I think I can. When are you seeing Randy? Does he know her car was found?"

"No, we haven't told him yet, but we will when he gets to the precinct. He knows my shift doesn't begin until eleven. We agreed to meet there at eleven-thirty, but I can go in early if you want to see the purse."

"I do if that isn't too much trouble for you. You probably had other plans for your morning."

"Not really. I went in early to catch up on paperwork. That's how I caught your call."

"Sorry about that, but I wanted you to hear my details before you spoke with Randy again. My husband watched our kids last night when I went over to Joanie's, and he just left to take them to pre-school. He knows how upset I am about my friend."

"It was good you contacted me. The information you've provided is extremely helpful. Why don't we head over there now, then, I'll drive you back here."

"Actually, I would appreciate that. My nerves are really on edge and maybe driving myself isn't a good idea. Thank you. I'll let you out the front door and come out through the garage."

***

"Good morning, Gretchen." Detective Harris strolled casually by her desk, setting down a full Starbucks cup of coffee on top of some papers. Gretchen looked up.

"Thanks, Butch. I could use another cup. It's been busy. The friend of the missing woman from last night called me bright and early. She was eager to talk before we see Randy Evans today. She's credible and very knowledgeable about Joanie Evans' habits and personality. I drove her here to identify the purse that was found in the locked vehicle at the state park. You did hear the car was found in the parking lot at the state park, didn't you?"

"Yeah. I was notified earlier this morning. You have had a busy morning. Let me sit down and hear the details before Evans shows up. Is he a suspect?" Butch sat down at his desk directly facing Gunderson's. The desks were shoved together so they could talk over cases together, and because detectives preferred their conversations not be overheard by others around them.

Gretchen filled her partner in on everything that Shannon had shared with her and acknowledged that she had identified the purse as Joanie's own.

"Shannon couldn't believe the purse didn't have at least one credit card or I.D. She insisted her friend would never drive a car or even go for a walk without an ID on her at any time. Shannon's only explanation was that Joanie may have taken a walk in the woods and put her keys and ID in her pocket. But then she wondered why Joanie wouldn't have taken the dog with her. She said he loved walks with Joanie."

"I take it you believe there was foul play, one way or another," Butch said. "Possibly, somebody grabbed her and took her ID to set up a way to ask for ransom. Or like you said, she went for a walk and kept it in her pocket. I don't see how her husband would factor into those scenarios, do you?" Harris asked.

"No, but he might have killed her and set it up to look like an abduction or missing persons, even an accident, if her body is found. Maybe it's possible he didn't think about an ID in her pocket. Maybe they met there to take a walk together. If that's the case, where are her car keys?" Gretchen wondered out loud.

"First things first, Gretchen: Where's the body? I thought I'd let you interview him today. Your female approach might encourage him to tell us the truth about what he knows or what he's done," Butch said.

"I wasn't planning on a female approach. I was going for 'tough as nails.' What do we know about the guy? How was he last night?"

"He seemed genuinely concerned, and at the time, I had no reason to believe he had anything to do with her disappearance," Butch said. "Her friend assured me it was unlike her not to have picked the kids up, or she would have contacted someone else in the family to do it. The kids are only two and three years old. One thing's for sure: Something happened to her. She doesn't fit the profile of a runaway, not at her age."

"Let's not alert Evans that he's under suspicion," Gunderson said. "We can show him the purse and tell him we found the car, then watch his reaction. It's all in the eyes."

19

A Suspect Appears

The two officers watched as Randy Evans followed a pretty girl in her late teens as she led him back to their desks. "Here he comes now, escorted by our young Miss Beck. If anyone can charm him into a false sense of security, it's her," Harris said with a grin.

"Watch it, Butch, she's practically jailbait. Just working here for the summer before she begins law enforcement at Sinclair College," Gunderson said. They watched as the two walked toward them, eyes mostly on the girl.

"Detectives, Mr. Evans is here to see you," Miss Beck said in her young, most professional voice.

"Ah, yes, thank you, Miss Beck," Butch Harris said. "Please have a seat, Mr. Evans. This is my partner, Detective Gunderson."

"Hello," Randy said, nodding in her direction. He appeared nervous and strained. Harris noticed he was wearing the same shirt and trousers from last night.

"Care for coffee?"

"I'd appreciate that. Just black, thanks," Evans answered without hesitation.

"Hey, Beck. Bring Mr. Evans a cup of coffee . . . *please*."

"Yes, sir," Miss Beck said in an assertive voice.

"We have some information to share with you," Harris began. "We found your wife's car." He looked closely at Randy's reaction. Nothing.

"It was locked with an empty purse was on the front seat." Again, both detectives studied Randy Evans' facial features. *Is that a bead of sweat on his brow?* Harris wondered. *Kind of funny he isn't jumping with some kind of emotion. Maybe he's in a standing coma?*

"We'd like you to identify the purse to be sure it belongs to her," Gunderson said.

Suddenly, Randy came alive. "Did you say you found the car and her purse? Where?" he said in a loud voice.

Geez, this guy is a bad actor, Harris thought. "Yeah, it was spotted after park hours last night by a Warren County sheriff's deputy. The deputy ran the plates and determined the car was registered to your wife. They've towed it to their official parking facility and have searched it thoroughly. There's no sign of blood."

Even under the circumstances, Randy Evans' reactions weren't normal. He slumped again into a kind of stupor and didn't display any further emotion whatsoever.

"After you look at the purse, it will be placed in the

evidence lab," Gunderson explained. She opened a desk drawer and removed the purse in a plastic zippered bag and laid it on top of her desk in front of Evans. He took a long look before saying anything.

"Yes, that's her purse. I gave it to her for Mothers' Day this year. It's practically new. She loves it." Evans' voice dropped. He picked up the plastic bag and looked at the colorful, cloth purse inside. Then he set it back down. "Is there anything in it?"

"Just a bill with her name on it."

At that, Evans seemed to react nervously as if he had forgotten something.

"Have you thought of anything else you want to share with us about your wife? Did she go to the state park often?" Detective Gunderson picked up her pen to take notes.

"She likes to walk the trails early in the morning. She likes her solitude and goes there to pray in nature," Randy said. "On warm Saturday afternoons, she sometimes takes the boys there to throw stones in the stream. They're not allowed to wade or anything. The water is shallow but there is a current from the dam, and the bottom is rocky. Then she takes them to a local ice cream store to get them away from the park." He shook his head and took a sip of coffee. "It seems like such a safe place. What could have happened to her, Detective Gunderson?" Mr. Evans sounded calm, not at all what they expected.

"Where were you all day yesterday?" Gunderson said, having decided to steer the questions into a more productive vein.

"I drove to work, made a few business calls, didn't take a lunch break outside the office. I was in a staff meeting between eleven and one and they provided sandwiches and drinks. I left work at five and stopped to pick up my dry cleaning, a prescription, and a gallon of milk. I no sooner walked in the door than the phone call came from the director of the nursery school."

"Did you speak with your wife during the day? How did you know to buy milk?"

"We usually catch up talking at lunch, but since I had a meeting, we didn't do that yesterday. She knew about the meeting. I picked up her prescription for Paxil and decided to get milk while I was at the drug store. With two little guys, we always can use more milk." Evans finished his coffee and glanced at Gunderson with squinty eyes as if he were assessing her reason for questioning him.

"Why was Mrs. Evans taking Paxil?" Gunderson asked.

"She's has panic attacks and suffers from anxiety since about the age of fourteen. I think she started seeing a counselor after I was sentenced to seven years in juvenile detention. But she couldn't take the Paxil while she was pregnant, and her two pregnancies practically ran together. The boys are just a year apart. During that time, her anxiety really mounted. So, the doctor recently put her back on it. My grandmother, Noni Parrish, has helped us out and so has Joanie's friend, Shannon. Unfortunately, my mother was rarely around." Evans didn't look at anyone directly.

"Okay, Mr. Evans," Detective Gunderson responded. "We wanted to bring you up to date with our findings. We'll be back in touch when we have more information for you. May I have your immediate boss' number, please?"

"Sure, Mr. Cassidy is on a family vacation until July first. He wasn't at the staff meeting, but I checked in with him immediately afterward. Minutes were faxed to him at his hotel. He's a great boss; doesn't micro-manage and when he gives you responsibility, he gives you authority, too, and assumes you'll complete whatever the task. I called him this morning to explain what was happening. He said I should take as much time off as I needed to handle the circumstances." Evans wrote Cassidy's name and number on the back of his business card and placed it on the desk in front of Detective Gunderson.

Gunderson stood up and extended her hand. "Thanks for coming in today, Mr. Evans. I'm sorry we don't have better news. We'll definitely stay close in touch." They shook hands. Detective Harris nodded in agreement, stood, and shook hands with Evans.

"Thank you both," Evans said. "Please call me day or night. I don't want to worry the boys, so I'll keep sending them to nursery school. They've noticed their mommy isn't around and keep asking for her. By the way, Joanie is without her meds. I can't imagine how she must be feeling . . . wherever she is."

Mr. Evans turned and walked away slowly with his

head down and hands in his pockets. As soon as he was out of the area, Gretchen said, "We have his fingerprints on the plastic bag with the purse, on his business card, and on his coffee cup. Want to run them?"

"Really, Gretchen? Of course, we should run them. I'll take them down to the lab, myself. But none of this places him with her in the park. Even so, his prints will serve as a comparison to any prints found."

"While you do that, I'll start contacting his witnesses. I'll call Cassidy first, then I suggest we go to the pharmacy and find out whether he really picked up her prescription and which doctor prescribes her meds."

"I'd like to talk to the preschool director. How about if we stop there after the pharmacy?"

"Great idea."

Just then Harris' phone rang, and he answered. "Harris, here." Gretchen paused to see who was calling. It was Kristy Cavanaugh, the park ranger at Caesar's Creek State Park who had discovered Joanie Evans' car in the parking lot.

"Hello, Detective Harris. I'm calling to tell you we've found a body and need someone to come and identify it. The Warren County Coroner's office is on the way to retrieve it. Do you want to wait until it's transported there?"

"Yes. That's a good idea. Mr. Evans just left us, but I will contact him to meet us at the coroner's office and ID it. Where did you find it, and do you think it's Mrs. Evans?"

"Put it this way: There's a driver's license in her bra. 'Joan Evans, D.O.B. 7/11/1981.' Park maintenance found the body an hour ago in a dumpster next to a small picnic area beside the creek. I waited for the Warren County Sheriff's deputy to get here before I called you. His name is Deputy Marv Peterson if you need to contact him."

"Thanks, Kristy, or should I call you, 'Ranger?'" He chuckled.

"Kristy will be just fine," she answered.

"Okay, call me, 'Butch.'"

"Have a nice day, Butch," Kristy said and hung up.

"Well, that just changed our itinerary for today," Harris said. "Call Evans and see if we can swing by his house and pick him up. He probably shouldn't be alone after he sees his wife's remains."

"Good idea. Why don't you get the car? I'll meet you out front with coffee refills."

***

Randy Evens answered on the second ring.

"Hello, Mr. Evans, this is Detective Gunderson again. Just after you left, we received news that something important has come up. Can we meet at your house?"

"Okay, but what's happened?" Evans asked.

"We're sorry to say but, we believe your wife's body has been found. We need you to go with us and identify it," Gunderson said, wondering if he would try to run.

"Wow, so soon? I mean, I can't believe she's dead. I wanted to think there was some other explanation. But, of course, I'll go." Evans' voice had a bewildered tone.

"Kind of a strange response, Butch?" Gretchen asked after telling Harris about it in the car.

"I'd say so. The first three words out of this new widower's mouth are 'wow' and 'so soon.' The man is strange," Butch said.

"Do you think he killed her and thought he disposed of her body where it wouldn't be found?" Gretchen asked.

"We have no evidence that places him in the park with her, let alone killing her," Butch said.

Gretchen sighed. "I'll stay in the car. You go up to the door and get Mr. Devoted Husband."

Not sure if Evans would even be there, Detective Harris knocked on the front door. He was surprised that Evans opened it immediately and stepped out. The three of them drove to the Warren County Coroner's office with little conversation. Detective Gunderson identified them to the deputy at the front desk.

"Good morning. . . please sign in." The deputy glanced past the detectives to Mr. Evans, looking at him while the three of them produced identification and signed their names. The officer kept Mr. Evans' ID and explained it would be returned to him when he signed out on the visitor's log. Gunderson and Harris were permitted to keep theirs as recognized Ohio law enforcement officers.

"Go through the double doors at the end of the hall. I'll buzz you into the morgue. Dr. York will greet you."

"Thanks," Harris said.

Once Dr. York was introduced, and led them into the morgue, it only took five minutes for the drama to be over. York removed the sheet from the body lying on the cold steel exam table. And Randy Evans saw the body of his wife. He clasped his hands tightly across the bridge of his nose and mouth as tears welled up in his eyes. His voice choked.

"Oh, my God. Joanie. . ." He brushed back wet hair from her forehead, then turned his back to her naked body.

"Why is she like that . . . with no clothes on, I mean."

"The medical examiner has to conduct a thorough autopsy. It's a typical procedure in an unlikely death. Even with suicides, blood tests are conducted to check for drugs or alcohol," Harris said.

Their stay was brief when it was clear Evans had seen enough. Gunderson followed him out of the secure area into the lobby.

"Is there anyone you want me to call?" she asked.

"No. Just drop me off at home. I honestly need to be alone. I'll call my grandmother to pick the kids up later this afternoon." He didn't mention Shannon. Gunderson decided she would make the call and notify her of her friend's death. She would also make herself available, in case Shannon wanted to talk.

They returned Evans to his home, and Gunderson got out of the vehicle along with him. "We'll stay in touch. Call us any time you need to talk," she said.

"Just catch the SOB who did this to my precious wife. If there's anything I can do to help, please feel free to ask. After Joanie's memorial, I'll ask my grandmother to stay with us. Todd and Eric will need all the love and attention they can get. Maybe going back to work will keep this horrible loss off my mind," Evans said.

Unfortunately, Gunderson decided to ask one more question: "Don't you think Shannon would be willing to help? She said the kids practically consider her their aunt." Then immediately, she realized she'd revealed too much when Randy froze and abruptly turned around.

"Did she call you and tell you that?" Randy knew no such conversation had taken place at the house.

"I wasn't at your house when you contacted the police about your wife being missing. I was in contact with Shannon to ask when she had last seen your wife," Gunderson said, trying to quickly erase her mistake.

"As a matter of fact, they *are* attached to Shannon," Randy said. "She has two little girls about their ages and probably was with Joanie at the park with the four kids the day before she disappeared. Do you suppose Joanie was stalked? The two women sat near the playground area about three times a week, as I recall. Tuesdays and Thursdays were after school. On Saturday mornings, when I played golf, they met there with coffee. Do you think someone at the park could have followed Joanie home?" Evans asked.

"It's possible, of course. The perpetrator must have known he or she could find her at the park and followed her there."

140

"Or, he could have followed her from the nursery school, right?"

"That, too. We'll track this person down. You just focus on your wife's memorial service and let us focus on catching her killer."

Gunderson got back into the unmarked car and shook her head.

"What's up?" Harris asked. "You're shaking your head; that's a bad sign. Buckle up and tell me what you're thinking."

"I screwed up. I disclosed my contact with Shannon this morning. At least I didn't say she called me and came to the precinct. I protected her on that. But when he said he was going to call his grandmother to pick up the boys, I asked if he was going to ask Shannon to help. I mistakenly told him Shannon said the kids think of her as their aunt. He asked how I knew that."

"How did you cover your blunder?"

"Just said I'd been in contact with her to see when she saw Joanie last. I didn't say how the contact was initiated. I think he bought it."

"Good. Where to now, partner?"

"Let's check out the nursery school and talk to the director before they close."

"Good idea. Let's see if grandma picks up the little guys, and if Shannon gets her own kids."

"Let's grab coffee on the way; my treat."

"I won't say 'no' to that."

141

20

On the Road Again

"Hello, Rosie. It is me, Travis. You won't believe why I'm calling."

"Hi, Travis. Is Stella, okay?"

"We're fine. This is a business call. Remember Randy Evans from eleven years ago? The 14-year-old who shot his father? Well, he's all grown up now and my son, Devon, is representing him. He's being charged with the murder of his wife, Joanie. She was his girlfriend at the time of his father's death. I'm calling you on Devon's behalf. He'll be lead counsel and we need your expertise."

"Oh, Travis! What happened to that young man? He hated the violence he grew up with and now you're saying he's resorted to it again?"

"We aren't certain. But we do know we need your assistance. He's being held in the Warren County Jail because that's the county where the crime was committed. Judge Robert Schuster has denied our motion for bail, citing Randy's prior juvenile history. Even though his conviction at fourteen cannot be presented by the state's attorney as evidence."

"He had such a bright future, Travis, with the education he obtained while he was incarcerated for seven years. The last I heard, he was happily married with two kids and a good job. How could this have happened?"

"Well, Rosie, he's denied killing her and states he doesn't remember meeting her at Caesar's Creek State Park, let alone shoving her off a steep embankment to her death. Is it possible to have amnesia for something like that?"

"There is a condition known as dissociative amnesia. It's usually associated with being a victim or witness to a crime, but not usually a perpetrator. I've hypnotized witnesses to assist them in recalling details regarding crimes in which they've taken part. Don't get me wrong. Those people weren't perpetrators, just victims or witnesses."

"You can actually do that? Hypnotize them to remember?"

"Yes. It doesn't always produce results, but it's worth a try. Small details can help detectives in their search for clues. For example, during the commission of an armed robbery, the victims will focus on the gun barrel pointed at them and not recall details about the appearance of the assailant or multiple assailants."

"That's logical, I suppose. Here's what they've got

so far: Her body was found in a small dumpster the day after Randy reported her missing. According to Randy, she failed to pick the kids up from nursery school and didn't show up that evening at home. At that point, he had no idea where she could be.

"The medical examiner determined she didn't plunge to her death. The cause was blunt force trauma to the back of her skull. She was hit from behind by a rock or something hard striking her in the back of her head. Secondary injuries included a compound fracture of her right femur and other fractures to her arms. No toxins were found in her blood. No skin was found beneath her fingernails to suggest she fought for her life. And there was no evidence of sexual assault or rape. The examiner stated when the park maintenance man found her body, she had been dead approximately twenty to twenty-four hours."

"What evidence did they find that led them to arrest Randy?"

"Mostly circumstantial. There was quite a storm the evening before she went missing. The morning after she disappeared, their muddy footprints were identified on the trail and stopped in front of a large boulder. Her footprints were not seen thereafter. One of her shoes was missing from her body and later was found wedged between a tree branch and a rock. His footprints were not seen on the trail returning to the bridge. However, there is reason to believe he attempted to climb down the slope to her but possibly changed his mind. A few small branches were broken off and were lying beneath a large oak tree about a third of the way down."

"So, it could have been an accident and he tried to rescue her?"

"Possible, but unlikely. They found her car keys in his dresser, and his muddy gym shoes in a wheelbarrow in his garage covered with mulch. Oh, and his fingerprints were on a padlock that laid on the ground beside the dumpster. The park ranger said the dumpster is usually locked to keep animals from invading it at night. But she also said that it's not uncommon for the maintenance crew to be in a rush and fail to lock it. The dumpster was next to a small picnic area on a cement slab, beside the stream. There is no evidence to suggest they sat on the picnic bench together. "

"Were there any witnesses or other suspects?" Rosie asked.

"Yes. A fisherman claimed to see a Jeep Cherokee speeding around the bend toward him as he was going down the winding, narrow road to fish. He saw two big men in the front seat and figured they were leaving the parking lot beside the dock where he was planning to set up. He wondered what their hurry was. He also noticed Joanie's car but assumed the passengers were hiking on one of the trails."

"I see," Rosie said. "How did they dismiss the two guys as suspects?"

"It turns out the two sets of large, fresh, footprints were seen on another trail. But the prints appeared to complete the rugged, two-mile trail ending back at the footbridge. No sign of interruptions. Kristy

Cavanaugh, the park ranger, told the detectives the men in the Cherokee were Bengals football players, Brock Bennett, and Tim Taylor. She said they jog that trail twice a week, then return to practice with their teammates by ten o'clock in the morning. When it isn't wet, they continue their cardio training by running up and down the steep, grassy slope to the top of the dam, about ten times. Under questioning, they said they prefer the grass which is more like turf than doing it on stadium steps in Cincinnati.

"Cavanaugh is the one who immediately notified the Warren County sheriff's department when she heard that maintenance found Joanie's body. As you probably know, rangers enforce park regulations and carry firearms. But, if they suspect illegal activity, they contact county authorities."

"I'll call Bucky and my mother as soon as we hang up. You can expect me there by Monday morning. Where should we meet?"

"Just come to the house and I'll provide you with discovery materials. We can have lunch with Devon, and you can head to the jail after we talk if you want."

"That sounds fine, Travis. Please give Stella a hug and tell her I look forward to seeing her soon."

"You bet, Rosie. Thanks a million. Devon will really appreciate your assistance. Give my best to Bucky."

Without hesitation, Rosie dialed her husband's cell phone.

"Hi Bucky, Travis called with a new case. Actually,

it's a new case involving an old case. Remember Randy Evans, the kid from eleven years ago?"

"Sure, I remember it well. What happened?"

"Well, it seems he's being charged with the murder of his wife. After growing up with such an abusive father, I would never have guessed he would turn to violence."

"Is that uncommon?"

"Not really. The cycle of violence can permeate the next generation. Especially if they haven't learned to handle anger by any other means. If they never have a role model who demonstrates alternative conflict resolution techniques. People really need to experience how to behave in order to know how to behave. Strangely, lots of behavior is learned.

"Anyway, Travis called because he and his son, Devon, want me to evaluate Randy Evans again. I would like to go down on Sunday and stay with Mom and Caleb for a couple of days. The only stumbling block would be if they are traveling. Marrying later in life, they are making up for lost time. Are you able to spring loose from campus?"

"Oh, geez, Rosie. I'm sorry to say I can't do that. The athletic department is holding a week-long, summer baseball camp for local kids, mostly from the inner city. They'll be staying in the dorms. I need to stay close by."

"Now I remember. You mentioned that a week or so ago, but I don't recall you telling me the dates. I'll call Mom as soon as we hang up. I plan to meet Travis on

Monday morning and get discovery materials. Then I'll consult with Devon who is representing Randy. And, of course, I will evaluate Randy at the Warren County Jail. I shouldn't be gone more than two or three days."

"Okay, let's talk more this evening, hon. Maybe by then, you'll have more details about your trip."

"I'll call my mother and let you know what we figure out. And, by the way, I think steaks on the grill are in order. What sides do you want?"

"Fresh corn, Rosie, and if you have the makings of a salad, that would be great."

"Sounds fantastic. Love you. Bye."

"Bye, hon."

Rosie dialed her mother and was surprised she picked up immediately. Her mother was usually involved in daily social or volunteer activities. Oftentimes, she didn't even answer her phone.

"Hi, Mom, how are you?"

"Hello, Rosie. I was just thinking about you."

"Well, you may see me soon, too. Travis just called and I'm being appointed to another case near you. It will be in Warren County. His son, Devon, is representing the defendant and I was hoping to stay with you and Caleb for a few days."

"What a nice surprise. It will be great to have you and Bucky here again."

"Bucky can't make it this time. He has a kids' baseball camp to direct all next week. That means Caleb is stuck with girl-talk," Rosie laughed.

"Caleb will enjoy pampering us. You know,

opening the wine, grilling chicken, tossing salad, and maybe taking us out for dinner one night. How soon can you get here?"

"I can drive down on Sunday afternoon. Should be there about four. That won't interfere with any plans, will it?"

"Absolutely not. Drive carefully. Can't wait, Rosie. I have a surprise for you."

"You won't tell me now? Bummer. I hate waiting for surprises. I'll let you know when I leave home. Hugs to Caleb. Love you."

"Love you too, sweetheart."

21

The Investigation Continues

The two detectives had just parked outside Shammy's Pharmacy and now entered the privately-owned drug store. They flashed their badges at the pharmacy counter and asked for the pharmacist.

"We're here regarding a homicide investigation. We need to know about prescriptions for a woman named Joan Evans. What can you tell us?"

"Do you have a subpoena?" Shammy asked. They noticed a diploma on the wall identifying Karl Shammy as a registered pharmacist and assumed he was the owner of the store.

"No, but we can get one, if necessary. We're here for the name of the physician who prescribed her medication and would appreciate your cooperation. Mrs. Evans is recently deceased and obviously cannot provide the information. If we need a subpoena, we can have one here in an hour," Harris said in a gruff voice. "But then we'd have no reason to 'appreciate your cooperation,' would we?" He gave Shammy a knowing smirk.

"I suppose I can tell you what you want to know. Sorry to hear about Mrs. Evans, She was a nice lady, courteous." Shammy looked up her prescription history. "She refills Paxil every three months. Her husband just picked up a refill last night. It's prescribed by Dr. Sherri Bernhardt. Dr. Bernhardt is a psychiatrist located about three blocks from here."

"Thank you. That's very helpful," Gunderson said as they turned and left.

"Well, that's unexpected," Harris said. "I assumed a primary care physician was prescribing the meds, not a shrink. Let's go check out this Dr. Bernhardt."

They pulled up to a small, white, frame two-story house with an unattached garage at the back of the driveway. The sign beside the front door read, "Dr. Sherri Bernhardt, D.O." There was nothing to identify the doctor as a psychiatrist. Three rocking chairs and two small tables were on the porch. A newspaper was lying on one of the cushioned chairs, obviously opened for reading. They tried the door which opened into a small reception area containing chairs, magazines, and children's building blocks on a side table. There were no patients in the waiting room. The receptionist looked up from behind the glass window.

"May I help you?"

"Yes, I'm Detective Harris, and this is my partner Detective Gunderson. We would like a few moments with Dr. Bernhardt, if it's convenient for her."

"Actually, she'll be out soon. Her counseling

session should end in ten minutes. May I ask what the nature of your call is about?"

"We are inquiring about medication and treatment of one of her patients," Gunderson explained.

"It's unlikely Dr Bernhardt will provide that information to you since it's confidential, as you're likely aware," the receptionist said in a firm voice.

Dr. Bernhardt took that moment to open the door of her office and walk into the waiting room with a plump, middle-aged woman. She noticed the officers, nodded, and continued talking to her patient, "Roxanne, please reschedule her in two weeks. Take care, now."

The patient approached the receptionist's window as the officers introduced themselves.

"Dr. Bernhardt, I'm Detective Harris, and this is my partner, Detective Gunderson. Might we have a few minutes of your time, privately? We're looking for information on one of your patients."

"Nice to meet you detectives, but I can't disclose any information without a subpoena," Dr. Bernhardt said in a pleasant tone of voice. Having rescheduled the patient, Roxanne closed her window, and the patient inserted the appointment card into her purse before quietly leaving.

"We understand that's the correct procedure under most circumstances. However, we're also here to inform you that Joan Evans is dead, murdered, and we're investigating a person of interest," Gunderson said. "So, time is of the essence."

Dr. Bernhardt immediately opened her office door and beckoned them inside. She took a seat in a high wingback chair. "I'm stunned. Please have a seat."

Detectives Harris and Gunderson sat on a love seat facing her and Gunderson explained what she could without adding much detail. "She was reported missing by her husband yesterday and her body was found this morning at Caesar's Creek State Park. While interviewing Mr. Evans, he mentioned she takes Paxil and has for many years. The pharmacist told us you are the prescribing physician. That's what led us here."

"Yes, I am the prescribing physician. But it seems that I am not disclosing information you don't already have. She's been in therapy with me off and on since her sophomore year in high school. Her anxiety became extremely elevated when she was about to marry. Then her meds were interrupted by two pregnancies, and therapy became more intensified. I've been seeing her every other week for some time now, but this morning, she was a no-show. I thought was totally out of character for Joanie, however, you've just answered that question. How truly awful." Dr. Bernhardt continued. "This is a hard one for me. I've grown quite fond of her. What on earth happened?"

"Did she ever express fear of her husband or any domestic abuse?" Gunderson asked.

"Now, that is a question I cannot answer without a subpoena. It goes beyond public knowledge such as you had from the pharmacy," Dr. Bernhardt explained.

"We understand. We'll request a subpoena, and

once we receive and review her records, we'll want to meet with you again."

"That will be fine." Dr. Bernhardt rose from her chair, appearing on the brink of tears. Gunderson and Harris closed the office door behind them and left to secure the subpoena from Judge Schuster.

***

A while later, Detective Gunderson was at her desk when the phone rang.

"Hello, Gretchen. This is Sid Hochwalt. Randy Evans has just been arrested for the murder of his wife. Two deputies are transporting him to the Warren County jail. I'll be prosecuting the Evans case and was just notified of your request for a subpoena for some doctor's records. May I ask, why?"

"Yes, but first, tell me the details of the arrest," Gunderson asked.

"We received an anonymous call that he purchased a one-way Delta Airlines ticket to Madrid. He was seen as a flight risk, so two deputies picked him up at his house without incident. Now, from what I hear, the deputies mirandized him and he immediately requested a call to his lawyer. It's likely he's making that call as we speak."

"Well, we didn't think he considered himself a suspect. He kept insisting that he didn't remember being with her after she took the kids to school. He certainly denied harming her. As for your question about the medical records, Joan Evans' husband told us she was on Paxil for panic attacks and anxiety, that sort of thing. We went to the pharmacy and got the name, then approached Dr. Sherri Bernhardt, regarding Mrs. Evans. She's requiring a subpoena to disclose confidential, doctor-patient records," Gunderson said.

"You will see to it that our office receives a copy, right?"

"Absolutely. You and the defense attorneys will get any evidence received, for sure."

"Thanks, Detective, I appreciate it." Hochwalt abruptly ended the call.

"Who was that?" Butch asked as he placed a mug of coffee on Gretchen's desk.

"Sid Hochwalt. He said Evans has been arrested while planning to leave the country and is at the Warren County jail. Sid wants Dr. Bernhardt's records, too. Word gets around fast, doesn't it?"

"I'm surprised about the arrest. I assumed we'd exercise the warrant," Butch laughed "Guess we're not fast enough today. I just got through asking the bailiff to have Judge Schuster sign off on the subpoena asap. He must have contacted Hochwalt's office to be sure it was all on the up and up."

"Sounds about right. Did you get the document?" Gretchen asked, sipping her coffee.

"I did. It's being faxed to Bernhardt's office, as we speak." Butch looked at his watch. "I think we still have time to swing by the nursery school. What do you think?"

"Sure. You drive." They headed down to the garage and found their vehicle.

"I'll call Shannon and see if I can stop by this evening and personally tell her about Joanie's body being found and the arrest of Randy Evans." Harris headed out onto the street.

"Well, if you're taking that responsibility, the least I can do is call Cassidy, the immediate boss of Evans. What a team, huh, Gunderson? If we were attorneys making big bucks, we could be called Harris and Gunderson, Attorneys at Law." Harris laughed and sped through a yellow light.

"Hey, buddy, number one. You just went through a yellow light. Number two, I have never wanted to be an attorney. Number three, if we were attorneys the sign would say Gunderson and Harris. Ha."

The two detectives parked their unmarked car in a side lot allocated for nursery school staff. Trying the nursery's side door, they found it was locked, so they walked around to the front. Gunderson reached forward and pushed a button to announce themselves. A friendly voice buzzed them in and a stern, older woman met them just inside the door. Her name tag identified her as Director Doris Mello. Standing in the hallway, Harris and Gunderson produced their identification.

"Good afternoon, detectives, how can I help you?" Director Mello asked.

"We would like to speak with you about the Joan Evans matter."

"I was expecting someone to contact me. We can talk privately in my office. Has something serious happened to Mrs. Evans?" Director Mello led them into her small, tidy office and sat down behind her desk. Two other seats were available.

"Yes. I'm afraid we have some bad news. Mrs. Evans' body was found at Caesar's Creek Park and her husband has been arrested as a suspect in her death."

"I thought something was happening. Their grandmother just picked the boys up which doesn't happen too regularly. She appeared a bit hurried. Ordinarily, she comes in and first observes them at play and usually doesn't rush them out of here like she did today. I can't believe this. Mrs. Evans is one of the most polite, helpful parents. She volunteers two half days a month and bakes cookies for special events. The little boys are a delight and always look clean. I just can't believe it. Those brothers will have to be even more protective of one another."

"Have you ever seen evidence of abuse toward the boys or Mrs. Evans?"

"No, I can't say that I have. There have been times when I wondered why Mrs. Evans didn't remove her sunglasses in the building. Three-year-old, Eric, has said a few strange things. Once he asked his teacher, Miss Molly, if it scares her when her boyfriend yells at her. Molly told him that her boyfriend doesn't yell at her, but it would be scary if he did. Eric said it scares him when his daddy yells at his mommy because supper isn't ready. He told her that he and his brother, Todd, run upstairs and close the door. He said they eat before their daddy gets home from work because mommy tells them he will be very tired and needs quiet."

"Who brings them to and from school?" Harris asked.

"Usually, Mrs. Evans transports them both ways. Her good friend, Shannon Conrad, has taken them home a few times when Mrs. Evans has a commitment. But she has also taken Shannon's girls home. Those two moms have a nice friendship. Mr. Evans' grandmother, Noni, gets them about one Friday a month. I think she keeps them for the weekend. She is such a sweet woman," Director Mello said.

Gunderson handed Director Mello her card. "If you think of anything else that you believe would be useful to us, please don't hesitate to call. And if you don't mind, we would like you not to share the information about Mrs. Evans' death."

"We appreciate your time. Thanks very much," Harris said. The detectives returned to their car, taking note of parents arriving to pick up their little ones.

"Let's go back to the station, then you can head home. I plan to catch up with Shannon yet later this evening," Gretchen said.

"Hopefully, Cassidy, Evans' boss, will return my call so we can get an idea of his performance at work, relationships with his co-workers, but especially, attendance at the meeting yesterday."

Gretchen dialed Shannon's number as Butch pulled into the parking lot beside the precinct. Surprisingly, Shannon picked up on the second ring.

"Hi Shannon, it's Gretchen Gunderson. Do you have a little time? I'd like to stop by for a few minutes."

"Oh no! Is it bad news? Don't tell me something's happened to Joanie. Yes, please come over."

"I'm on my way." She looked at Butch. "Does my name sound like 'bad news?'"

***

"Would you care for something to drink?" Shannon asked after welcoming Detective Gunderson into her living room.

"I'm fine, Shannon. I do have news about Joanie. I'm sorry to tell you that her body was found this morning at Caesar's Creek Park. Her husband was just arrested for her murder."

Shannon put her head in her hands and wept. "I can't believe it. She was my best friend and the sweetest woman I've ever known. She was so committed to Randy. And she waited all those years for him to get out of juvenile detention. He wasn't out but three months before they got married. Then bingo, two kids, two years in a row. How *could* he?!"

"Did she ever tell you she was unhappy or that he was mentally or physically abusive?"

"Not exactly. But it was easy to see he was extremely controlling. Yet she never said a bad word about him. When we met at the park to watch the kids play, she was always conscious about the time. She said he would be upset if she didn't get home and have dinner ready. I used to wonder why she could never relax."

"Did you know she was on medication for anxiety?" asked Gunderson.

"Yes, I did know that. She said it was her calming

medicine. She never drank wine or anything alcoholic saying it didn't mix with her meds. But I always thought she could use a little wine. But all she would order was sparkling water when we had lunch out. She was very weight conscious and said Randy didn't want to be married to a 'whale.' Once, I asked her if he called her that. She nodded, then changed the subject. I couldn't get her to speak of it again. I can tell you this: Joanie returned to her pre-pregnancy weight quicker than any other mother I know." Tears were now streaming down her face and Shannon reached for a tissue.

"One last question, Shannon. Did you meet Joanie and the kids in the park on Saturday mornings?"

"Yes, we would meet but every other week she would leave the kids with me while she saw a psychiatrist for counseling. She called her 'Dr. Sherri.' She said the doctor would not refill her medication if she didn't participate in counseling. I do know that Randy was not aware she was in counseling. He knew she was on meds, but he would have been furious if he knew she was telling a doctor or anyone about their personal life. I vowed that I would never let him know, and he never caught me with his kids on Saturday, because he played golf when the weather was good and indoor tennis when it was cold or rainy. Joanie and the kids were expected to go to his company's softball games on Saturday afternoons. It was kind of a rigid schedule, if you ask me."

"Thank you, Shannon. I won't stay any longer and I'm deeply sorry for your loss. Again, I appreciate you sharing the information with me when you were at Evans' house last evening. You will likely be called as a state witness at trial. Do you know what that means?"

"It means the prosecutor will want me to testify, right?" Shannon's voice was shaky.

"Yes. That's right. His name is Sid Hochwalt. He'll probably be in touch with you. I'll let him know we've talked. Our interview becomes part of a discovery packet. It holds all information gathered in the case by both the defense attorneys and the prosecutor. Yours will be categorized as a witness statement. He may ask you to write something out."

She stood to leave, and Shannon approached her for a hug. "Thank you for personally coming over to tell me about Joanie. I assume that if Randy goes to prison, Noni Parrish will become guardian of the two children. Even though she's Randy's grandmother, she has always been a great supporter of Joanie, too. I don't think he appreciates what she has done for his family. It would have been nice if he had included Joanie's parents in their lives, but he never did. His own mother was rarely in the picture. Joanie couldn't understand how his mother could leave her son in juvenile detention without making a point to visit him as often as possible. I guess she remarried and left town soon after he was committed.

"It's going to be hard for the little boys to lose both parents at once, too," Gunderson said." But at least their routine won't change much assuming Mrs. Parrish keeps them at their school. Which, in this case, would be helpful so they have one thing that doesn't change in their lives."

She patted Shannon's hand as she walked out the door.

22

Rosie's Casework Begins

Rosie drove up to the lovely house her mother and new husband were now making their home. Parking curbside, she climbed out with her suitcase and headed for the front door.

"Hi, mom," Rosie said, entering the foyer, putting her suitcase and briefcase down on the ceramic tile, and extending her arms to hug her mother.

"Hello, sweetie. I'm so happy to see you even though it's only for work this time. Did Jocko stay home with Bucky?"

"Yes. They're inseparable now. A little male bonding going on. Where's your other half?"

"He's napping upstairs. He said to let him know when you arrive, and he'll make us piña coladas. I think he's hooked on those tropical foo-foo drinks." They laughed together. It felt good to be with her, again, comforting really. They had always gotten along well.

"It's kind of early in the day for drinks, so you might as well let him sleep a bit longer."

"All right," her mother said. "Why not put your

things in the guest room and freshen up, if you want. I'll be in the sunroom."

"Okay, I'll only be a few minutes. I may put in a quick call to Travis Gump."

***

"Hi Travis. I'm here," Rosie said. "What are the plans for tomorrow?"

"Hey, Rosie, good to hear from you . . . come to the office in Lincoln Park about nine. Devon and I will give you witness statements, police reports, and other evidence to review. We can have lunch at Mama DiSalvo's. Then you can spend the afternoon with Randy. Does that work for you?"

"It does. Please tell Stella I'm looking forward to seeing her, too."

"Will do. Get some rest and enjoy your time with your mom and step-dad."

***

Just before nine the following morning, Rosie parked by Travis' building and went inside to the reception area.

"Good morning, Rosie. So nice to see you, and thanks again, for making the trip." Travis greeted her by the front desk and escorted her back to his office where tall and lanky, Devon, waited.

"Hi, Devon. I haven't seen you in eleven years. You were just a five-foot-eight, slender, running back in high school then. Now, look at you! A full-fledged, defense attorney. Where did the years go?"

"Who knows, Rosie. And after all those hours

studying in small, dimly lit cubicles, now I wear reading glasses! You should have told me being grown-up was such fun. But, really, I'm grateful Dad gave me an opportunity to join his law firm. I bypassed the public defender stage most of my attorney friends are facing now."

Travis smiled at his son. "I'm glad to have him with us, Rosie," Travis said. "Devon is extremely bright and competent. He'll represent Randy Evans well."

"I haven't the slightest worry. I think his horn-rimmed glasses make him look distinguished . . . very professional and I'm looking forward to sharing the psychological aspects of our defendant with both of you."

"One recent development occurred since we last spoke on the phone," Travis said. "Randy purchased a one-way plane ticket to Madrid for the evening following his wife's memorial service. That's when they decided to pick him up. He originally said the little boys would stay with his grandmother. We thought he intended to work through his grief . . . just not in Spain."

"Does that imply he knows, or now remembers, he killed her and is skipping out of the country, Rosie?" Devon asked.

"I can't know his motive until I've met with him once or twice. I assume you've interviewed him. What do you think?" she said.

"We've both interviewed him, within a couple hours of his arrest. He was distraught, of course, and didn't admit his plan was to leave the country. He said his boss, Cassidy, wanted him to meet with a television producer about filming ads in Spain about their Ohio company. When we confronted him with it being a one-way ticket, he said it was because he couldn't know a return date at this time. The company wants to hire young, talented, Spanish-speaking computer engineers and it takes time to find them. He thinks the only reason he's being held without bond is that his boss, Cassidy is still on vacation. We haven't been able to reach him to verify Randy's story yet. So far, Cassidy hasn't returned any of our calls."

"Let me have the materials and use your conference room to review them," Rosie said.

"Sure thing; right this way."

***

Let's see, Rosie thought as she began reading everything: discovery materials; statements from Joanie Evans' best friend, Shannon Conrad; and the director of the nursery school, Doris Mello. The witness reports were prepared by detectives Gretchen Gunderson and Butch Harris. After reading them, Rosie thought the documents were thorough and answered many questions in her mind. She yellow highlighted items she would question Randy about when she interviewed him.

Reports from the Caesar's Creek State Park ranger, and the Warren County sheriff's deputy were also there along with statements submitted by three witnesses from the crime scene: Two professional Bengals football players who saw a red truck speeding out of the park, and a park maintenance man who found Joanie's body. Rosie noted there was no direct statement from Randy Evans himself, yet he must have been interviewed by the detectives after his arrest. Why wasn't this report among the others? She decided to inquire about it after lunch.

Rosie left her materials spread out on the conference table, stood and stretched, then sipped her coffee. She wondered if Randy would remember her, or if she needed to establish a rapport as though it was their first meeting. His mental status was of top concern.

Devon tapped lightly on the door and entered. "How's it going? Need anything else?" he inquired.

"Not unless you have a written statement by Randy. Did he remain silent at your request or isn't anything here because he didn't say anything incriminating?" she asked.

"He hasn't made a statement to the detectives or written anything yet. The first thing he did after being mirandized was to ask for a call to his lawyer. I went down and introduced myself as Travis Gump's associate. We talked and he claimed innocence. He said he loved his wife and doesn't remember being with her that morning. His purpose for going to Madrid can be verified by his boss. That's it for initial contact. He'll be arraigned in front of Judge Schuster, and we'll plead 'not guilty' and go from there."

"Okay. I will make a few business calls until you're ready for lunch. I'll find Shannon's telephone number in the discovery materials and will set up a telephone conference call with her," Rosie explained.

"We've informed the jail that you'll be there at one-thirty to see Randy. I hope that fits your schedule. This evening, my father would like you to come over and have dinner with Stella and him. My wife, Brenda, and I will be there, too. Is that, okay?" Devon asked.

"It works perfectly. I look forward to meeting your wife."

23

Is Randy Competent?

Rosie spoke to the deputy at the visitation window. "Hi. I am Dr. Klein, here to evaluate Randy Evans," she explained.

"Yes, Dr. Klein. We're expecting you. Please show your ID, sign the visitors' log, and I'll buzz you through," Deputy Thomas said.

Well, this is a lot less formal than at the Montgomery or Lucas County Jails, Rosie thought as she complied with his request.

"They're bringing Mr. Evans down to our big visitation room. You should have plenty of room there. The smaller one is occupied," Thomas said, leading her down the corridor.

"Thank you; I appreciate it."

When they reached the room, Rosie put her materials on a table and sat facing the glass door. She determined that with Randy's back to the door, he would be less distracted. She watched as he entered the room, escorted by a deputy who released his handcuffs, nodded at Rosie, and left them alone in the room, locking the door as he left. Randy looked haggard and in need of some hygiene attention. He took a seat across the table from Rosie and folded his hands in his lap.

"Hello, Randy. I'm Dr. Klein. Do you remember me?"

"I think so. I know you were involved with me when I shot my dad years ago. I can't remember much about that time in my life, though. You're working with my attorneys, right?"

"Well, they did request me to see you; the court has appointed me to speak to you and assist your lawyers in your defense. However, nothing you say to me is confidential. I need you to sign a release of information that you understand what I'm telling you. I'm expected to render a report to the judge, prosecutor, and defense attorneys regarding your competency to stand trial. It seems you've declared no memory of the events resulting in your arrest. Is that true?"

Rosie slid the release form and a pen across the table to Randy. Without a word, he signed the document and slid it back to her.

"When I first reported Joanie missing, I had no memory whatsoever of what happened to her. Now, I don't know if I'm dreaming or if I'm beginning to put that awful day together, but when I saw her body in the morgue on that cold, steel slab, it jarred something in my mind. I'm starting to remember bits and pieces. But I can't believe I'd hurt the love of my life, yet I can't explain what happened to her.

"I was told they found her set of car keys in my dresser drawer and muddy shoes of mine in the wheelbarrow out in our garage. But I don't remember coming home or putting those things there. Fingerprints on a padlock? How can that be, Dr. Klein? Was I with Joanie in the park? Sometimes we walked there to be alone. Toddlers don't give you much privacy at home, you know. But if I *was* with her, I don't remember it."

"I understand. What visions are you seeing in your mind?"

"I see her tumbling down a steep, wooded ravine. I see myself sliding sideways down after her. That's all. Do you suppose I'm imagining it since they told me she fell to her death?"

"It could be that memories are surfacing in bits and pieces. They can be triggered by something you see, hear, feel, or even smell. Time will tell. I'm giving you a composition notebook. I would like you to write your thoughts, visions, and anything else you believe is relevant in it. You can even use it as a sketchbook if you want. Drawing releases feeling sometimes."

"See these scratches on the palms of my hands, Dr. Klein? They could be from grabbing hold of branches when I went down to help my wife. No one has seen them but you. My hands weren't examined when they handed me this orange suit and took away my clothes and shoes. But how can my fingerprints be on a padlock beneath the dumpster where her body was found?"

"Well, Randy, it definitely places you at the scene, doesn't it?"

"Dr. Klein, you didn't say 'scene of the crime' like the detectives describe it. Could it be just a horrible accident and not a crime at all?"

"I can't determine that, Randy. A medical examiner is capable of discerning things like that from the body. Is that what you're thinking, Randy? Do you suppose you were there, and she fell? I don't want to put words into your mouth. Just take me through your day as you recall it," Rosie said.

"My original memories go like this: I got up, put my slippers on, and went out to the curb to get the newspaper. I sat on a stool at the kitchen counter and drank a cup of coffee and I read the sports section. Joanie was at the table with the two boys helping to get their shoes on. They were eating cereal. When they finished, she grabbed their backpacks and gave me a peck on the cheek, like she always does. She ushered the boys out the door and said she would see me later. I quickly told her I had a lunch meeting and wouldn't talk to her until evening. Then I let Champ out into the backyard.

"Okay. What happened next?"

"I read a little more, had a breakfast bar, and went upstairs to shower and get ready for work. I remember having a headache and taking a hot shower hoping it would stop. Probably had a little too much to drink the night before. I figured Joanie would let the dog in when she got back. I got in my truck and drove to the coffee shop across from the office. Took a black coffee to go and walked across the street to work. The next thing I remember is coming through our front door to a silent, empty house."

"Those are your original memories? You don't remember your day at work?"

"No, I don't. The next thing I remember after coming into the house is getting a call from Mrs. Mello, the nursery school director, to pick up the boys. I brought them home and called Shannon Conrad to see if she knew where Joanie was. I called my grandmother, Noni. No one had heard from her all day. Shannon arrived and I decided to call the police to report her missing."

"I'm going to ask you a few questions unrelated to your current circumstances." Then Rosie went through a line of questioning that measures a person's ability to recall short-term and long-term memories.

From Randy Evans' interview, Rosie ascertained his approximate cognitive ability. His sentence structure, vocabulary, grammar, and educational background suggested an above-average intelligence and achievement. Long-term and short-term memory, except for the day of his wife's death were intact. He showed no signs of visual or auditory hallucinations other than the vague vision of his wife tumbling down the hill, and his attempt to help her. Was he delusional? Was he malingering, deliberately distorting the truth? She couldn't tell. But if she repeated some questions, Rosie might ascertain a contradiction or inconsistency in his responses which could mean he was being dishonest in his answers or at least distorting them.

"Thank you, Randy," she finally said after completing the final inquiry into his relationships and recollections of the day his wife died. "Now I need to ask you some additional questions regarding the charges against you and your ability to assist your attorneys in your own defense and if you understand the charges against you."

Rosie proceeded to ask Randy to explain what charges he was facing and if he was found guilty, what sentence or sentences were likely to be imposed. He was able to explain all possible consequences, including the likely years of incarceration.

She asked him if he knew the difference between aggravated murder and second-degree murder. He was quick to explain his understanding of those charges to her satisfaction. He indicated that both terms mean killing, but second-degree murder could be unintentional or unplanned while the penalty for aggravated murder could result in the death penalty. When asked how the death penalty was imposed, he asked for more information.

"The jury has to unanimously find you guilty," she said. "Are you aware of the lesser charges such as abuse of a corpse, or obstruction of justice?"

His descriptions were simple and accurate, but he had no knowledge of their sentencing guidelines. Dr. Rosie concluded that Randy Evans could assist his attorneys in terms of his intellectual ability, but she wondered just how useful his help would be if he couldn't accurately remember the incident or events that followed.

She asked him if detectives had read him his Miranda rights, or if he had signed the form indicating agreement. He stated, yes, they did, and he had signed. He also said he had asked to call his old attorney from eleven years ago and that's how he came to be represented by Devon and Travis Gump.

"I see. Well, that's all we need to do for today, but I'll be back tomorrow. Will you think about everything we've discussed, and perhaps more details will surface in your mind before we meet again. In the meantime, is there anyone you want me to speak to who could be useful in your defense?"

"Have you talked to my sister or my brother?" Randy asked. "They could help you understand our childhood and maybe have some thoughts that would help. I would also like to see Susie and Roger if it's possible."

"I'll follow up and find out, Randy. Until then, try to get some sleep. I'll see you tomorrow."

Rosie drove to Devon's Lincoln Park Office and found a space in the visitor's lot beside the building. It was beginning to drizzle a warm rain, so she grabbed her briefcase and made a dash to the double doors. She wasn't sure whether either of the Gump attorneys would be available, but she was certain her workspace would be set up by then.

"Good afternoon. May I help you, Dr. Klein?" inquired the pretty, plump receptionist.

"Yes. Thank you. I was hoping to have a few

minutes with Devon."

"I believe he assumed you would be coming here after you saw his client. Let me buzz him."

Devon came into the reception area and extended his hand. "Hi Rosie. Come on back and tell us how it went with Evans. Dad is just winding up a conference call with the prosecutor."

They shook hands and Rosie walked beside Devon to a corner office at the end of the corridor. The office was spacious with a sitting area in front of tinted floor-to-ceiling windows. Travis' back was to them as he hung up the phone. He turned to see them arrive and indicated for her to have a seat. Four chairs nestled around a low mahogany coffee table in the center. A carafe of coffee and three mugs bearing the Gump logo sat on a wooden tray.

"Coffee, Rosie?" Travis asked as he swiveled his chair around toward them.

"Thank you. That would be nice. I just drink it black."

"What did you think of Randy Evans?" Devon asked.

"I found him to be cooperative yet guarded. He offered information as I requested but provided no spontaneous answers. I think I need to speak to Shannon Conrad. She might have the most insight into the Evans couple's relationship and any problems he and his wife may have been having."

"That can easily be arranged. When would you

like to see her? I know she'll be glad to come here," Devon said.

"Tomorrow, if possible," Rosie said.

"What do you think about Randy's story?" Devon asked. "Is he malingering in terms of having no recall being with her that morning?" Devon had experience with defendants who feigned memory loss, making it impossible to get to the truth, and extremely difficult to defend them.

"I'm not sure," Rosie said. "I hope when I see him tomorrow, some additional memories will be triggered. He wants me to talk to his sister and brother. Is that feasible?" Rosie asked.

"We can make it happen. Do you want to see them, and Shannon Conrad, prior to meeting with Randy again?" Devon asked.

"I think so. Then, assuming I have their permission, I can use what they tell me, to launch a more specific dialogue about his wife, his relationships, and so on. From his behavior, verbal and non-verbal, it appears he'll have no difficulty conducting himself appropriately in the courtroom."

"Let's ask Claire, our receptionist, to call them and get them over here tomorrow," Travis suggested. He buzzed Claire and explained the request to set up meetings with Randy's brother and sister, and the friend, Shannon Conrad.

After Rosie shared information, she had gleaned from her interview with Randy, Travis and Devon found it interesting that Randy Evans was beginning to believe he tried to be her *hero*, not her killer. As for scratches on the palms of his hands, it was curious. There was no evidence under Joanie's fingernails to suggest she had fought anyone off. Perhaps, his story was plausible to that extent.

Eventually, Rosie stood and said, "I'm going to my mother's for a little while. Where do you want to meet for dinner?"

"Stella and I thought we'd start at our house for drinks, then go together to the Paragon. You'll love their steak, stewed tomatoes, and crunchy onion rings. Would you like to join us, Devon? Rosie can meet your main squeeze."

"Sorry, she has class on Monday night. First-year law student at the University of Dayton, Rosie," Devon said. "But I can join you as a single, Dad."

"Of course, you're welcome. Come to the house at five-thirty, both of you." Travis said with a laugh.

On Rosie's way out, Claire told her she had just scheduled Shannon Conrad at eight-thirty the following morning. "Hope that isn't too early. She said she'll take her kids to nursery school and head on over here. Susie and Roger will come together at nine-thirty."

"Sounds perfect, Claire. Thank you for arranging the appointments so promptly," Rosie replied and waved as she left the office.

24

The Plot Thickens

Rosie glanced at the clock. It was ten minutes past eight. "Good morning, Claire," she said to the younger woman at the front desk, priding herself on being twenty minutes early. She liked being somewhere well ahead of time and was equally impressed that Claire was at her post and not off somewhere getting coffee. She assumed Claire's workday began at eight.

"Good morning, Dr. Klein," Claire said. "Shannon Conrad called for you. She can't make it here today because her kids are sick. She asked if you would either call her or feel free to go to her house and talk."

"Well, I think a conference call will work. I don't want to take germs into the jail and have Randy pass them on to other inmates. Viruses really spread in closed environments like that."

"Why don't you make yourself comfortable in the conference room. There are sesame seed bagels, butter, and cream cheese on the table," Claire said.

"What do you take in your coffee?"

"Just black," Rosie told her and headed to the conference room. Claire brought a short, squatty carafe of coffee as Rosie took out her legal pad and pen.

"Why don't you have something to eat, Dr. Klein? Shannon's appointment isn't till eight-thirty. You still have a few minutes. I'll get her on the line and buzz you," Claire said.

"Thank you. I'll use the time to think about my line of questioning."

Rosie drank coffee and jotted down a few ideas. She wanted to pursue the subject of Joan Evans' relationship with her husband and believed if anyone knew private details, it would be Shannon. She also wanted to know more about Randy Evans' use of alcohol and involvement with his kids.

Shannon's Interview:

Claire buzzed to say Shannon was on the line. Rosie thanked her and picked up the phone.

"Good morning, Shannon. Sorry to hear your kids aren't feeling well. Do you have time to talk, or should we reschedule?"

"Good morning, Dr. Klein. Sorry, I couldn't come in today," Shannon said. "This time is good. The girls are snuggled together under a blanket and engrossed in cartoons. Our usual rule is: If you don't have a fever and aren't throwing up, you go to school.

But I'm letting them off the hook this time because they really wanted to go on a field trip today, so I don't think they are faking stomach aches and headaches. By the way, you sound just like Detective Gunderson," she laughed.

"I read Detective Gunderson's report, Shannon, and I'm so glad you provided personal details about your friend. May I ask, what prompted you to look around the house when Mr. Evans left to look for her?"

"I helped myself to a cup of herbal tea to calm my nerves. Since I carry my own teabags, all I require is hot water. I was putting my empty cup into the dishwasher, and that's when I noticed her mug with lipstick on it. Somehow it triggered doubts in my mind. You see, my friend, Joanie suffers from OCD. You know, obsessive-compulsive disorder. She would *never* have left lipstick on the rim of her mug. She would have washed it and put it away rather than place it in the dishwasher to begin with. OCD people can't stand to see things out of order or untidy."

"Well, you're a very observant person and obviously a dedicated friend. I read that you and Joanie often met at the park with your children and watched them play several times a week. Did you share personal aspects of your lives, too, or just the common things about raising little ones?"

"We shared all kinds of thoughts, fears, and blessings. We attended a Bible study at church and lots of times talked about our lessons. She was very insecure, Dr. Klein. Her husband was so controlling, she couldn't let him know that instead of meeting me sometimes, she went for counseling on Saturdays. He knew she was on medication for anxiety but expected her to keep their private lives to herself. He didn't realize that counseling was a 'must' if the doctor was going to continue prescribing her meds."

"Do you have any ideas as to what made her feel insecure?"

"Yes. She waited for Randy all those years while he was in juvenile detention. His letters made her feel needed. She began to believe she was lucky to have him and didn't think she could make it on her own. They were married as soon as he got out. And he's kept her barefoot and pregnant, so to speak. She never told me he hit her, but she always made excuses about her bruises when I asked about them."

"I've spoken with Randy Evans," Rosie said. "Do you think they would have arranged to meet each other at the park that morning?" Rosie asked.

"Actually, I think it's possible. As I mentioned before, she wanted to talk to him and there is never much privacy with little ones underfoot. By the time they went to bed, she told me he was often drunk. She could never talk with him then."

"So, your understanding is that he was drunk just about every evening?"

"I can't say for sure. One night a week he plays basketball at the church. He doesn't attend services himself, but he lets his wife and kids go so their family qualifies for church activities. The boys were christened there. Randy's brother and sister, Susie and Roger, are their godparents."

"Has Joanie ever said how he treats her when he's drinking?"

"Joanie said she avoids him by going upstairs with the boys and reading to them. He'll fall asleep, or you might say, passes out in his recliner with the television tuned to sports."

"How much does Noni Parrish, or Randy's siblings know about his behavior? Were you Joanie's only confidant?"

"She was afraid to say anything to Susie or Roger. Not that she thought they would tell their brother, but if either one would slip, then she would pay the price."

"I understand. How about Noni?"

"Noni knew more because the kids stayed at her house. They would say things at times like they couldn't wake up their dad. Their mom would be out running an errand for him, and he was supposed to be watching them. But he would be asleep in his chair, and they weren't allowed to get into the refrigerator by themselves. So, they would try to wake him up to get them something, and they never could."

"You said, 'she was running errands for him?'"

"Yes. Unless it was for him, Joanie wasn't allowed out of the house after he came home from work. If he needed something, he would demand she go get it, but she had to leave one kid behind. I think Randy was paranoid that she would leave him, and he knew she would never take off without both boys. If it was near their bedtime, he had her leave them both. Stupid. If she wanted to leave, she had all day to do it."

"She never talked about leaving him, did she?"

"No. She didn't believe in divorce. Aside from her strong religious beliefs, she figured he wouldn't pay child support and he might fight for the kids by saying she was nuts because he could use the fact that she took anxiety meds against her."

"So, you have reason to believe he was with her that morning?"

"I don't know. She wanted to plead with him not to be so harsh with the boys and cut down drinking in front of them. Maybe they went to the park to walk and talk."

"Maybe. In what ways was he harsh?"

"He used a paddle to spank the boys with their pants down or make them sit in a dark closet for long periods of time to think about whatever they did wrong. It broke her heart. What little kids don't do things wrong sometimes? Nothing big. Maybe spill milk or push and shove each other like boys do," Shannon said. "And one other thing: On weekends he was drinking to the point of passing out. She didn't want the children to know, so she told them he was napping."

"Do you know Susie and Roger? Was Randy close to his siblings?"

"They would come over for cookouts occasionally,

but Joanie's side of the family was never invited. His grandmother, Noni, was like a grandma to Joanie and she often came over." Just then, Shannon was interrupted by the girls and told them to quiet down.

"Thank you, Shannon. You've been immensely helpful. Feel free to contact me if you have anything else to share. I'm terribly sorry about the loss of your friend."

"Thank you, Dr. Klein. I can tell you're a compassionate person. You do remind me of Detective Gunderson. You talk like her, too. She also told me to call anytime."

Rosie hung up, refilled her coffee, and reached for a bagel. As she spread it with blueberry jam, she began to think about her next interview with Susie Evans. Susie had lived through the tragic death of her father and the long-term incarceration of her brother. Roger had been away in the military, and their mother had been a mess. Susie had been very young at the time and only got to visit Randy at Christmas time.

Claire buzzed Rosie to say that Susie was in the waiting room.

"I'll come out and get her. Thank you, Claire." Within minutes, Rosie greeted her.

Susie's Interview:

"Good morning, Susie. I'm Dr. Klein." She was looking at a pretty, slender, young woman standing in the corner leafing through an Oprah magazine. Susie looked up and smiled.

"Hi, Dr. Klein."

"Come on back to the conference room." They walked side by side. Susie was as tall as Rosie even though Rosie wore two-inch pumps.

"Care for a cup of coffee or water?" Rosie asked.

"Yes, thanks. Cream and sugar, please." Rosie poured coffee from the carafe and passed Susie cream, sugar, and a spoon.

"Thank you for coming in, Susie. Just call me Rosie. I know this must be a difficult time for you and your family."

"It's terribly difficult, Rosie. I can't believe Joanie is gone, and I can't believe my brother had anything to do with it. We adored Joanie. She stood by Randy the whole time he was in juvenile detention. Their kids are so sweet. I'm their godmother. If Randy goes to prison, how would I ever take care of them? I'm only twenty-one."

"Don't worry about that, Susie. I understand Roger is married and is also their godfather."

"That's true. Our mom and stepfather are never around. Our grandmother, Noni, is always available to help, though, particularly since our grandpa died last year. He was such a nice man."

"Is there anything you would like to tell me about your brother? I'm a psychologist and will be helping his lawyers prepare his defense. Are you aware of any problems he has had since getting out of juvenile?"

"Not really. He loved Joanie. He has a job and plays sports. I was ten when our dad died. Randy doesn't remind me of him at all, though. Randy doesn't cuss or beat Joanie. But our dad could be mean. He often hit our mom so hard she would end up in the emergency room. We always had to lie and say she fell off her bike and got hurt by the handlebars. Truthfully, he punched her in the stomach with his fist."

"Wow. Did you ever see him hit her?"

"Once I did. I was supposed to be headed up to my room. Mom, Randy, and I had just walked in the door from school. Our house had an open loft upstairs. When I heard him yelling, I laid down on the carpet and looked down through the slats. Yes, I saw him hit her twice with his fist. I covered my mouth to keep quiet. She was holding her stomach and laid in a ball on the living room floor and didn't move for the longest time. Dad told Randy to watch me so he could take mom to the emergency room. Sometime in the middle of the night, dad came back home, but Mom was in the hospital for a few days. We never talked about it again."

"Did somebody in authority interview you after that?"

"A lady from Children's Protective Services came over and talked to me and Randy. Roger wasn't home. He was much older, so I don't think they worried about him. But he was a witness to it, too. Randy and I said mom fell off her bike. They believed us, I guess. It must not have occurred to them that it was dark outside when the supposed 'accident' happened. But why would she be out riding at night?"

"I can understand why it's hard for you to believe Randy couldn't be abusive to his wife or kids."

"How could he be, after hating dad for hurting our mom?"

"Do you have a boyfriend, Susie?"

"Yes, a really nice guy. If he ever gets mad or yells at me, he apologizes later. He even gets me flowers and promises not to yell again."

"I see. Does he yell often?"

"He's not perfect by any means. But at least he's sorry and everything is nice most of the time. I'm not complaining."

"Thank you for coming in to talk with me, Susie." Rosie stood and Susie followed. They walked back to the reception area where Roger was sitting, waiting for his appointment.

Little does she know it, Rosie thought, *but I suspect Susie is on the same path as her mother and Joanie. Why doesn't she see she's already in a dangerous pattern? Why doesn't she know that it's never okay to excuse controlling behavior on the part of a partner in a relationship?*

"Hi sis," Roger said to Susie. She gave him a hug.

"Hi there, bro. You're going to like Dr. Rosie."

"I'm sure I will." They laughed and Susie waved good-bye.

"Hi, Roger. I'm happy to meet you," Rosie said shaking hands.

"Glad to be here to help my brother in any way I can."

"Come on back." Rosie opened the door to the hallway, and he followed her into the conference room.

"Do you care for water or coffee?" Rosie asked.

"Black coffee will be great. At this time of the morning, I need a caffeine boost."

Roger seated himself across the table from Rosie's materials. She sat down and buzzed the front desk. "Please bring us another carafe of coffee, Claire, no condiments needed." Claire quickly brought the freshly brewed pot and quietly exited the room.

Roger's Interview:

"So, Roger, I understand you live in Hilton Head," Rosie said. "I take it you're no longer in the Marines?"

"Actually, I'm in the Marine Reserves. I did my four years and decided to commit to being a reservist. It's just one weekend a month at Parris Island and two weeks in the summer. My wife works as a civilian on base. She's a cook in the officers' dining room. That's how we met. She was working in our mess hall, but since then, she's been promoted. The officers love her cooking. In high school, she was in culinary arts. It was a charter high school. Honestly, her pies are the best."

"I'm curious as to your impression of your brother's marriage to Joanie. Did you see them often?"

"I'm the kids' godfather and feel badly that because of the distance between us, my wife, Grace, and I haven't gotten up to see them much. After my four years of active duty, I used my sign-on bonus of ten grand for college. I graduated with an associate degree in hospitality. We hope to own our own restaurant someday and are saving to purchase one here on the Island. This is a tourist hot spot. People love coming to the Island from all over the world. Europeans love it, and they like our American food," Roger said.

"That's wonderful. Now, Roger, I'm talking to you today to gather facts. You do realize that Randy is the prime suspect in the murder of his wife, don't you?" Rosie asked. "The circumstantial evidence places him where her body was found on the day *before* it was found. He initially claimed to have no memory of being with her at the park and certainly not of harming her.

"After being arrested and charged with murder, he said her body in the morgue triggered some visions and memories. He thinks it's possible that she fell, and he believes he attempted to help her. Only that would not explain why he wouldn't have called for an ambulance. or why he went on to work that morning."

"Wow. I had no idea of all that, Dr. Klein," Roger said. His shock seemed genuine.

"Apparently, he's become a heavy, daily drinker. Were you aware of that?" she asked.

"No, I wasn't. We were with them this past Christmas. Mom and her husband had us all over for Christmas Eve. I figured he was drinking to celebrate the occasion. I know he has a good job, so how much of a problem is his drinking?" Roger asked.

"I haven't spoken to his boss yet who is supposedly out of town on vacation. Joanie's friend, Shannon Conrad, didn't mention hearing about any work-related problems. Here is a question for us to begin: How soon after his release from juvenile detention did you see him?"

"I saw him that same day. We knew ahead of time that he was being released. Grace and I came up and spent a long weekend with him at mom's house. She and her new husband bought a condo at Nantucket Reserve in Centerville. There was a spare bedroom for Randy. It was a peaceful environment for him to ease back into society.

"You know, he went into juvenile as a young teenager and came out as a young man. They had a deck off the dining room that sat high above the grassy bank of a large, kidney-shaped pond. We could hear frogs and the sounds of water streaming from a fountain that sat in the middle of the pond. It was peaceful. We all thought it would do him good. Mom also had a hot tub. We both sat in it enjoying beer and cigars. I remember Randy being relieved to be out and able to get on with his life. He talked about an internship he was starting at NCR. Joanie came over for dinner that night and they shared their plans to buy an engagement ring and get married."

"How has being raised by an abusive father factored into the way you treat your own wife and kids?" Rosie asked.

"I learned real discipline in the Marines. I

learned how to respond to aggressive acts toward me there, too. I learned how *not* to respond, I should say. It was great to learn impulse control and how to keep my emotions in check.

"If anything, my wife will tell you that if we get into a heated discussion, it aggravates her that I will walk away and not engage. My father *never* walked away. In fact, he was the one who always initiated the aggression. We never had a role model to teach us how to treat women respectfully or handle conflict, disappointment, or frustration appropriately," Roger said.

"After Randy and Joanie had the boys, did you ever know him to act verbally or physically abusive toward them or toward Joanie?" Rosie asked.

"Let's just say, Randy and I differ on the subject. I will *not* physically spank my son, but Randy thinks differently. I believe in using other methods of discipline.

"Grace and I took parenting classes offered to expectant parents at church. They taught us that discipline is intended to teach. You never know what your kids are learning when you spank them. Some learn to be sneaky and avoid being caught. Some learn that it only hurts briefly, and better than a suffering a day or weeklong punishment of some denied privilege."

"Sounds like you and Grace have healthy attitudes toward child-rearing. What did you see in terms of Randy's relationship with Joanie?"

"We didn't learn anything good about marriage from our parents. They had no mutual interests or friends. He yelled and she jumped. She had no input whatsoever into decisions made about our routines or how money was spent.

"My wife's parents are totally different. They plan everything together. They planned how many kids to have and how to raise them in a God-centered home. From what I can tell, my dad was not happy when my sister Susie arrived on the scene. He actually blamed my mother! I believe a man needs to take responsibility for his actions. My father always blamed someone else for his, mostly our mom, but sometimes us, for anything that didn't produce the results he expected.

"I must admit. I do see some of that attitude in my little brother. He blamed Joanie for getting pregnant the second time. From what I could tell, he controlled the money because he felt it was his right since he earned it."

"How could you tell that?"

"One time we talked about them visiting us, and he flat out said they couldn't afford it. I could tell from the look on Joanie's face that she had an opinion to share, but she didn't dare open her mouth. In the kitchen, she told Grace she would love to bring the boys down to visit sometime. She said she thought walking on the ocean's edge on the beach at Hilton Head would be wonderful."

"The only thing I have regrets about is leaving the house at eighteen. I left my brother in the position of protecting our mother and sister because I just couldn't stand my dad's rages any longer. I wasn't thinking about the family, just about escaping. It was selfish of me.

"Going into the Marines instead of the Air Force like my dad wanted me to do, was a form of retaliation toward him. I can't know all that Randy endured in juvenile all those years. But my guess is that it hardened him, and it's possible that he can't let go of the need to defend himself against all attacks. His perception probably isn't clear as to what poses a threat. He obviously doesn't know how to handle stress. He may think that anyone disagreeing with him is a threat, a danger to his ego, maybe?"

"That's good insight, Roger. I appreciate your honesty. I don't think you should beat yourself up about leaving at eighteen. You could not have predicted what would happen next. Thank you for coming in to speak with me today. If there's anything else on your mind, here's my business card. Feel free to contact me anytime."

Roger nodded his head in agreement. "Thank you, Dr. Rosie, I hope this will help my brother."

25

A New Case on the Horizon

Rosie stood up and stretched and thought about her next move. She could use her time to gather materials or call her mother for some quality time. She opted to balance her emotions after the sad Randy Evans case interviews by giving her mother a call."

"Hi, mom? I'm free for lunch. Can we meet somewhere?"

"Wonderful, dear. My bridge friends are dying to meet you. Can we meet at Walnut Grove Country Club at noon?

"Sure," Rosie said, "That's out east a few miles on I-35, right?"

"Yes," her mom said.

"That works. See you soon."

Rosie was glad for the distraction and loved being with her mother, an uplifting personality. She assumed dinner would be with Travis, Stella, and Devon to discuss her opinion of Randy Evans. Was he malingering? Did he deliberately shove his wife ? If so, did he mean to kill her? Or was it a horrible accident? It was so horrible that he had no memory of the event. She would think about it later. For now, her mind would rest.

Rosie drove to Walnut Grove and met her mother in the foyer. They hugged and proceeded into the dining room to join her mom's three bridge-playing friends.

"Everyone . . . this is my daughter, Rosie," Esther said. Her friends looked up, smiled, and greeted her in unison with versions of: "Oh, it's so nice to finally meet you, Rosie,"

Lunch proceeded with mostly small talk although they were intrigued by Rosie's career path. However, she took her professional hat off and put on her baseball hat, figuratively speaking. She inquired about their lives and relationships with her mother. They assured her that her mother was a remarkable, talented woman herself. They could see how she produced such a beautiful, talented daughter.

After a pleasant ninety minutes, Rosie excused herself from the table saying she had to drive a half-hour to the Warren County jail in Lebanon. She and her mother embraced.

"See you around eight-thirty tonight, Mom." Then, she turned to the others. "It was nice meeting you all. I know my mother is in good hands. . . and I wish you all 'great hands,' too." Inwardly she laughed at her own clever joke about their card-playing. "May you each have a grand slam this afternoon." The four ladies laughed together easily.

"I'm impressed with your daughter's humor," one of them said to Rosie's mom, "and her bridge knowledge, too. Let us know if she ever wants to play cards."

***

On the drive to Lebanon, Rosie's phone rang. She was stopped at a traffic light and felt safe to answer it.

"Hello. Is this Dr. Rosie Klein?" inquired a strong, female voice.

"Yes. This is Dr. Klein," Rosie said. She put her phone on speaker.

"I'm McKenna Day, an assistant prosecutor in Lucas County. I received your name from a mutual colleague, Matthew Murphy. He couldn't say enough about your qualifications, professionalism, and particularly your thoroughness. He said you are at the top of our list of experts and would provide an honest opinion regardless of who appointed you."

"Well, that's quite a kind vote of confidence," Rosie. "I'll be sure to thank him."

"Dr. Klein, I'm prosecuting an extremely complicated murder case and would like to have you appointed to evaluate the defendant's legal sanity, competency, and whether he actually is suffering from post-traumatic stress disorder . . . you know, 'PTSD.' He states he shot his wife as she came toward him, because he thought she was an Iraqi woman with a weapon hidden in her apron, maybe explosives. In other words, the defense says he was sleepwalking or hallucinating from PTSD. We need to know for sure."

"Well, I'm winding down a case in Warren County and will be home by Thursday. Can we meet to talk on Friday at the prosecutor's office?"

"That works great, Dr. Klein. I can have you appointed by Judge Benson this afternoon and will have materials for you to review. Does ten-thirty work for you?"

"Absolutely, and just call me Rosie."

"Thanks, Rosie. Just call me McKenna," she laughed. "I look forward to meeting you."

26

Memories Emerge

Rosie walked quickly from the public parking garage to the jail and through the security detail. Just after she seated herself in the visitation room, Randy was brought in by a deputy who released his handcuffs. He appeared weary with a scruffy beard, bloodshot eyes, and messy hair.

"Good afternoon, Randy. I see that you've met with your lawyer this morning. His name was on the visitor's log."

"Yeah. He seems nice, but obviously, he's not as experienced as his father, Travis."

"I'll probably ask you some of the same questions he did. Sorry for the repetition. Have any more memories emerged regarding that day at the park?"

"No. But, Gump was very interested in the scratches on the palms of my hands and the fact that Joan's fingernails didn't have any signs of skin underneath them. He thought that might prove I was telling the truth."

"Has he spoken to your boss, Mr. Cassidy, to validate your purpose for having a one-way ticket to Madrid?"

"He didn't mention it. But then I'm so nervous, I honestly forgot to ask him. You've got to believe me, Dr. Klein. It was for a business trip, and it was purchased for me at least a month ago. I don't know why it wasn't a round-trip ticket. Maybe he planned to send me on to a conference in Vienna. In no way, was I planning on killing my wife and running away, especially without my boys."

"I understand. But I'm not the one to convince, obviously. The prosecutor will present all the information to the twelve jurors and one alternate. My role is to determine whether you can help your lawyers defend you. I see no reason why you can't. Can you think of anything that could prevent you from assisting in your own defense?"

"No. Just nerves, and I can't sleep. There's a lot of snoring and guards flashing lights in our cells every night. At least, my two cellmates are quiet. They seem to like me okay. They're both pleading self-defense in each of their own cases. None of us knew each other before we became cellmates. But we're all fighting murder raps. They're not related to the victims, though, just me."

"Assuming your memories of Joanie slipping and falling down that steep slope are accurate and assuming you slid down to rescue her, help me understand why you would hide her body and not report the accident immediately. Actually, you *never* reported it."

"I can't answer that. I've racked my brain trying to figure out what I did and didn't do. I think for sure that I didn't remember any of it when I called the police to say she was missing. Possibly I left to get help and someone else discovered the body and hid it in the dumpster."

"I'm sorry, Randy, but in all honesty, that's not true. Your fingerprints were on the padlock beneath her body in the dumpster."

Randy put his head down on his arms and sobbed loudly. He cried out, "I'm *not* a killer! I loved her."

"Randy, there are times when good people act impulsively when faced with unexpected, stressful situations. Do you recall why you might have gone to the park or whether you argued?"

"I can't be sure. Let me think about it. Can you give me a few minutes?"

"Absolutely. Take all the time you need. I'll read the witness reports." Dr. Rosie could hear Randy breathing heavily and glanced at him. He wiped his eyes and looked up at the ceiling with his hands folded as if in prayer.

Minutes later, Rosie broke the silence. "When you left the park, did you see any other cars coming down the narrow road?"

"I can't remember driving out of the park . . . oh, wait. I *did* drive up a narrow, paved road. Two guys in a jeep were coming down toward the parking lot. Why?"

"The two guys were Bengals football players who

jog the trails as a work-out. They identified your red truck."

"I think you're right about good people acting in bad ways sometimes. You once told me I was a good person, back when I shot my father to protect my mother. Do you still think so?"

"Yes, I do, Randy, and I remember that, too."

"I remember Joanie asked me the night before it happened that she wanted to take a walk and talk about our future. Let me think." Randy's face was turned away from Rosie. "I have to admit, I was drinking too much. I was afraid she was going to tell me she wanted a divorce. She always begged me not to drink in front of the kids. I tried, but when I pass this neighborhood bar, Kremers, on the way home from work, guys from work stop in for a beer or two, and I just go in with them. I don't know why. I'm deeply sorry, now. I shoulda listened to her."

"You thought she might be asking for a divorce that morning?"

"Yeah. I was always the one who threatened to divorce her when she nagged me. Back then, she didn't believe in divorce. I guess I thought she might of changed her mind, you know, I kinda felt desperate."

"But you don't know that for sure. When you were hiking, you don't recall her asking for a divorce, right?"

"No. Oh, no. She wanted me to *listen*. She was frustrated and pointing a finger at me." His voice elevated, "Oh, dear Lord. I remember something! I grabbed her wrist and pulled her toward me." His eyes opened wide with the memory. "Then, I don't know why, but I shoved her backwards, and she slipped! Honest to God, she slipped! Her heels went out and she went backwards down the steep wooded slope. Oh, God!" he said in a tormented tone of voice. "I couldn't get down there. There was no place to put my feet. I had to run back down the trail. By the time I finally got to the bottom by her, she was flat on her back, eyes wide open. There was a lot of blood underneath her head. I could see she was gone. I remember those eyes staring up at me." Randy could hardly breathe. He crossed his arms, grabbed his chest and shook his head in disbelief.

Rosie gave him a moment, realizing the shock of such memories finally returning. After a while, she said softly, "Randy, go on if you can. It's important."

He sobbed and said, "She was lying at the base of the hill. There was a small picnic area nearby with one picnic table on cement. The dumpster was beside it. It was unlocked. I removed the padlock which was just hanging loose and lifted the lid. Then, I tossed in the padlock, too. I picked up her lifeless body and placed it as gently as I could in the bottom of the shallow dumpster. It was almost like a white coffin. I can see it now in my mind."

"What happened next?"

"I took her car keys from her jeans pocket. I don't know why I did that. Then I followed a narrow trail that ran across the bridge, over the stream, to the parking lot. I made sure her car was locked but I left her purse on the passenger seat where she put it. Then, I. .I. . don't know, guess I panicked. I jumped into my truck and drove out as fast as I could . . . just to get out of there."

"You didn't realize you had been seen?"

"No. I wasn't thinking clearly. I went home to change clothes. Now I remember putting my muddy shoes in the wheelbarrow. I've done that before. Then I drove to work and just forgot about everything."

"Randy, with your confession, there won't be a trial. The prosecutor will decide what to charge you with based on the evidence, including your version of events. The defense may dispute the charges, or they may agree. Judge Schuster will set a date for a sentencing hearing. Both the prosecutor and your attorney will address the court with their positions. You'll have an opportunity to make a statement and people who know you and Joanie will have an opportunity to speak to the judge. You will hear what they have to say, good and bad, and they will hear your story. The judge will set a date for sentencing and will take all information under advisement. Do you understand?"

"Yeah . . . I understand. . . I did it. I killed my wife," Randy's voice wavered. "I want to make a statement to the judge. This is just like last time when I shot my father. Only this time, the outcome will determine where I spend the rest of my life . . . and if I'll ever see my boys again outside prison walls." His head was bowed low. "You know, Dr. Rosie, maybe they would be better off without me. I have nothing to live for at this point."

"Randy, don't think that way. You don't have a

crystal ball to see what purpose your life has. Maybe it's time to trust God. Has the medic been in to see you?" Randy shook his head.

"I'll ask the medic to prescribe an anti-depressant." She waited a moment. "May I get the prison chaplain in touch with you?"

"Yeah, I'd like that. I can't go on feeling this heavy burden of guilt," Randy confessed. "I feel so ashamed!"

She sat quietly while he processed what he had just told her.

27

What Happened in Juvie

Realizing that he had just faced the truth, Rosie spoke softly. "Randy, before I go, I have one I need to talk with you about one more thing. You acknowledged that since you left juvenile, you've had a short fuse. What was your temper like before you shot your father?"

"I was sort of mild. I liked music," he said. "I studied and obeyed rules at school and home. I was a good kid. My dad didn't realize how hard I tried to get his approval. I was not an angry person except when I saw him hurt my mother and when he smacked my brother and me around. He usually left my little sister alone. My friends were from good homes and were like me. I wasn't surrounded by angry or hostile kids."

"So, what changed after you went into juvie? What happened to change your behavior and your attitude?"

He was silent. Then, slowly he began to open up about his past. "I never told anyone but I was sexually and mentally abused in juvie. I came out broken with so much anger and fear. You hear a lot about correction officers hurting kids, but most abuses came from older inmates. The physical abuse was everywhere, too. It's a tough place to be.

"When I was fifteen, I had to be the 'boyfriend' of the oldest and strongest one there. No one else messed with me because of that. But I don't need to explain to you what that meant, do I? You know what I mean . . . the price I paid?"

"No, Randy, you don't have to go into detail. I am so extremely sorry. Did the officers in charge know what was going on?

"They had to know. And the guards did other cruel things, like locking me up in solitary for three days at a time. Minimal food and water; little light and no heat. One time, they thought I stole a cell phone, but I couldn't tell them I was set up by a gang in there to take the blame. There were things like that. It's hard to get guards to believe you in a place like that. Without confessing, you pay the price."

"Randy, we need to have your attorney come over and listen to your story. Stay here. I will ask the guard to let you wait here while I call Attorney Gump."

"Okay, and thanks, Dr. Klein. It kinda feels good to get this off my mind, but honestly, you've got to believe me about Joanie. I remembered a little more last night in my cell. And some things surfaced just now as we talked here. But my mind has been totally confused, and my heart is broken. I've destroyed our lives. My precious boys deserve better."

Rosie slid a pencil and a legal pad across the table to Randy. She got up and tapped on the glass window in the door with her car keys. The deputy unlocked the door and she asked him to keep Randy Evans in the visitation room. "His attorney will be coming to visit him soon."

She turned around and spoke to Randy. "You might want to jot down what you've just told me, so you don't leave anything out when Attorney Gump gets here, okay?"

"Yeah, that's a good idea. Maybe I should write out the order of the events that morning, too."

"Yes. Do that and I'll do the same. I'll give my version of what you just told me to Attorney Gump later today." Rosie closed the door gently and walked out of the building. She called Devon Gump's office. His receptionist, Claire, answered with a cheery voice.

"Claire, this is Rosie Klein. Is Devon Gump available to speak?" She put Rosie's call through to Devon.

"Devon, I urge you to get over to the Warren County Jail as soon as you can. I know it's a thirty-minute drive, but I have Randy waiting in the visitation room. He has a confession to make. I hesitated sending him back to gen pop. I honestly think he needs to be put on suicide watch at this point. I also want to contact the chaplain and jail medic."

"Rosie, I can make it happen and will be out the door in ten minutes. Thank you. See you at dinner tonight?"

"Yes. I'm heading to your dad and Stella's house right now. I know Stella is expecting me."

28

Time of Respite

Stella answered the doorbell and threw her arms around Rosie. "It means so much to have you here with us. I'm sorry Bucky couldn't make the trip. How have things been going, so far?"

As Rosie brought her up to date, Stella led Rosie outside to the patio where a pitcher of Sangria and four glasses sat, along with a tray of cheeses, olives, summer sausage, grapes, and crackers.

"My forensic work has so many surprises," Rosie said, "Here I was in the middle of evaluating Randy Evans' competency, and the next thing I knew, he was confessing! He didn't murder his wife, as in first-degree planned murder. It sounds more like it was accidental in the heat of an argument. That would reduce the charge to manslaughter and probably obstruction of justice for hiding the body," Rosie speculated as she helped herself to a handful of grapes.

Stella poured Rosie a glass of Sangria and hung an orange slice on the rim. "You have got to be kidding.

He's confessed? Does Devon know?" She handed the glass to her dear college friend, kicked her shoes off, and sat down beside her.

"Yes, Devon just went down to interview him. Where is Travis?"

"Travis is on the golf course, or on the way home from the club. They'll probably start planning strategy tonight after Devon drives back from seeing Randy."

"I need to let Bucky know I'll be home by dinner time tomorrow. I don't think I'll need to see Randy again if we talk business tonight."

"Speak of the devil," said Stella as Travis walked out onto the patio. He gave her a kiss on the cheek and acknowledged Rosie.

"Hi, ladies, Devon just told me the news. Our guy confessed to causing the death of his wife. Causing the death is not the same as planning and executing a murder. I don't have to tell you that, do I?" Travis asked Rosie.

"No. So, will you be contacting the friendly prosecutor and explaining the change of circumstances in the case? You'll probably discuss appropriate charges?"

"All of the above. I do need you to complete a report we can submit to Judge Schuster and the prosecutor's office. It'll be interesting to see if Randy gives Devon the same details as he gave to you. You really think he's a danger to himself?"

"I do, especially if he sees no hope in ever being with his boys again. I'll call the medic and ask for antidepressants to be prescribed. The chaplain may be helpful to assuage some of Randy's guilt and shame."

"Now, we wait," Travis said. "Meanwhile, until Devon arrives, let's enjoy the evening together. Tell me more college stories about my Stella." For the next hour, they relaxed and laughed together. It was good to be among friends.

A while later, Rosie asked to be excused for a few minutes. She stepped into the kitchen and called her mother. "Hi mom. How was the rest of your afternoon with your friends?"

"It was great, Rosie," her mother replied, "They were so impressed with you and couldn't stop talking. To be quite honest, it was distracting to play a hand of bridge with questions and comments going on." They both laughed. It was easy between them.

"Since I can't see you this evening, can we have breakfast before I head back home? What's your schedule? Of course, Caleb is welcome too."

"I look forward to it, dear. Unfortunately, Caleb has a midmorning tee time."

"You don't need to wait up. I will be home by ten, I'm sure."

"That's not late for me. I usually read until eleven. We can have a nightcap."

"Okay. Talk later."

Next, Rosie dialed Bucky. He answered and she could hear barking in the background. "Hi Bucky. How's your camp going?"

"It's been very encouraging to see those young

men and women striving to secure their futures in high school and college sports. How has your case been?"

"I'm pretty well wrapped up here at Travis and Stella's house. We're having a semi-professional dinner together. Devon is joining us soon. I'll share my professional opinion and findings about the Randy Evans case with them and complete a report for the Court once I get home. I'll see my mother in the morning, then I'll be on my way home."

"Does that mean I'll see my sweetheart tomorrow night?"

"Absolutely. How's *my* sweetheart been, and Jocko, too, of course? I heard him in the background."

"He's definitely noticed your absence. Other than that, he is fine. We both miss you."

"I should be home by four o'clock. How about you, when will you be home?"

"I'll be here; I don't want to keep my best gal waiting. Drive carefully. Don't let your case distract you on the highway."

"I won't. Thanks for the reminder. Love you. Bye."

"Bye, Rosie. And tell your mom and stepdad I said hello."

"Will do." Rosie hung up and returned to the patio where Devon was standing beside his father. Stella was seated at the table, listening to their conversation.

"Hey, Rosie. Can we take time to talk about Randy Evans?" Devon asked, who had just arrived. They joined Stella beneath the umbrella and Devon began to share his visit with Randy.

"Randy will be on suicide watch until the sentencing hearing," Travis said. "Oh, and, by the way, I contacted Frank Winslow, one of the assistant prosecutors on the Evans case. Sid Hochwalt is meeting with the grand jury on another case and is unavailable. Frank and I are meeting in the morning. Is there any chance you could join us? You are most able to answer some of Winslow's questions regarding Evans' state of mind."

"Sure. No problem. I'm available. Where and when?" Rosie asked. She reminded herself to cancel breakfast with her mother knowing she would understand.

"He's coming to my office at ten o'clock. You don't need to be there early. We're discussing everything now. How about you, Dad? Would you like to sit in on the meeting?"

"Yes. I will but, I want you to take the lead, Devon. I can fill Frank in on the juvenile history even though it won't be admissible evidence at trial. It seems to me, though, it still helps the defendant. What do you think, Rosie?" Travis asked.

"Absolutely. This is one of those rare cases where childhood abuse by several sources and no intervention has led this young man to suffer severe emotional distress, but it's not an excuse for what he did. Is that your take, too, Devon, that he lost control and accidentally pushed her? Or do you believe he deliberately shoved her down the cliff?"

"From my interview with him this afternoon, I

think they argued, and he felt provoked or threatened as she pointed her finger in his face, and maybe her tone of voice. Again, no excuse for the violent reaction, but it's an explanation as to his perception. He overreacted because of the years he suffered being bullied and also the physical abuse," Devon said.

"Also, new information came to my attention when I spoke with Winslow. He received a statement from Detectives Gunderson and Harris stating that Randy Evans' boss, Mr. Cassidy, *did* purchase a ticket to Madrid for Randy. He was to go on to another meeting in Vienna and that ticket was waiting for him at the office yesterday. The return was to be from Vienna to Cincinnati and had not been booked yet."

"Well," Travis said, "I guess none of that will factor into the matter at hand. But it does speak to his credibility. That's one thing truthful that he always maintained to be the truth, right?"

Rosie and Devon nodded yes. "What we do need to deal with is his motive in placing her in the dumpster and attempting to hide all evidence of his involvement," Devon said, scratching his head. "I think perhaps at that moment in time, his desperate, survival instinct kicked in. He was probably thinking there was no way he was ever going back to a place of incarceration. Probably something he felt that juvie was. Did you ask him, Rosie?"

"We didn't get beyond his memories of pushing her and his supposed attempt to help her. He had no explanation for his behavior the rest of the day. He swore he didn't remember any of it when he picked up the kids from daycare and then called Shannon Conrad, his grandmother, Noni Parrish, and the police," Rosie said.

"What does matter here is the fact there is no evidence of premeditation," Devon said.

"Very likely, but additional charges will be forthcoming," Travis said. "You can't hide a corpse and physical evidence without being charged with abuse of a corpse or obstruction of justice."

"I will definitely be prepared to do that," Devon said.

"I spoke to Randy about what he would say to Judge Schuster and the family," Rosie said. "I hope to meet with him prior to that hearing."

***

That night, Rosie and her mother enjoyed their nightcap, had coffee and a bagel in the morning, and hugged good-bye with promises to get together again soon. Rosie planned to drive the 175-mile trip home to her husband and Jocko while processing thoughts about the case. There was always work to be done, but she would be glad to get home.

29

Dayton Bound - Again

O n Tuesday, Rosie was back in Dayton and had just settled behind her desk when the phone rang in the outer office. Within a minute, her secretary was patching a call through to her.

"Hi Rosie. It's Travis Gump. Is this a good time to talk?"

"Hi Travis. I assume you're calling with news about the Randy Evans sentencing hearing.

"Yes, I'm calling to ask you to be there. The sentencing hearing is scheduled for two weeks from Friday. Your report has been entered into evidence and will serve as your direct testimony. I doubt the prosecutor will cross-examine you, but I'll ask if you've found any mitigating factors that Judge Schuster should hear prior to his sentencing recommendation. You can share your findings at that time."

"Okay, sounds good," Rosie replied. "I'll be there."

"Also, mixing a little pleasure with business, we're having a charity golf outing with proceeds going to the Cystic Fibrosis Foundation. One of our judge's daughters died from cystic fibrosis so we've decided to make it our charity cause this year. I'd love you to bring your clubs and play. A number of lawyers and judges will be there which is being held at my country club this year. It would be good for you to meet them."

"I'd love to," she said.

"Would Bucky be interested in playing? It's a scramble format, so no one needs to be an outstanding golfer. I know he took the sport up after he met you and he's athletic. Bet he can hit a mile-long drive, right?"

"Absolutely, but I doubt he'll want to play even though I'll invite him. Is there something else he can do to assist? Once before he stood on the tee and sold hole-in-one chances." They laughed easily at the mental picture.

"I'll fax you the information. It's the day following the sentencing, so maybe you could make it a long weekend here. If you want to see Randy one more time, Devon has offered to arrange it."

"That'll be fine. I assume Devon will want to meet with me, too."

"Yes. Actually, it would work if you could plan on coming to the office after you have interviewed Evans."

"Sure, as soon as we hang up, I'll call my mother and arrange to stay at her house. Tell Stella I look forward to seeing her."

"Your mother and her husband are welcome to come to dinner the evening of the golf outing. Some of the lawyers play in a band and they'll be entertaining us."

"Sounds wonderful," Rosie said. "Be seeing you soon."

Just as she hung up, Ruth tapped lightly on the door and walked in. Plunking down in one of the plush, wingback chairs, she put her feet up on the ottoman.

"So, boss lady, what's going on? I feel as if we never have a chance to catch up. How's your personal life?"

"My personal life is great. I need to go back to Warren County for the Randy Evans sentencing hearing, scheduled in two weeks. I hope Bucky can go with me this time. We've been invited to play in a charity golf outing sponsored by the Dayton Bar Association. My mother will be thrilled to see Bucky. His charm has her practically swooning," The two women laughed.

"So, what about you, Ruth? What have you been up to since I've been gone?"

"I have a concert coming up and would like you and Bucky to attend. It will be at the Toledo Museum of Art following a reception with appetizers and drinks. We will be singing patriotic songs and Southern gospel hymns. I know those are your favorite."

"Sounds like fun, Ruth. How much are the tickets?"

"I am gifting them to you, Rosie. You are a tremendous boss and a dear friend."

The phone rang, again, and Ruth jumped up. "Well, nice chat; back to work."

Rosie called Bucky to share events of the day and suggest they go to supper at Alfie's.

"Hi Rosie," he answered cheerfully. "How's my best gal?"

"You mean your *only* gal, right?"

"Of course! To what do I owe the pleasure? I only saw you a couple of hours ago."

"How would you like to go to mom and Caleb's with me in two weeks? Travis called to tell me when he needs me to testify in the Evans case, then asked us to play in a charity golf outing. There is a dinner with entertainment. Don't feel pressure to play in the tournament. On the other hand, you can if you like. I would welcome you on my team."

"Sure, I'd love to go. Can I let you know in a few days whether I want to participate in the golf outing? I'll see about getting some practice at the driving range. Maybe I should just sell hole-in-one tickets again."

"Do whatever you are comfortable doing. I'm thrilled you'll accompany me. Jocko can stay at mom's when we're away from her house. By the way, I'd like to have a filet mignon at Alfie's tonight. How does that strike you?"

"Okay, and speaking of strikes, you should see the pitcher I just recruited for the baseball team. He's tall and wiry and has a huge wingspread for balls hit anywhere near him."

"Congratulations. I take it you're in the mood to celebrate then."

"Absolutely," Bucky replied exuberantly.

"Great I'm about to call my mom to make our plans to visit. Then I'll head home, walk Jocko, and see you around six."

"Sounds like a plan, Rosie, see you at home."

Rosie made the next call to her mother to make arrangements and continued on with her workday.

I am so blessed to have such wonderful family and friends, she thought. *I am one happy woman.*

30

Reunion

The trip to Dayton was an easy drive. Knowing they would see Rosie's mom and her husband soon, made it even more pleasant. Arriving at the condo, they parked and carried one suitcase apiece upstairs with Jocko leading them on his leash. Rosie's mom answered the door on their first ring.

"So nice to see you again, Bucky," Esther said as she greeted her new son-in-law with a hug.

"The pleasure is all mine," Bucky said, hugging her back.

"Hi, mom." Rosie said while she waited for the hug she knew was coming. "Where's Caleb?"

"He is on the nineteenth hole, hoping we'll join him for a late lunch," Esther answered.

"Ahh, the nineteenth hole," Bucky grinned with appreciation as the women laughed.

"Right, where are the men enjoying it?" Rosie asked

"No matter where it is, I say we take him up on his

offer," Bucky said, "What do you think, ladies?"

"Fine with me," Rosie said. "Mom, is it okay with you?"

"Of course! Jocko can have the run of the house while we're gone, dear. He seems to be getting older, isn't he?" Esther smiled. "Just like the rest of us. Well, let's be on our way. I'll drive." She grabbed her keys.

Rosie didn't want to think about losing Jocko, but her mother was right. Rosie admitted she had noticed how slowly Jocko was moving now on their daily walks.

***

Caleb was seated at a table in the mixed grill. There was a 'men's only' grill area adjacent to their locker room where the men wandered around in shower towels. It wasn't a good spot for their gathering either since it was a place where women were not permitted. That would have excluded the very two women he wanted to sit with. Caleb now stood and shook hands with Bucky.

"Good to see you. Did you bring your clubs?"

"As a matter of fact, I did. Rosie said she would be occupied with court-related stuff, but also invited me to play in a charity outing. So, I need to practice, that's for sure," he laughed.

Caleb held out the chair for his wife, Esther. Bucky followed suit for Rosie. They enjoyed a leisurely lunch that would double as dinner for the older couple. Travis and Stella were expecting Rosie and Bucky at six p.m., so the younger couple settled for a bowl of lobster bisque and fresh, warm bread.

***

Devon and his wife, Brenda, were sitting at a table by the pool along with his father, Travis, and Stella. When Rosie and Bucky arrived, Stella answered the door and led them outside to the group where she introduced Bucky and Rosie to Brenda.

"Glad to meet you, Bucky," Devon said.

Devon began outlining the pending procedures to Rosie. Out of courtesy, she didn't interrupt the young lawyer to mention how familiar she was with sentencing hearings. When he completed his explanations, Rosie simply told him she would meet one more time with Randy Evans and hear what he planned to say at the hearing.

"Devon, rest assured Rosie will be prepared to testify if you need her," Travis said, "and she'll have Randy geared up to speak on his own behalf, too, if you want."

"I have no doubts, Dad," Devon said. "I must admit that anything we say or do at this point will unlikely influence Judge Schuster's recommendation which he's probably already decided upon. But, in the United States of America, everyone is entitled to a proper defense and has the right to be heard. But I do have one question: Although his prior conviction as a juvenile would not have been allowed in a jury trial, do you believe Judge Schuster will factor that into his opinion?"

Travis thought a brief moment about how to answer his son, then responded. "Rosie can present the circumstances of his childhood. That is considered a mitigating factor in his defense. But the juvenile conviction simply can't be held against him in the determination of sentencing in an adult court of common pleas," Travis said.

"Okay, everyone, time to enjoy a casual dinner together," Stella chimed in.

They put aside thoughts of Randy Evans and joined Stella in catching up on Bucky's career and plans he might have in pursuing a second career as a golf professional.

"Very funny," Bucky said. "If I didn't make it in baseball, how would I ever make it in golf. How's your game, Devon?"

Devon just laughed.

Rosie addressed Devon's wife, Brenda. "I understand you're in law school. Do you plan on joining the Gump firm at some point?"

"Not really, unless they expand their legal services to include family law. I aspire to be a family law judge after I practice for seven years. Obviously, that's now a long-term ten-year plan. It could even take longer if my education is prolonged by the births of our twins."

"Twins? Is that an *announcement*?" Stella spoke up in animated tones.

Devon reached for Brenda's hand. "You got it, grandma. Didn't you wonder why Brenda was putting on weight when she's one of the busiest, active women you know? We were looking for the right time to tell you."

"How wonderful! We're delighted, Devon," Travis said. "Let us know how we can help. Anything you need to help Brenda stay on track with her education, just ask."

The evening ended on a high note with Bucky and Rosie inviting Travis and Stella to join them for a week on Hilton Head Island in September.

31

Final Evaluation

Rosie took a seat with her back to the wall. Although Randy Evans posed no threat to her physical safety, her heart raced, remembering an incident years ago when one inmate had ripped an earring out of her earlobe. It had been painful, and she had sought the help of Dr. Seifer, her downtown landlord to get over the traumatic memory. He had assured her that the periodic intrusive recollections would eventually subside. Now, she used a thought-stopping technique she had been taught by her psychiatrist in their sessions. He reminded her to use a calming exercise, one she had even taught her own hypervigilant, anxious clients in the past.

"Stop it," Rosie said out loud to herself, then found something else to distract her vivid memories. She pictured herself on the beach at Saint Martin walking hand in hand with Bucky. She even added their dog, Jocko, in her thoughts even though he had not really accompanied them on their honeymoon.

Just then, the guard opened the door and released Randy Evans' handcuffs. She immediately noticed how meek he appeared. As Evans took his seat, the interview began.

"Good morning, Randy. Are you prepared for the hearing?"

"Yes, Dr. Klein. I'm glad to see you. How are you?

"Fine, Randy, thanks for asking," Rosie said. "How are things with you?"

"Well, my brother, Roger, and our sister, Susie, came to see me. They were both encouraging. Roger and his wife are taking guardianship of my boys and are planning to move into my house so the boys will be comfortable and not have to adjust to a new environment. With everything they've been through, I'm glad Roger and Susie still want to have a relationship with me, in spite of the terrible things I've done."

"Why, that's wonderful," Rosie said. "That will be a tremendous help to your young sons, won't it?"

"Yeah. I also wish I could see my grandmother, Noni. But Roger said she isn't feeling well. Her heart isn't that strong anymore. She plans on writing to me though and sends her love. Nice, huh? We lost my grandpa Adam last year which has been stressful for her and the rest of the family. He was such a great role model."

"I understand," Rosie said. "How did he pass?"

"He had a sudden heart attack, then arrested in the hospital. He was in a coma on life support for nineteen days which took a toll on everybody, especially my grandmother. It was horrible to see him lying there day after day. At least he died peacefully, without pain."

"That's a good thing, Randy," Rosie agreed. "I'm so sorry for your tremendous loss, too."

"Do you think I'll see him in heaven . . . or is that not where I'm gonna end up?"

"Making amends with others and your personal relationship with the Lord will determine where you spend eternity. It seems to me that believing in God is already helping you feel less isolated than you did when we met a few weeks ago. Is that so?"

"You're right about that. Even though memories keep flooding in, I have people to talk to. I don't think I could live with myself if it weren't for them. I think I deserve whatever sentence Judge Schuster imposes. I have to own up to what I did."

"I'm glad to hear that, Randy."

"Honestly, Dr. Rosie, I hated how my father treated Mom and us. I hated the way I was abused in juvie all those years. But I don't understand how I turned out to be just like my old man: mean, irritable, controlling, and abusive. Thank God, I didn't seriously hurt my boys, Todd or Eric. And I hate myself for what happened to Joanie. But the worst thing, and something I'd never forgive myself for causing, is if their memories of me would be filled with fear and hatred." He looked at her, then hung his head down. "What am I saying? They'll hate me for causing the death of their mother."

Randy barely got the words out before he put his head down on his arms and wept out loud. Rosie sat quietly, knowing he needed time to grieve. Finally, he sighed and sat upright in his chair. She watched his face and when it was appropriate, spoke again.

"Did you write what you plan to say to the judge and others who will be sitting in the courtroom?"

"Yes," Randy said, wiping his hands on his clothes and pulling a folded sheet of notebook paper from his breast pocket. He handed it to Rosie. "Will you read it, Dr. Klein? I can't do it now," he sounded truly sad and forlorn.

"Certainly. Shall I read it out loud?" Rosie asked.

"Yeah, if you don't mind," Randy responded.

She read the statement out loud, then looked at him. "It sounds good, Randy. Did the medic prescribe the Zoloft I recommended to calm your anxiety? And have you been taking it?"

"I have and it's been helping. Regardless of the collapse you just witnessed, my moods are better. I don't know why, but something about your presence just let me have this meltdown. I'm glad you understand. You know, a guy can't show weakness in prison. The weak are like sheep thrown to the wolves."

"Well, after reading your speech, I don't think you're a danger to yourself any longer. Am I correct?" Rosie asked.

"Yes, completely. I'm clinging to the hope that my boys will one day be reconciled with me. I plan to fill a lot of journals and write to them and the others often."

Rosie stood and Randy followed. She shook his hand. "See you at the hearing, Randy. I'm recommending anger management classes as part of your rehabilitation program. Your fellow inmates will respect you when they see how successful you'll manage stress and confrontation from them and from the guards."

"Thank you, Dr. Klein. I'll never forget your kindness. I just hope I'm not sent to a maximum-security prison. Is it okay, if I let you know where I'm housed and keep you posted on my progress?"

"Absolutely. I'm going to advise the medic to take you off suicide watch but keep you on your meds for the next six months. I also applaud you for choosing to trust God to direct your path in life from now on, and for wanting to serve a purpose in prison. Self-respect will develop, and you'll have something to offer your sons when they grow up."

The guard unlocked the door and led Randy out in handcuffs. Rosie collected her materials, took a deep breath, and sighed. She thought back to the time Randy was fourteen years old, and how tragic his life had become. Her sorrow stayed with her for a while after she left the building.

In the car, she decided to call Bucky. *Maybe it'll lighten my mood,* she thought.

He answered on the second ring.

"Hi, Bucky. I'm through interviewing my inmate. Just heading to Travis and Devon's office to brief them on my opinion of their client's state of mind. It shouldn't take long."

"We're just sitting in your mom's kitchen waiting

to hear from you. How about meeting us at the Peasant Stock? Invite the Gumps, if you want. Their office is nearby."

"You know, I need some quiet family time and the Peasant Stock is a perfect place. Last time I was here, you weren't with me and most of my time was spent with the Gumps, and Randy Evans. If you don't mind, I'm not going to ask them tonight."

"Okay, sweetie. Let us know when you're on the way, Bye for now," Bucky said.

"Good deal. Love you." Rosie hung up.

She drove directly from the Warren County Jail to the Gump offices in Kettering. In her mind, she processed her opinion of her morning meeting with Randy Evans as she listened to light jazz and her mood began to lighten.

32

The Evans Hearing

Randy Evans sat quietly between his attorneys, Devon, and Travis Gump. Twelve jurors were seated in the jury box waiting to see if they would be needed should a trial be called to commence. Prosecutor Frank Winslow sat at a table across the aisle with two assistants seated to his right. Roger and Susie Evans were sitting two rows behind their brother and a few reporters were in the back row just inside the doors. Bailiff Williams, a tall, muscular, stern-looking, middle-aged man, announced the entrance of Judge Schuster.

"Please rise."

Everyone in the courtroom respectfully stood as Judge Schuster took his seat behind the bench; he gestured for them to be seated.

"Would the representatives for the defense, and the State of Ohio, now approach the bench?" Judge Schuster requested firmly.

Devon Gump and Frank Winslow immediately

stood and stepped forward as directed. The court reporter, seated nearby, was not privy to their conversation. It was assumed by all that the judge was requesting confirmation that the prior agreement was still in place. Once confirmed by both attorneys, Judge Schuster announced: "Please be seated gentlemen."

"As you both know, this jury has been selected in the event a trial will proceed should the agreement between the State of Ohio represented by Attorney Winslow, and the defendant, represented by Devon Gump be nullified," the judge said. It would be highly unusual for that to happen, however, since Judge Schuster was known for his thoroughness and was always prepared.

"Attorney Winslow," the judge intoned, "On behalf of the State of Ohio, you may begin your final statement to this court."

Attorney Winslow moved swiftly to the podium which was positioned in the center of the aisle directly below the judge's bench.

"Your honor, the State of Ohio has agreed to a plea of second-degree murder and obstruction of justice by the defendant, Randy Evans. In so doing, we are recommending he be sentenced to the maximum number of years according to the Ohio statute for his offenses, to be served concurrently. Joan Evans experienced a violent death at the hands of her husband, Randy Evans. His children are deprived of being nurtured, loved, and raised by their mother. Mrs. Evans was highly respected and appreciated by her community, and her life was prematurely torn away from her loved ones and friends. Thank you for your consideration, your honor." Attorney Winslow closed his folder and returned to his seat without glancing toward the defense table. He failed to notice the gasping sound of Randy Evan's sister, Susie.

Judge Schuster quickly responded. "The agreement to the charges has been noted as is the recommendation for sentencing. The jury is now excused." He looked at the jury members, most with placid expressions, a few with looks of disappointment. "The court thanks you for your service." An officer of the court opened the side door and all jurors filed out quietly.

Devon Gump stood and announced: "Your honor, on behalf of the defense, we would like to begin by hearing the testimony of Dr. Rosie Klein."

"Your expert witness may take the oath and be seated," Judge Schuster answered. I assume the prosecutor has reviewed her credentials and has acknowledged her as an expert witness."

"No objections, your honor," Frank Winslow answered. "The prosecutor's office frequently refers criminal cases to Dr. Klein, and we recognize her expertise," he said.

Rosie approached the witness stand and faced the bailiff. She placed her hand on the Bible and said, "I do" to the question of whether she was willing to tell the truth, the whole truth, and nothing but the truth, so help her God. She seated herself with her materials in front of her.

Devon stood closely in front of Dr. Klein and began his line of questioning. "Dr. Klein, how long have you known the defendant, Randy Evans?"

"I met Randy Evans when I was appointed to evaluate him for shooting his father. That was approximately eleven years ago. He was fourteen years old, and his case was heard in the juvenile court of Montgomery County, Ohio."

"Can you tell the court what circumstances led to Randy Evans shooting his father?"

"Yes. For years, Mr. Evans' mother suffered severe mental and physical abuse by his father, Colonel Evans. On the day of the shooting, Mr. Evans' older brother, Roger, turned eighteen and left on that same day for the United States Marine Corp. Randy did not think he could possibly protect his mother, his little sister, or himself with his older, stronger brother gone from the house. He was totally intimidated by his father's anger toward them and planned to defend himself as his father came up the stairs that day, angered by what he perceived was his older son's betrayal.

"Randy Evans could not remember any time when he was *not* harshly punished for small, childhood violation of rules. He fully expected his father's conduct to continue. On that particular day, he feared for all of their lives and felt completely helpless with his brother gone. That is why he armed himself with a gun and planned to defend himself that day."

"What was the result of his decision to shoot his father that day?"

"He was sentenced to juvenile detention until he turned twenty-one years of age."

"What happened to Randy Evans during his years in the juvenile detention center?"

"Some good things occured but some terrible things happened to him. He received his high school diploma and completed an associate degree in graphic arts during his time there. However, he also suffered mental, physical, and sexual abuse at the hands of older inmates that he endured over seven years, and which has scarred him to this day.

"Throughout his detention, an older gang member repeatedly raped him. When that inmate aged out of the facility, Randy was passed on to another gang member for a fee. The second gang member actually "bought" Randy from the first gang member as a sex slave."

"How did you come to find out this information, Dr. Klein?"

"At the request of Attorney Devon Gump, I was appointed by Warren County Court of Common Pleas, Criminal Division, to evaluate Mr. Evans' competency to stand trial on the charge of murdering his wife. During my clinical interviews with Mr. Evans, he disclosed this information to me. An investigative reporter, who I cannot identify to the court, confirmed Mr. Evans' version of his bondage to the gang members. He was apprised of the information by an anonymous informant who was incarcerated with Mr. Evans, and a detention officer who no longer works for the facility."

"Since Mr. Evans pled to causing the death of his

wife, but denied planning to *deliberately* kill her, how did your assignment change?"

"It became two-fold in nature. First, I still needed to determine if he understood the charges against him, and secondly, I needed to determine if he could assist in his own defense. These factors determine competency. It did not appear that those capabilities were significantly impaired. However initially, he had amnesia for the actual event and the remainder of the first day following his wife's disappearance. This meant he could not adequately defend his alleged actions the day of his wife's death."

"Initially? Does it mean that his memories returned Dr. Klein?" asked Attorney Gump.

"Following her death, what he initially described did not coincide with the physical evidence found at the scene of her death, nor in his home. Upon identifying his wife's remains in the morgue, vivid memories began to surface regarding the incident on the park's trail."

"Is it common for amnesia to occur when someone experiences a traumatic event involving a person he or she loves?" Devon Gump asked.

"It can happen and is not uncommon," responded Dr. Klein.

"What about partial memories to surface?"

"Some memories can return quickly while others may return more gradually or not until a lengthy period of time has passed. The 'sleeper effect' is a syndrome involving memories that surface much later under uniquely similar circumstances. For instance, if someone's childhood abuse began at three years of age, that repressed memory may surface when the person's *own* child turns three years of age," Dr. Klein explained. "I have seen many clients whose memories of horrible incidents emerged years later. Once the process of healing begins, more memories are recalled, and their treatment is usually intense and definitely not short-term."

"For purposes of this hearing, your assignment was to look at significant mitigating factors that would be useful to Judge Schuster as he determines appropriate sentences. Of course, there are recognized sentencing mandates that limit his flexibility. Would that be correct, Dr. Klein? Was that your purpose?"

"That is correct."

"Do you discern mitigating factors for this hearing? And if, so, would you please share them now."

"Yes. There are factors I would like to share with the court. In families where domestic violence goes unnoticed or unreported, all family members experience emotional turmoil. As a result, mental, social, and emotional growth are stifled. Children learn to handle their feelings, and their social environment, by observing the adults' responses to daily circumstances of life. That includes the manner in which parents, and authority figures, handle positive and negative emotions. How young people act at home is the behavior that will develop at school and in social situations. They learn how to gain attention in positive and negative ways. They learn how to avoid negative consequences in ways that are both healthy or unhealthy," Dr. Klein explained. She stopped and looked at him.

"Go on, please," Attorney Gump advised.

"When Randy Evans went to juvenile detention, he began to feel sadness, abandonment, fear, and anxiety. He felt abandoned by his mother after rescuing her from a life of misery at the hands of his father, yet she hardly ever came to see him. Lieutenant Colonel Evans was never charged with domestic violence, so when he died, he had an impeccable record with the Air Force, which was something Randy Evans knew to be untrue.

"Mrs. Evans proceeded to redecorate her home with insurance money received from the United States Air Force and remarried within two years, leaving the area with her daughter, Susie, Randy's younger sister. His mother occasionally sent postcards from glamorous vacation spots. Her visits to her son occurred at Christmas only and only at the urging of Randy's grandmother, Noni. His grandmother was the only one who consistently visited him and showed unconditional love. His childhood sweetheart, Joanie, sometimes came with Noni. She waited for him for seven years."

Dr. Klein continued. "As Randy became subjected to life-endangering abuse, he became filled with anger and rage. He felt desperate with no one to trust or turn to. He was released from juvenile detention with arrested development, no skills to deal with his emotions, and no knowledge as to how to demonstrate appropriate behaviors under stress. He and Joanie married soon after his release and soon had two children. He wanted to be in control of everyone to maintain control of himself. He vowed no one would ever take advantage of him again. He felt his manhood was threatened by what most couples would see as simple, differences of opinion. He also failed to form deep, meaningful relationships with others because he feared rejection. So, he turned to alcohol to numb his feelings of insecurity and help repress his anger."

"One last question, Dr. Klein: Do you see Randy Evans as capable of rehabilitation?"

"Yes, I do. For the time being, I am requesting that the prison medic at his permanent facility keep him on anti-anxiety medication for the first six months. Mr. Evans' hope is to serve his time and learn skills to be a loving father and grandfather upon his release. As for now, sir, I also strongly recommend anger management classes and Alcoholics Anonymous sessions.

"Although Mr. Evans knows the root causes of his bitterness and anger, he still needs to acquire new responses to help deal with unexpected verbal or physical confrontations. As he progresses, I believe he will be able to encourage other inmates to deal honestly with their issues. Inmates need to see him 'walk the talk' before they will respect his opinion and want solutions he has to offer."

"Thank you, Dr. Klein. I have no further questions," Attorney Gump concluded.

Judge Schuster spoke next. "Does the prosecution have anything to ask of this witness?"

"No, your honor. We do not. The State rests. We thank Dr. Klein for her time today," Attorney Winslow responded.

"Dr. Klein, you may step down," Judge Schuster said and nodded in her direction.

"Do you have any other witnesses who wish to speak today, Attorney Gump? The judge asked.

"Your honor, we have no other witnesses to speak on Mr. Evans' behalf, however, he, himself would like to speak. He has prepared a statement." Devon Gump returned to his seat beside Randy Evans and patted him on the shoulder.

At that moment, Roger Evans, the defendant's brother, stood, and addressed the Judge. "Your Honor, I am not on any list of witnesses to be heard today. But, as the defendant's brother, I would appreciate the chance to explain something to the Court, if that is possible, sir."

"You may approach the podium," Judge Schuster answered,

Randy glanced quizzically toward his brother who walked to the front of the courtroom, cleared his throat, and spoke in a clear, strong voice.

"I am Roger Evans, Randy's older brother. I take some responsibility for what has happened to him from the day I joined the Marines. I thought only of myself at that time, and not about the ramifications that my actions would have on my mother, brother, and sister.

"The discipline and training I received in the Marine Corps equipped me to have a meaningful, successful life. You cannot call what happened to my brother, 'discipline' in any form. What my brother suffered was brutal punishment not only by our father but at the hands of much older, stronger juvenile offenders and correction officers.

"His childhood sweetheart, Joanie, waited for him for seven years, and they married immediately upon his release at the age of twenty-one. Randy had no idea how to develop and maintain an adult relationship with anyone, let alone a wife and small sons. I just wanted to paint a picture of a very bright, victimized adolescent who then resorted to a life of pain and ultimately, sorrow. He deserves whatever consideration you can give him. Thank you, your honor, for hearing me."

"Your testimony has been noted," the judge said. "You may return to your seat, Mr. Evans." Roger Evans nodded his head toward his brother, then slowly returned to his seat beside Susie, their sister.

When Randy had first entered the courtroom, he hadn't seen any of his family members, now he noticed his mother seated in the back row with Roger's wife, Grace. He became overwhelmed with mixed emotions: Shame, anger, deep remorse, and love. He had been extremely surprised and grateful to hear Roger speak on his behalf which gave Randy more confidence to provide his own statement to the court.

"The defendant may now step up to the podium," Judge Schuster stated firmly.

Randy Evans positioned himself directly in front of Judge Schuster's bench. He was dressed in khaki pants, brown tie shoes, a light blue, Oxford cloth, button-down collar shirt, and navy sports jacket. He was clean-shaven with short, blonde hair and a receding hairline. He cleared his throat and began:

"Your honor, thank you for the privilege of speaking this morning. I'm not here to attempt to justify what I did. I'm not asking for mercy. I'm simply apologizing to Joanie's parents, and my family for taking away their beloved, Joanie. I don't expect their forgiveness."

"I am also grateful for the reduced charges, not because I deserve them, but because it means I may one day see my boys graduate from high school or college. That possibility now gives me hope."

With his thumb, he wiped a few tears from the corner of his right eye. Then he placed both hands on the podium and straightened his shoulders. He cleared his throat and continued.

"I will use my time in positive ways and plan to help other inmates in any way I can. No one was there to help me in juvenile, but that taught me how important it is for someone to help others who find themselves in hard times. Now, the best I can do is to let God use me as his servant to help the people I'll be spending my life with in the years ahead. In some small way, it might help Him to forgive me. I am so sorry for all that has happened. Thank you, sir, for allowing me to speak." Randy folded his paper and returned to his seat.

"We'll convene at one o'clock for sentencing," Judge Schuster said as he banged his gavel on the wooden ledge.

"Court dismissed," the bailiff announced.

A deputy handcuffed Randy's wrists and as he was led out of the courtroom, he glanced over his shoulder at his brother, sister, and mom. He knew Noni Parrish, their grandmother, was in the hospital with a mild heart attack, and couldn't be there. She would have, though, if she could have been. At this moment in time, all he could do was hope his family would return for the sentencing. Then, maybe he could give them a hug goodbye.

33

The Sentencing

Rosie met Bucky for lunch at The Golden Lamb. He was already seated with fresh hot bread and water sitting on the table.

"Hmmm. Bread and water. How appropriate," Rosie commented. "At least, in this day and age, Randy Evans will receive better meals than he did in juvie, right Bucky?" Rosie asked.

"I thought your testimony was outstanding, Rosie. The Judge doesn't have much leeway in terms of sentencing though, does he?"

"No, he doesn't. But hopefully, the institution he goes to will have the services I've recommended: Anger management and alcohol treatment. Even though he won't be drinking in prison, he still needs support therapy. He still needs to understand how to handle stress without self-medicating because that temptation will always be there. There's a distinct difference between being 'dry' and being sober. Dry means you don't drink or use whatever your drug of choice is. But you tend to take on a victim posture. Sober, on the other hand, means, you still don't drink but you experience the joy of a new day and don't take it for granted."

"Good to know. Thanks for pointing out the difference. As for the joy of your lunch with me, what would you like to order?"

"A gyro salad would hit the spot. How about you?"

The server approached and Bucky ordered for both of them. "Two gyro salads, please," he stated with a smile.

***

Court convened precisely at one o'clock just as Judge Schuster had stated. Bailiff Williams announced, "Court is in session. Please rise." Everyone in the courtroom stood.

Judge Schuster took his seat and said, "You may be seated." Cameras were never allowed in Schuster's courtroom, however, reporters were there taking notes. Eventually, they would leave to wait outside on the steps for the defense attorney and prosecutor to emerge after the session, all hoping to get exclusive statements to announce on their breaking five o'clock news.

"The defendant will stand," Judge Schuster commanded. He looked at the young man now standing with his hands folded one over the other in front of him, his head bowed. There was a momentary silence before the judge spoke again.

"In the matter of the State of Ohio vs. Randy Evans, the Court finds you guilty of second-degree murder. You are sentenced to fifteen years to life and will be eligible for parole upon completion of two-thirds of your sentence."

Randy Evans didn't move.

"On the charge of obstruction of justice, the Court sentences you to time served. The circumstances surrounding the obstruction, have led this Court to consider it a gross misdemeanor with the guideline stating there may be a sentence of less than a year. In this case, the obstruction was the disposing of the body of the deceased and not reporting it to the explanation of temporary amnesia factored into that conclusion. Obstruction was not found to be the outcome when the defendant denied recalling the event at the time making the missing persons' report.

Randy still hadn't moved, but his head seemed to hang slightly higher.

"Your family may now approach." As his gavel struck the stand, the judge announced: "Court dismissed."

Devon and Travis shook their client's hand. The deputy stood aside as Roger and Susie quickly approached to hug their brother and offer encouragement.

"Hey, Randy," Roger said giving him a bear hug. Randy's mother followed slowly, close behind.

Rosie was standing in the back of the courtroom with Bucky by her side. She noticed Grace weeping silently just inside the courtroom doors. Rosie held back her own tears as she and Bucky left discreetly trying to avoid the reporters.

"The sentence gives Randy a chance to restart

his life after serving ten years with good behavior," Rosie said to Bucky. "That means he'll have a chance to rebuild a relationship with his sons again."

"He's suffered a lot in his life," Bucky said. "Hopefully, he'll see the road ahead as a positive path and this time take the right fork in the road. He'll still be young enough, when he gets out, that he can still have a very meaningful life."

***

Late that evening, Rosie and Bucky arrived home and took their suitcases out of the car along with Jocko who had been quiet during the entire drive back.

"It was nice having an early dinner with Mom and Caleb, wasn't it?" Rosie asked.

"Yes, and it's nice being home with my best girl, too." Bucky held his arm firmly around Rosie's shoulders as he opened the front door. She released Jocko's leash.

"Tomorrow I have to oversee another baseball camp. What does your day look like?" he asked as they stepped into the foyer.

"I have clients at my Summerhill office and will spend a few minutes catching up with Ruth. I need to follow-up with McKenna Day and see what the prosecutor's office needs from me in the upcoming Scott Larson murder case," Rosie said. "Oh, and I see Dr. Seifer at noon. When we scheduled the appointment, I was apprehensive about fulfilling my obligations on the Randy Evans case. But now I'm thrilled I can report to him that not only did I use the thought-stopping techniques to reduce anxiety - and that was in privacy - but I think I presented myself quite professionally on the stand. Do you agree?" she asked.

"Honey, you were spectacular on the stand, and I assume you managed well in your last interview with Evans, too," Bucky replied warmly.

The evening was ending on a note of optimism. Rosie felt a sense of security. She had her sweet, supportive husband, her devoted dog, and a renewed pride and self-confidence. *I'm still one blessed woman,* she thought as they turned out the lights and headed to the bedroom for a good night's sleep.

Part Two

34

The Scott Larson Case

Rosie just arrived home when her phone rang. She answered and heard a low, pleasant-sounding voice on the line.

"Dr. Klein? This is McKenna Day from the prosecutor's office. Is this a convenient time to talk? I'd like to set up an appointment to meet with you and talk about a case for you to assess."

Rosie kicked off her shoes, put her briefcase on the ottoman, and plunked down in her chair. "Certainly I can talk. When do you have in mind to get together?"

"At your earliest convenience," McKenna responded.

"Well, how is tomorrow? Does ten o'clock work for you?"

"That would be fantastic, Dr. Klein. I assume you know where we're located."

"Yes, I do, and please call me Rosie. I look forward to meeting you, McKenna."

"The pleasure is mine. See you tomorrow."

Jocko rose from his position next to Rosie's feet.

She could tell he was responding to Bucky's presence as her husband came in the door with flowers in his hand. She stood to greet him and thank him for the flowers. The evening progressed with good wine, good food, great conversation, warm feelings, and true gratitude for finding one another.

***

The following morning, Rosie stopped by her office to connect with Ruth, her trusted office manager, and check the week's schedule of appointments. Ruth had coffee and chocolate croissants waiting for her beloved boss.

"Good morning, Ruthie," Rosie said spotting the sweet treats. "Well, thank you for my favorite morning delicacy. Are you nonchalantly putting in a request for a raise?" They both laughed in an easy way they had developed over the years.

"Just want you to know how glad I am to have you back, boss," Ruth said. "The long periods of quiet between phone calls when you're away, make the days long and boring," Ruth explained.

"Well, I'm not here for long today either, Ruthie. Will you fill me in on our week's schedule? Then I'm off to meet an assistant prosecutor, McKenna Day, about a new murder case."

"You have three appointments on Tuesday morning and two women's groups on Wednesday. You aren't teaching summer school at U.T. this year, are you?"

"No. My Tuesday and Thursday afternoons are open until mid-August. If I get a referral for a custody evaluation, feel free to schedule the initial appointments for any parents on Tuesday and Thursday mornings, and family sessions in the afternoons."

"You're working too hard, boss."

"I think I may take Fridays off. I can use them for report writing or telephone consults. Just cross them out of the appointment book until further notice, okay?"

"Sounds like a plan, boss. Tell me about your new murder case."

"Supposedly the defendant shot his wife because he mistook her for an Iraqi woman armed with explosives as she walked toward him. According to the defense, he was either hallucinating or wide-awake sleepwalking. He's an Army veteran but never actually served during Desert Storm nor during any wartime. But he's pleading Not Guilty by Reason of Insanity and Post Traumatic Stress Disorder.

"Sounds complicated."

"I'll check back with you later, Ruthie. Meanwhile, please contact Jake Morgan, the attorney for the defendant. His name is Scott Larson. See if he has any discovery materials ready for me to review."

***

Rosie entered the parking garage and was greeted by her favorite valet, Geoff, who was always smiling. She handed him her keys, and a five-dollar bill. Geoff was a graduate student at the University and always appreciated her generosity.

"Be back in a couple hours, Geoff."

"Sure thing, Dr. Klein. I'll have your car ready."

Rosie walked two blocks to the Lucas County Courthouse where the prosecutor's office was located. She placed her purse and briefcase on the conveyer belt in the lobby and stepped through the metal detector. The deputy standing nearby appeared familiar, but she wasn't quite sure where she had seen him before. He addressed her by name and waved her on toward the elevators.

As Rosie exited the elevator on the third floor, a familiar face greeted her. It was Bart Meyer, who had replaced Matthew Murphy as Lucas County Prosecutor when Matt had decided to become a juvenile court judge. Matt had personally invited Rosie to his swearing-in ceremony which she had attended. He had stepped down as Lucas County Prosecutor because he hoped to make a difference in young defendants' lives.

"My goal is to rehabilitate them early in life, so they won't appear in adult criminal court in years to come," he had told her at that time.

"Hi, Dr. Klein. How have you been?" Bart greeted her. "I assume you're here to meet with McKenna Day on the Scott Larson case."

"I'm fine, Bart and yes, I'm here to see McKenna Day. How have you been?"

"We have a new baby. If you see bags under my eyes, you'll know why," he laughed.

"Congratulates to you and Carolyn. Please tell her for me. Is he a 'junior?'"

"Actually, he's Bart Meyer, the third. I'm the

junior."

"I see."

Bart entered the elevator as she exited. "I'll be joining you in a few minutes. First, I'm expected in Judge Kimble's chambers for a quick meeting."

Rosie nodded and approached the receptionist's desk. "Hi, Arlene. I'd like to see McKenna Day, please. She's expecting me." Rosie didn't need to introduce herself because Arlene had manned the receptionist's desk for as long as Rosie could remember and always greeted her with a smile.

At that moment, McKenna Day, a tall, statuesque brunette, entered the lobby.

"Hello, Rosie. I'm McKenna. Come on back, please."

Rosie took a seat facing McKenna's desk. "Care for a coffee or water?" she asked.

"I never turn down a cup of coffee at this hour of the day. Black, please, and thanks." The carafe was on McKenna's desk and she poured Rosie a mugful.

"Thank you. I appreciate it," Rosie said.

"Getting right to it, then. We've accumulated discovery materials for you. We have police reports, emergency personnel reports, Scott Larson's statements to the detectives, and forensics from the crime scene. Mrs. Larson was dead on arrival. There were no witnesses," her tone was warm but official.

"We're still waiting for the defendant's medical and military records as well as his college transcripts. He attended college on the G.I. Bill after serving eight years in the United States Army. Larson graduated first in his class with a bachelor-of-science degree in nursing. He's been employed as an emergency room nurse at Toledo Hospital for ten years. That's where he met his second wife, Olivia, the one he killed.

"His first wife, Alexis Jackson, divorced him soon after he received his degree. They met while he was in college. She was his psychology professor and twelve years older than him. The detectives have submitted reports of their conversations with Dr. Jackson," McKenna explained, "but you may still want to interview her."

"Okay, I will do that. I assume her contact information is listed in the detectives' reports. Did they have children?"

"No children. But listen to this: As soon as Scott's divorce was final, he and Olivia were married by the hospital chaplain, Samuel Christoff. It's been said that Olivia had no idea Scott was married before, let alone divorced. Reverend Christoff is also waiting to hear from you. He thought highly of Olivia and is heartbroken over her death. She was only thirty-one years old. Scott is forty-two."

"I can understand his feelings. What was Olivia's job?"

"She worked two twelve-hour shifts on weekends in the emergency room. At that hospital, two long twelve-hour weekend shifts is equivalent to thirty-six hours and considered full time. She was shot at home on a Friday morning just after her husband returned from a nine p.m. to seven a.m. night shift. He worked four ten-hour shifts during the week.

"The crime scene looked like she was getting ready to leave for college classes. She was working on a master's degree in nursing at Wayne State University in Detroit, an hour's drive away on Wednesdays and Fridays. Her backpack and purse were on the kitchen counter along with two plates of chocolate chip cookies. One was covered in foil, the other was obviously for Scott.

"Apparently, Olivia was known to be a great baker. She made cookies for co-workers at the hospital, friends, and her husband. On the morning she died, he walked into the kitchen from the garage, spotted the plates of cookies, and took a bite out of one.

"She entered the kitchen from the hallway which was dark. The kitchen shades were closed. One light was on above the stove and one ceiling light above the counter.

"Scott told detectives that she startled him. He was exhausted from working all night. When she suddenly appeared, he hallucinated and mistook her for an Iraqi assailant. Reacting quickly, he grabbed the gun from his jacket pocket and shot her once in the abdomen."

"Why was he carrying a gun?" Rosie asked.

"He claimed he always carried the gun because it was dark when he entered the hospital from the adjacent parking garage. According to him, the neighborhood isn't great and is where the homeless and drug addicts gather at night."

"Did he render CPR?"

"That's what he *said* he did, but there was no sign of blood on his clothing or shoes. There was quite a pool of blood around her body, but no sign that he knelt anywhere near her. She must have clutched her stomach when she was hit and slumped onto her right side. Her hands and the sleeves of her shirt were bloody. She was wearing an apron. Apparently, her routine was to wear an apron when she baked, then hang it near the laundry room door on her way out to the car. A friend of hers reported that to the detectives."

"How tragic. Where is he being held now?" Rosie asked.

"He's being held in the psych unit at St. Stephen's Hospital. It was determined not to place him in Toledo Hospital where they both were employed. Right now, he's being evaluated by a psychologist selected by the defense. *Your* evaluation will serve as a second opinion. You can bet he will practice what to say to you after being seen by the first psychologist. Larson is very smart and very clever. He wants us to believe he suffers from PTSD and was trained to shoot on sight. It's true that Iraqi women were forced to carry weapons or explosives either in their aprons or covered over by them at outdoor markets.

"But get this: He left the army just *before* Desert Storm broke out. He was in Korea during peacetime. He served in the military police (MP) who got special training. You know, MP's are held to higher standards than even our civilian officers."

There was a light tap on the door and Bart Meyer stepped in, closing it behind him. He was carrying his own coffee and a clipboard.

"Good morning, ladies. I assume you've brought Dr. Klein up to date, McKenna. Rosie, any questions, you need me to answer?" He pulled up a chair and sat down.

"We were discussing details of the crime and possible witness interviews," McKenna said. "Rosie wants to speak to Alexis, his previous wife, as well as Olivia's close friends, coworkers, and Reverend Christoff."

"Good. You have a reputation for thoroughness, Rosie. This time you'll also have the benefit of reviewing the defense psychologist's findings. Dr. Pendleton is also highly respected but was their second choice. That's because their first choice - Dr. Rosie Klein - was already appointed by Judge Brown at the request of *our* office." They all laughed.

"I think I'll begin by reviewing the materials and interviewing Alexis Jackson and go from there. I'm eager to see the defendant's medical, academic, and military records," Rosie explained as she stood up. "Just let me know when you receive them."

McKenna and Bart stood and shook Rosie's hand. Bart held the door and McKenna returned to her desk. "As soon as those materials come in, I'll have a courier bring them to you, Rosie. As far as I know, Dr. Pendleton has not requested them yet. As you know, it's our obligation to share all discovery with the defense

35

The First Wife

Dr. Alexis Jackson entered the waiting room and approached the front desk where Ruth was at the computer. "Good morning. I'm Alexis Jackson, here to see Dr. Klein."

"Hello, Dr. Jackson," Ruth said looking up. "She's expecting you. Just tap on the door and go right into her office. Do you care for coffee or water?"

"Thank you, no, I've brought my own thermos," she said. Then tapped on the door and heard Rosie call out to her.

"Come right in," Rosie said. She was used to Ruth's customary modus operandi. If a visitor was not welcome, that knock would not be permitted. Ruth protected Rosie's privacy at all costs.

"You must be Alexis Jackson," Rosie said upon seeing the neatly dressed woman.

"I am, and assume you are Dr. Klein."

"Call me Rosie. Please be seated. Thank you for taking time out of your schedule to meet with me."

"Not a problem, and please call me, 'Alexis.' The Spring term has ended, and I'm footloose and fancy-free, as they say; no more 'Doctor Jackson' for a while."

"Are you aware as to why I've requested this meeting? Have you met with Dr. Pendleton?"

"No. He hasn't requested to see me, but I'm glad you did, Rosie. I have a lot to share with you about Scott Larson."

"It's good to have your cooperation, Alexis. He's charged with the murder of his wife, Olivia. The defense alleges that he is not guilty. They contend he is Not Guilty by Reason of Insanity and that he suffers from Post-Traumatic-Stress-Disorder, you know, PTSD. According to them, he reacted spontaneously to halt an intruder whom he did not recognize."

"That's bull crap, and I can prove it," Alexis Jackson said, becoming more animated, almost angry. "I've lived with him, slept with him, and never saw *any* visible signs of PTSD. He always slept like a baby and studied hard for hours on end. I'll give him that. There were never signs of distractibility. We were close until I married him. During all that time, he never once complained about flashbacks, nor overreacted to sounds.

"Really . . . how interesting."

"Shall I go on about Mr. Scott Larson?"

"Absolutely," Rosie said and grabbed the carafe to top off her coffee.

"I was his professor for child and abnormal psychology. He was an exceptionally bright, highly motivated student. Being twelve years older than Scott, I'm not proud to say that he set me up from the day he entered my classroom. First, he flattered me. Then, he praised my teaching methods and said I was the best professor in the department. He asked if he could stay after class to pick my brain for help researching a medical topic on a paper he was writing. Guess what the topic was, Rosie?"

"I give up," Rosie responded.

"PTSD. . . can you believe it? He said he wanted to reenlist in the Army as an army nurse once he graduated. It's true that PTSD is prevalent among men and women who have completed duty in a war zone. They've seen friends and other soldiers killed or severely injured with loss of limbs, sometimes sight. They, themselves have suffered physical, mental, and emotional afflictions."

"Did Scott say he served in a war zone or that he suffered from PTSD?"

"He told me that when he was in high school, he'd heard about the prisoners being released from Iran . . . that they came home with horror stories of their treatment. He wished he could have helped them both medically and emotionally. He said that's what influenced him to join the military rather than to go directly into college. He aspired to become a nurse or medic but lacked a degree at that time. He was in the military police but left to become an emergency room nurse. That's what he *said*. I believed him at the time. Stupid me!"

"Sounds logical. Why wouldn't you believe your student? He sounded very motivated, didn't he? Is he also smart?"

"He's brilliant. That's how he beats the system in every way imaginable. Oh, and he mentioned that if he had stayed in the military without a degree, he would have been stuck in the military police. That's what he was doing when he left the service."

"How did your relationship progress from professor-student to marriage?"

"Instead of getting together in the classroom, we agreed to meet in the student cafeteria. It was quite noisy, so I suggested we move to the faculty dining room. That was my first mistake."

"Why, what happened?"

"I could see the disapproving looks of my colleagues in the faculty dining room. So, I suggested we meet at a coffee shop off-campus. Well, then we decided it was easier for us to go there in my car since it was parked in the faculty lot nearby, whereas Scott's car was way out in a student lot, and he had another class to attend later on. If he lost that parking spot, he'd be stuck half a mile further from the building. Using my car made sense."

"As you reflect on this, what is your take on his motives? Did he fall in love with you?"

"No. He set me up from the beginning. He was living on the G.I. bill and his rent was being raised each year. The bill paid for his tuition and fees, but his housing was not. He had car and insurance payments to make. And unbeknownst to me, he owed fifteen grand on three credit cards. His second tour of duty had been in South Korea where he spent gobs of money on electronic equipment like keyboards and computers. He took scuba lessons, got certified to teach, and bought expensive camera equipment. He used his pay for everything but paying off bills."

"Did you fall in love with him?"

"At the time, I thought I did. I'm ashamed to say I was coming out of another relationship with an unavailable, older married man. He was the chairman of one of our departments. If you don't mind, I won't say which department. I was lonely and my biological clock was ticking. I thought perhaps I could have it all: career and family. At first, Scott seemed like a breath of fresh air. It appeared that he had little baggage. He'd not been married. He had no child support. He was ambitious and seemed self-disciplined. He respected and admired me."

"I understand; so, what happened next?"

"The quarter ended. It looked as if we would not have reason to get together anymore. His paper received an A-plus and he honestly earned an A in each of the courses he was taking from me. Here I was an abnormal psychology professor, and I didn't see the writing on the wall. Scott was a sociopath. He took no responsibility for any of the poor decisions made during his youth. He only shared with me a few choices he made that got him punished by law enforcement and his coaches. He blamed others for everything else. If he could beat the system, he bragged about it and repeated the behavior until he was caught. There was no shame or guilt or remorse for hurting others."

"What do you mean by his being punished by his coaches or law enforcement?"

"Even though he was a bit older, he successfully became a walk-on on the football team. Later, he was benched for six football games during his senior year for violating curfew, using alcohol and pot, and letting his grades drop below a C average. He thought the curfew of eleven p.m. on weekends was stupid, and that his classes were boring. Teachers didn't motivate him. As far as alcohol was concerned, he wasn't the one to buy it, nor was he driving the car. So, he reasoned, nothing was his fault. His friend bought it and another friend drove them to Walden Pond where they sat and drank. The vodka at his girlfriend's house was sitting unused, and her father didn't miss it. Besides, he admitted that he replaced its bottle level with water so no one knew."

"Is there more?" Rosie asked.

Alexis wiped a tear from her eye and took a sip of whatever she had in her thermos. "He suddenly proposed to me saying he couldn't bear being away from me. He said I was the best thing that ever happened to him, and he couldn't wait for his family to meet me."

"Were you shocked or expecting it?"

"I was stunned. Scott turned to me on a park bench and produced a five-carat diamond ring. He said it had been his mother's and once she divorced his dad, she wanted Scott to have it for the girl of his dreams."

"What did you say?"

"I told him I would have to think about it. I thought our age difference might disturb him as we grew older, and I didn't think he was prepared to start a family. But if I were going to have a child, it needed to be soon. Besides, I was tenured at the university and didn't want to move away. He planned to reenlist in the army and finish a twenty-year career as a nurse."

"Did he offer to change his plans?"

"He said he understood but didn't talk about the army issue. He did agree to have one child and said he hoped it would be a girl and looked exactly like her mother. I was touched, to say the least."

"I assume you agreed to marry him, and so you did, correct?"

"That was my second mistake. We went to Pennsylvania for a long weekend, so he could meet my parents. He charmed them, of course, and they never mentioned concern about the differences in our ages. I wasn't surprised. They live in a log home on ten wooded acres. My dad is retired from Owens Illinois. Are you familiar with the company?"

"Yes. I am. How did he end up in Pennsylvania?"

"When my dad was fifty-five, they transferred him to Clarion, Pennsylvania, and when he was sixty-two, they offered him a buyout. By that time, I was attending Clarion State College and lived at home in a loft apartment above their three-car garage. I remember it being lovely in the winter with snow on the ground and on the tree branches, just glistening. It's one of my favorite memories. But I left there for graduate school in Ohio, and have been at the University of Toledo since receiving my Ph.D."

"Then what happened?"

"I never met Scott's parents. His mother was deceased, and his father was all but non-existent. We had a small, intimate wedding with my parents in attendance and my best friend as maid of honor. Scott asked a classmate of his to stand up for him. The minister at the First Baptist Church married us after we completed three premarital counseling sessions. Reluctantly, Scott participated, but let it be known that he knew all he needed to know about marriage. I should have known better but our marital troubles started soon after that. By then, I knew I had made a big mistake.

"Later, in the throes of our divorce, I found out that Scott's father had abandoned them years before and Scott's mother died mysteriously in a fire when he was only a senior in high school. The fire investigators thought the fire was set to disguise a home invasion, but they lived in a very modest bungalow that sat behind a large Victorian home near the Toledo Museum of Art. Why would *anyone* bother to rob a *bungalow* instead of any of the wealthier houses in the neighborhood? Anyway, by then, Scott was angry with me and claimed his mother wanted her ring back. I hired a private detective who found out all the details I've just told you. I also decided to keep the ring."

"My goodness, Alexis, that is really quite a history.

How long did you live together?"

"He moved into my house off Berdan near Douglas, after we married. It had a breezeway leading to an unattached garage. He put a gas heater out there and kept his personal things in the garage. In the summer, he had a window air-conditioner. I never questioned him spending so much time secluded in there. He always said it was easier for him to study without interruption.

"Funny, it never bothered him studying near me when we first met. Back then, if I was teaching, he stayed in my office. If I was in my office, he sat as nearby as he could be. Usually, he found an empty classroom. When I got pregnant after five months, he seemed genuinely happy that he was going to be a dad. But unfortunately, I miscarried after the first trimester. We were just about to decorate a bedroom to use as a nursery. After I lost the baby, things changed. He became moody and started skipping early morning classes. At night he removed himself to the garage and told me to lock the doors and not wait up. He would give me a peck on the cheek, grab the house keys and his backpack, and slip out the back door. I had no idea what was really going on out there until much later."

"What exactly was happening?"

"He was entertaining underage, neighborhood girls. They would slip out of their bedrooms and walk down the alley to the backside of the garage. I found pictures he took of them in provocative poses. He wasn't very discreet. He left them in a binder that sat

269

on his desk. He may have been priming them, Rosie."

"It does sound suspicious. How did you react?"

"I just decided to let it play out for a while. I was miserable from losing the baby and couldn't fathom losing my husband as well. Not to say how embarrassing it would be for my family to know.

"Finally, just before his senior year in college, I decided the relationship held nothing more for me. There was no intimacy and very little communication. He constantly criticized my cooking. He complained about his classes. He even complained about a small, part-time job he had on the weekends as a valet in a parking garage downtown. He complained that his service wasn't appreciated and tips were skimpy at best."

Whoa. Rosie thought. *I wonder if my favorite valet, Geoff, might have worked with Scott?* It made sense since they were both in school. Could it be that James had even parked her car on a Saturday morning? *I'll have to ask Geoff. I won't leave any stone unturned.*

36

The Rest of the Story

D r. Alexis Jackson was silent for a moment after telling Rosie about the collapse of her marriage to Scott Larsen. Thinking of all the details brought back an amount of emotional pain.

"So, did you have a game plan?" Dr. Klein asked.

"Finally, I decided to see an attorney and begin putting my affairs in order. Fortunately, we had not combined our finances. While I was pregnant, he asked for his name to be on the deed of the house saying that if anything happened to me, he would raise our child in the house. I'm not sure why I waivered at that time. But it was just before I miscarried. I think I told him my lawyer suggested we wait until after the baby was born so the baby's name could be mentioned in the transaction. My will would state that Scott would have the house and be the executor for anything left by me to our child. That quieted him down."

"You were smart to tell him that. Had you really seen an attorney about a will at that point?"

"No, but truthfully, I was going to do it. Then I began noticing Scott's dramatic change of heart toward me. It started when I became pregnant. I didn't know if it was because I was gaining weight, or if he was really afraid of becoming a father and didn't want to tell me. He wanted me to stay in the house when I wasn't teaching. He didn't want to take walks anymore, or even let me go to the store. He preferred to take care of all errands alone. I thought maybe he was ashamed of me. After I lost the baby, he was worse than ever."

"Sounds controlling."

"Absolutely. That's when I began preparing divorce papers. As I did, the answer came to me. He didn't want me to be seen by the young girls walking in our neighborhood or at the corner market. He probably had portrayed me in a negative light, or maybe even denied I was his wife. Finally, I told him I was going to my parents' house in Pennsylvania for the weekend. But I didn't leave town. I stayed nearby at my best friend's house, the one who stood up for me at our wedding. I hired a private investigator to watch the house. He told me exactly what was going on and who went in and out.

"Scott also had several men about his age come over. They had out-of-state license plates and one night, soon after they arrived, three teenage girls came over, too. The investigator thought they looked to be about fifteen, definitely underage. One walked and two came by bicycles. The men left about two a.m. and the girls remained until dawn. He figured they told their mothers they were staying at one another's houses.

"On Monday morning, before I was to return home, the investigator looked in the trash outback. There were a couple of Jack Daniels bottles, a half a dozen coke cans, an empty half-gallon of orange juice, a pack of Virginia Slims menthol, and a pack of Lucky Strikes."

"That must have been very difficult for you to face, Alexis."

"It was humiliating. And hard to tell my parents about what was happening. Scott graduated in May of 1995. Then he began to process paperwork for re-enlisting in the Army. He also had to prepare to take the nurses' state license exam. He could only be a nurse in the military if he were already licensed. I told him I was going to Pennsylvania for a month and would return to teach classes for the second summer session. I knew he would like total privacy to study for his exam and also told him he was welcome to come up and visit me if he liked. He said he appreciated my understanding and would stay in touch daily. I left him with our cat, Lilly, figuring it would make him feel confident that I would be coming back and that I trusted him. He knew how much I loved that cat. Unfortunately, the day I left was the last time I ever saw my precious Lilly alive again." Alexis began to weep.

"I am so sorry. What happened to her?"

"Scott was served with divorce papers while I was gone, and an eviction notice was posted on the door approximately four weeks after I left. By then, I knew his exam date had passed, so I felt no guilt. If he had studied and prepared, the test was behind him. If he put it off for no good reason and partied in my absence, then I couldn't be any part of that. I waited to hear from him.

"He was stunned by my actions and called to beg me to reconsider. He said he would be shipping out soon and it made no sense to get divorced. What I realized later is that he believed the Army would see him as more stable if he were a married man. He felt it would help his career. But when he realized I was truly over him, he cursed and yelled, then drowned my Lilly. He also trashed the house and left the day before my summer session was to begin. What he didn't know is that I did not plan to teach and intended to remain in Pennsylvania just to be safe. My best friend found Lilly's body when she went over to take the cat home with her. She was planning to take care of Lilly until I returned for fall quarter."

Rosie reached a hand out to console her. "You went through hell, didn't you?"

"Yes, you might say that," Alexis responded.

"Two last questions, Alexis. Did Scott own any weapons, and did you ever see him after you filed for divorce?"

"He had two guns and kept them under his side of the bed within reach. Once when he appeared agitated or frustrated about life, I saw him put a gun into his backpack and head to school for a night class. I questioned him, and he made up the excuse that there had been some vandalism near the university. I don't know whether he ever put the gun back under the bed. I tried to find out more about his mother's death, but he said he couldn't talk about it. I asked him why he never told me she was deceased, and he said he thought he *had* told me when he gave me the ring. Honestly, Rosie, he made me think she had just given him the ring for our engagement. But by that time, she had already been dead for years. I don't even know if the ring was truly hers or if he stole it, or *where* it came from. As for your second question, I only saw him at our divorce hearing. We never even spoke."

"Well, you have certainly filled in many gaps, Alexis. It must be terribly difficult to relive your history with him. I can't thank you enough. Please feel free to contact me anytime you want to talk more about it." Rosie stood and faced her. She took both of Alexis' hands in her own and squeezed them gently.

"I would love to stay in touch," Alexis said. "Coffee, perhaps, when this case is over for you."

"Great idea. I'm downtown every week unless you would prefer meeting closer to the university. You mentioned a coffee shop that you frequented with Scott. Would that work for you?" Rosie inquired.

"That will be fine. Let me know when you'd like to get together, and I will put it on my calendar. Don't you teach too?"

"Yes, on Tuesday and Thursday afternoons. I'll be doing reports and phone calls on Fridays for a while. All other appointments are in Summerhill," Rosie answered.

As they walked through the waiting area, Rosie noticed another younger woman obviously waiting to speak with her. Not recognizing her as a regular client, Rosie assumed she must be connected to Olivia, Scott Larson's second wife.

Saying goodbye to Alexis, she introduced herself to the new woman. "Hello. I'm Rosie Klein. Are you waiting to see me?"

37

Meeting Another Witness

When Alexis Jackson left, there were three women in the office lobby, and Ruth spoke up. "Dr. Klein, this is Reneé Rapton. She worked with Olivia Larson at the hospital and was also taking classes with her at the university. They were both working on masters' degrees in nursing."

Reneé stood up and shook hands with Rosie. "Hello," she said.

"It's so nice of you to agree to speak with me, Renee," Rosie said. "I'm really sorry about the loss of your friend." Her voice was filled with sympathy.

"Thank you. I'm happy to help in any way I can. Olivia's death was such a shock to all of us who worked with her. Only a few students at the university really knew us since we attended classes only two days a week; the others take classes more frequently, maybe four or five days a week."

Rosie invited Reneé into her office and closed the door. Both women took seats.   Reneé had an air of urgency about her, almost as if she *needed* to talk about her friend.

"So, how long did you know Olivia?" Rosie asked.

"I think we both started the exhaustive weekend shifts about the same time, so about two years. We hit it off right away, even took our breaks together. When we realized we were taking the same courses at the university, we began sitting together. We even hoped to be lab partners in future classes requiring lab time."

Reneé's eyes teared up as she continued. "Olivia was the kindest person, Dr. Klein. She baked cookies for the staff, offered transportation if someone's car was unavailable. Everyone just loved Olivia. We hoped to complete our masters' degrees and go on to become nurse practitioners. We even talked about counseling people in an office like yours, someday," Renee now began to weep openly. The pain was still fresh; she had lost someone close to her.

Rosie handed her a tissue and asked: "Did she discuss her marriage with you?

"Olivia occasionally made comments which made me believe her husband would just as soon she stay home and have babies. But she defended him by explaining that he was much older. However, I noticed small things, like when she left classes, she literally ran to her car to get home. I couldn't help but think she was afraid he would be mad at her for some reason, even if she got home hours before he did. We were an hour away from home, but she wanted to have dinner ready for him. Once she mentioned she felt sorry for him because he worked ten-hour shifts."

"Are you married, Reneé?"

"I'm engaged. He's very supportive.

"Didn't you and Olivia work twelve-hour shifts?" Rosie asked.

"Yes. Sometimes we worked three in a row. Her husband, Scott, always had a day off after only two days of ten-hour shifts. That's why I couldn't really understand her concern. But he resented her taking a class in the late afternoon on his day off even though they had lunch together. On Fridays, she always rushed home from class. She said it was his fourth day of working and she needed everything at home to be perfect. I don't know that he *required* it, but I do know he didn't help with anything. She cooked, cleaned, did their laundry, and grocery shopping. Personally, I didn't understand it."

"No mention of physical abuse?" Rosie asked.

"She let me believe everything in their marriage was perfect. Hard to believe, don't you think?"

"Perhaps she was simply a private person. Did you talk about what you wanted in your own marriage?"

"We talked about a lot of stuff. I didn't see her as a 'private' person. I saw her as a quiet person, a bit on the shy side, and very nervous when it came to taking tests. She was driven to do her best. Anything less than an A would have devastated her. As far as marriage, yes, I did talk about what I hoped my marriage would be. She was my confidante. I love my fiancé, but he's not perfect; who is, really? Maybe, Jesus, right?" Renee said.

"Right. I take it you never met Scott, did you?"

"Only once. He took an extra eight-hour shift on a Saturday and came up to our floor to trade cars for some reason. She was in a room with a patient, and I was sitting at the nurse's station. He approached me and introduced himself as her husband. He was very handsome with intense blue eyes. She knew he was coming and had left her keys at the desk for him. I thought he might still ask to see her, you know, kind of like you want to say 'hi' or something? But no, not him. In sort of a disgruntled tone of voice, he said he couldn't wait to see her, that he was through with his shift and heading home. So, we exchanged keys, he nodded, turned, and left. Never said 'it was nice to meet you' and 'thank you.' Just nothing. I thought that was rude."

"Did he know you were friends?"

"He looked at my name tag. I assumed he knew I was her friend. Now that you ask, I can't be sure she talked about us working together or going to school together. Maybe he didn't know my name. Either way, he wasted no time leaving and didn't feel the need to say 'boo.'" Reneé laughed. It was the first time her mood was anything but somber.

"Thank you, Reneé. You've been very helpful. Is there anyone else from the hospital or college that you think I should speak to?" Rosie asked.

"Olivia had a special relationship with our chaplain, Samuel Christoff. She often asked him to visit patients who seemed to need to talk with him, or maybe have some prayer. The chaplain is only permitted to enter someone's room if requested to visit by the patient or a family member. If they do, then nurses are allowed to ask chaplains to visit. A patient rarely turned down a visit with Chaplain Christoff if Olivia encouraged them to see him."

"I'm going to interview Chaplain Christoff, then. I assume you feel the same way your friend did when it comes to the value of a patient seeing a chaplain," Rosie said.

"I do and am glad you'll be meeting him. He is a wonderful, caring person. As I've said, Olivia and I are very interested in mental health. He made us feel as though we would be terrific counselors."

Rosie handed a card to her. "Call me if you have any information to add."

"I will," Reneé said. "It was really nice to meet you."

38

A Turn of Events

The plaque on the door read: "Dr. Samuel Christoff" in white letters. Rosie tapped on it. A deep voice responded.

"Come on in."

Rosie entered the small office adjacent to the hospital chapel and introduced herself.

"Good morning, I'm Rosie Klein, here to speak with Chaplain Christoff."

"That would be me," the man said. Rosie looked at the youthful and slender, tall gentleman as he stood and extended his hand. Rosie shook it firmly.

How much younger he is than what I expected, she thought.

"Good afternoon to you, too," he said.

"Should I address you as 'reverend' or 'doctor?'" Rosie asked.

"Actually, most people just call me 'Sam.' How about yourself, Dr. Klein?"

"Most people call me 'Rosie.'" They laughed easily

and he sat back down. She followed his lead while noticing piles of paper covering his desktop.

"What brings you in today, Rosie?"

"I've been appointed to evaluate Scott Larson and understand that you had a close relationship with his deceased wife, Olivia."

"Ah, yes. How very sad. She was so compassionate, and the patients loved her. She will be sorely missed among our staff, too. She made each of us feel special and needed."

"So, I've heard. I'm interested in any information you can provide about her marriage, and your opinion of Scott Larson."

"Well, I'm not a psychologist like yourself. I don't claim to know anything more about the human mind, one's motivation, or one's emotional state of being other than what I gather from a simple conversation. The truth is that I rarely saw Mr. Larson and almost never held a conversation with him. During his shift, he usually remained in the emergency room during his lunch break or would eat meals outside the hospital. I can't ever remember seeing him in the cafeteria. He, actually, appeared to be a very intense, private person."

"I see," Rosie said. "Did you have occasion to see patients in the emergency room area? I've heard there are times when a shortage of hospital beds keeps patients on gurneys in the halls of the emergency room."

"Yes, that happens upon occasion. There are times I'm requested to see families of patients waiting for answers about their loved ones' conditions. If a doctor thought a critically ill, or injured patient, wasn't going to make it, I might be called to comfort the spouse, parent, or family member. It might even be for a friend or professional colleague if the patient is a firefighter or law enforcement officer," Sam explained. But, if you're wondering if Scott Larson ever requested my presence, the answer is no," he said with a solemn tone.

"Was your relationship with Olivia personal or professional in respect of pastor-client confidentiality?"

"Professional, though we had no confidentiality agreement. I don't know exactly what I would do if subpoenaed to appear in the trial. I would probably have to consult an attorney, although I don't have much to say about Olivia beyond her position here at Toledo Hospital. Our chats were about the needs of her patients, and what we could do to comfort them. Some wanted to know if they were going to hell, and they would confess their sins privately to me. Others voiced concerns about family members and wanted me to help them after they were gone."

"Did you ever notice any bruises on Olivia, or notice if she was acting upset or despondent in any manner? Did she ever confide in you about being discontent in her marriage?"

"I can't say I saw any evidence of *physical* abuse, and Olivia never complained about Scott to me. However, I was led to believe he did not support her ambition to become a physician's assistant or, perhaps, a nurse practitioner. I did notice once or twice some difficulty in their spending time together. Just small things, like the toss of a head if I saw them talking together. Just a feeling. In my profession, you can tell a lot from body language. The problem was not because of her graduate courses, I don't believe, but because of their totally different work schedules. They worked opposite shifts."

"I see," Rosie said.

"Oh, one thing I do know for certain, Rosie, Olivia was baptized last year. Scott was off work, but didn't attend. A few of our close medical colleagues came to the ceremony. She felt an urgency to have me baptize her. She'd been 'sprinkled' before but wanted to be immersed. Our baptismal font is behind the chapel in a small prayer room with padded pews and stained-glass windows. I would be glad to show it to you if you have time."

What the heck. . . I might as well take a look, Rosie thought. *Pastor Sam seems like a truly caring man.* "Sure, that would be nice. I'd like to see it," Rosie answered.

Sam opened the side door of his office and led her through the chapel. She couldn't help but notice a large cross made of oak mounted on the wall with a padded kneeling rail in front of it. They walked across the chapel floor, and he slid open a narrow door allowing them to enter the baptismal room.

Brilliant light streamed through the stained-glass windows and left Rosie standing in awe. The room held six small pews where guests could view baptisms or just pray silently on other occasions.

"What a lovely room. It must have given Olivia a

real sense of peace to be baptized here," Rosie said.

"It did. We're planning a private memorial service to be held here for the staff who knew and loved her."

As they stepped back into his office, Rosie handed Sam her card.

"Thank you for your time. If you have any other thoughts about her, please call."

"I will. And thank you for taking an interest in the deceased and not just the perpetrator. So often it seems that's all investigators want to talk about."

***

A short drive later, Rosie entered her Summerhill office and noticed Ruth was on the phone. She raised her hand to flag Rosie down as she was hanging up.

"Hey boss, you won't believe this. That call was from the prosecutor's office. You are supposed to call Bart Meyer there at your earliest convenience. I think that should be right away, Rosie. Something important has come up about the Larson case."

"Okay, please buzz me when you have him on the line but let me kick off my shoes first and sit down. And could I trouble you for a cup of herbal tea? I have had my fill of caffeine today," Rosie said.

"Funny you should ask! Fine minds must work in this office. I just put plain water through the coffee machine with no coffee grounds. Something must have told me that tea would hit the spot."

A short time later, Ruth walked in and placed Rosie's favorite beautiful little ceramic cup and saucer on her desk. The boss was stretching her arms high above her head, thinking about walking Jocko in the moonlight later in the evening. Bucky would be meeting three local high school athletic directors for dinner so she would have time to herself. At his dinner meetings, he always encouraged the directors to apply for athletic scholarships to help their most talented young male and female athletes, especially those striving to play in division one sports. Her quiet evening would give her a chance to disengage from work responsibilities and bask in the moonlight with her dog beside her.

"Thank you, Ruth. I've always known you to be a multi-talented woman who can multi-task exceptionally well. So, do you have Bart Meyer on the phone yet? Ha! Just kidding."

Ruth looked at her boss with a knowing smile. Despite constant stressors in Dr. Rosie's life, she always tried joking and staying joyful to keep the atmosphere light. It was one of the reasons Ruth loved working for her.

A short time later, Ruth buzzed Rosie with the prosecutor on the line. Rosie put her cup of tea down and grabbed a pen and legal pad, assuming she would need to take notes of this important conversation.

"Good afternoon, Rosie. I hope you're sitting down. Dr. Pendleton has just completed his evaluation and has concluded that Scott Larson did *not* suffer from PTSD and was *not* legally insane at the time of the crime's commission. Therefore, the defense team has withdrawn their plea. So, you've just been relieved of your duty for that portion of the case.

"*However,* we've turned down their request for a plea bargain, so he *will* be tried for first-degree murder. Following a guilty verdict, which I am confident will be rendered by the jury, *your* opinion will factor into the ultimate sentencing of the defendant.

"Keeping all that in mind, I am forwarding Dr. Pendleton's report to you and am requesting that you evaluate Larson immediately following his conviction. According to Ohio law, prior to his sentencing hearing, he is entitled to at least one psychological evaluation meant to ascertain mitigating factors leading to the commission of the crime. Your findings will be reviewed by Judge Brown and will factor into his sentencing determination."

"Really, Bart? I don't quite understand why they didn't wait for my findings and opinion," Rosie replied.

"Well, you and I both know that if the psychologist or psychiatrist for the defense renders a professional opinion *favoring the position* of the prosecution, like this one does, it puts the defense in a very bad position. They know your reputation for fairness, but they must have had an extremely weak case. It's as if their 'Hail Mary pass' just got intercepted.

"You may know that Pendleton is thought to be very defense-oriented, but I must say, he is also smart and shrewd. He saw right through Larson's story."

"Well, frankly," Rosie said, "I'm not surprised that Pendleton saw right through Larson's act. Larson most certainly knew the wrongfulness of his action at the time of the offense. In my opinion, it's quite likely that he reviewed Larson's military records, as I did, and saw no evidence for the rationale of a PTSD claim.

"On another note, Bart, let me tell you about the three-character witnesses I've interviewed for Olivia, not Scott, before we hang up," Rosie said. "I recently talked with Dr. Alexis Jackson, Larson's first wife, who provided quite a history of Larson's life from his second Army stint until their divorce. A second person was a friend of Olivia's. Her name is Renee Rapton who shared her experiences about Olivia at work and at the university where they were pursuing masters' degrees at the same time. Finally, I saw Chaplain Christoff at the hospital, and learned a few things from him."

"That's great, Rosie, you have a good jump on your assignment. Let me know if you need anything else. I'll let you know when the jury's verdict is in. Then I'll wait for your report. The trial begins on Monday and will likely last two weeks, maybe less. It will all depend on a couple of things. I honestly can't imagine what the defense could possibly present to support this scum bag. He certainly won't use Dr. Pendleton's report since that was related to the Not Guilty by Reason of Insanity plea. As far as the jury goes, I doubt they'll deliberate very long."

"I agree. Their defense will be flimsy. I'll wait to hear from you. Is McKenna Day still on your team?"

"Yes. She'll be first chair. I'll be in her support position. One of us will be in touch. Oh, I almost forgot, Larson will be held at the Lucas County Jail. He's being moved there from the hospital as we speak. Now there is no excuse for him to remain at St. Stephen's since we know he has no mental health diagnosis.

"Well, good talking to you, Rosie. I'll look forward to your report after the trial. I expect it will tell the true story of the real Scott Larson."

39

Meeting Scott Larson

Rosie pulled into the parking garage adjacent to her downtown office. As usual, Geoff greeted her with a smile and opened her car door. It suddenly occurred to her to inquire if Scott Larson had ever worked with him on weekends. When Alexis had told her that Larson sometimes worked at a downtown parking garage after they had married, Rosie had tucked the information into the back of her mind. Now was the opportunity to corroborate the information.

"Good morning, Geoff. It's good to see you. I have a question. Do you recall working with a man named Scott Larson on weekends? It was a while back, maybe nine or ten years ago when you worked here during high school."

"No, can't say that I do. Not here, but there *was* a Scott Larson in one of my undergraduate psychology classes a while back. He was a vet, quite a bit older than me. We were seated in elevated rows, and he sat on the aisle across from me. I liked to be on the aisle to slip out if I had a shift here at the garage. I assume he also had somewhere to go, too."

"Okay, I was just wondering. Anything else strike you about him?" Rosie asked.

"Yeah, actually. He always put his backpack on the seat beside him which meant no one could sit there. I never saw him open it, and he carried his textbook and notebook under his arm; always had a pen behind his ear. I always wondered what was in the backpack."

"Well, thank you, Geoff. I'll be back in a couple of hours." Rosie handed Geoff a ten-dollar bill and walked briskly down the sidewalk to the Lucas County Jail. With a wave and a nod, she acknowledged numerous lawyers and other court personnel as they headed to coffee shops or early lunches.

"Good morning," she said to the deputy behind the sliding glass partition. He raised his head and smiled.

"I am here to see Scott Larson," Rosie said while signing the visitor's log. As usual, she looked at the list of previous professional visitors. No one had come to see Larson yet today. His transfer occurred before the weekend, and this was only Monday. She surmised his legal team had no interest in breaking up their weekend to come downtown. They were on salary with little incentive to work more than their weekday hours.

She was permitted to enter the secure area and took the elevator to the third floor. Larson was already seated in the conference room facing the door. The corrections officer was standing with handcuffs hanging from his belt and arms crossed near the door. He told her to go on into the room but quietly cautioned: "He doesn't plan on talking to you today." Rosie acknowledged the comment, then walked in the door.

"Good morning, Mr. Larson, I'm Dr. Rosie Klein. I'm here to assist the court in your sentencing. Can we talk?" Rosie stayed standing on the other side of the table.

"No. I won't sign anything, and I won't talk to you until I get the go-ahead from my lawyers." Larson clenched his fists and leaned forward, looking her square in the eyes. "I was *not* told you'd be coming today, or any time. I've already talked to a shrink, and it got me nowhere. No use talkin' to any more docs," Larson said firmly.

Rosie remained standing with her briefcase in her left hand. Now she stepped forward and placed her right hand on the table between them. "That's perfectly understandable from your point of view. I'll return once you're more comfortable talking to me, or at least when you're willing to participate in an interview. Meanwhile, you might want to think about what you'll say to the judge at your hearing. That is, if you *choose* to speak." Rosie didn't wait for an answer. She cautiously turned her back and opened the unlocked door. The deputy took the cuffs off his belt and entered the room to escort the prisoner back to the cell block.

She was fuming. It had been a waste of time trying to evaluate Scott Larson. She suspected his lawyers wouldn't like his refusal either. She was their only hope to avoid the harshest of sentences. Larson had no idea what a bad choice he had just made. She decided not to call them, assuming they would hear from their client soon enough. And she wasn't going to return again unless she got the go-ahead from Larson's attorneys.

I don't like wasting time, she thought. Pulling out her cell phone, she called her office. "Hi, Ruth. I'm going to grab some lunch and hang out at my downtown office for awhile."

"What's going on? Ordinarily, you're only there on Fridays."

"Yeah, well, I ran into a minor roadblock this morning. Scott Larson refused to talk to me, saying he wanted his attorneys to okay it first."

"We've heard it all, now, haven't we?" Ruth replied.

"You might say that. I have paperwork to do and could use a cup of fresh coffee. I'll stay here in case I get a call to return to the jail this afternoon."

"Speak of the devil, Rosie, the phone's ringing. I can see from the caller ID it's from Morgan and Associates, Larson's attorney. Let me put you on hold, okay?"

"Sure," Rosie said.

Ruth came back on the line within minutes. "You can probably guess what Attorney Morgan had to say. He apologized profusely for his client's unwillingness to cooperate. He assured me that if you go back, you can complete your evaluation without any more interruptions. He also accepted part of the blame by explaining he had not adequately prepared

Larson for another psychologist's interview. He apologized for that."

"Well, I'll take him at his word, but I'm going to let Larson wait for an hour or so. I need to grab a bite to eat. Call Morgan back and let him know how much I appreciate his quick response. Oh, and ask if he has any other material, he would like me to review. His office is also in Summerhill, and I could pick it up as I head home.

"Consider it done. Good luck, and don't rush through lunch. After all, Larson isn't going anyplace, and he's inconvenienced you, to say the least," Ruth said. "You're really good not to hold grudges, boss, but then that's why you've got such a great reputation."

"If you say so, Ruth, whatever you say," Rosie smiled, deflecting the praise.

40

Larson's Scheme

R osie approached the plexiglass window where the same visitation officer now sat eating his lunch.

"Hi, I'm back to see Scott Larson," she said as she signed the visitor's log for the second time today. She noticed Jake Morgan's signature below her first signature on the sheet. He obviously had been to see Larson just after she left earlier and had obviously instructed Larson that Rosie's visit could only help him. *Good thing, too, or I wouldn't have come back to see this inmate on a bet.*

Deputy Poole wiped his mouth and slid open the window. "I'm sorry Dr. Klein, but the visitation area upstairs isn't available. I can place you on the first floor across from the booking area," he explained apologetically.

"That'll work fine. Thank you."

The deputy got on the phone to arrange for Scott Larson to be brought downstairs. Rosie placed her briefcase on the conveyer belt which took it inside while she stepped through the metal detector. She heard the buzzing sound of the door unlocking and entered, then grabbed her materials. She listened for the buzz to permit her to open the second door. She looked up at the overhead camera which let officers see who was in the hallway. They now allowed her to enter the booking area.

Four large deputies stood before her. It appeared two of them were escorting men for fingerprinting. Two other officers were filling out paperwork to complete prisoners' bookings.

Larson was being escorted down the hall and into a very small visitation room. She followed him. He wore jailhouse scrubs in khaki green.

Wonder why his uniform isn't orange like others I've seen, she wondered. No sooner had she taken a seat, than Larson asked if they could sit elsewhere.

"It's way too noisy in this hallway. There's an area around the corner with more privacy. I don't want to have to listen to those guards for the next hour."

"If it's okay with the officer in charge of you, it's fine with me," she said. Standing, she opened the door and Larson followed her.

"Bronson, it's too noisy here," Larson addressed the large guard. "Okay if we use one of the rooms around the corner?"

"I guess so," Deputy Bronson said. He led them down the hall and unlocked a room similar in size but in a much quieter area.

Hmm, he sure is familiar with the officer in charge

PHYLLIS K. WALTERS

of transporting him, Rosie thought. *He's addressed him by name, but at least it wasn't his first name.* She noticed a pen in Larson's right breast pocket. That too, made her wonder. *Why is he permitted to carry an object that could be used as a weapon?*

Bronson left them alone and returned to the main hallway. Rosie took out her legal pad and a consent-to-release form. Scott just stared at her with his arms crossed in front of his chest.

"I'm Dr. Rosie Klein. I need you to understand that what we discuss today is not confidential. The information will be provided to the judge, your attorney, and the prosecuting attorney. It is meant to assist the court in the determination of your sentence. Do you understand and agree? If so, please sign this form."

"All right. I understand. I'll sign the stupid thing. But I think you're trying to trick me, aren't' you? You work for the prosecutor's office, right?"

"No, I don't. Number one: I'm not trying to trick you. I will ask you to explain some details about your childhood, your past, your education, your military, and your career histories. Secondly, I was appointed by the *court*. The prosecutor's office did request that I evaluate you, and your attorney agreed. Now, may we proceed?" Her voice was strong and steady. She looked at him directly. He stared back, then looked down at the paper. Larson signed the consent form and leaned back in his chair with arms straight out, palms down on the table.

298

"Okay doc, shoot." He laughed and returned to an upward position. "I mean, start your questions."

Rosie began by asking him about his childhood and family. When she came to the loss of his mother, he paused for several minutes. With head down, he told her the same story he told his first wife, Alexis, about the mysterious fire that took his mother's life. "It made me a homeless orphan," he said, sounding wounded.

"And your father?" Rosie asked without emotion.

"I already told you, he left for God knows where."

"When did your mother die, and what did you do next?"

"She died in September of my senior year. I was the quarterback of my high school football team. It upset me, okay? Booze was the only thing that helped. So, I got benched. My grades fell, and any chance of a scholarship to play football in college went with them."

"Did you lose everything in the fire?" Rosie asked.

"Not exactly. My mother died of smoke inhalation. She was wearing diamond earrings and had rings on her fingers which I got. My stupid first wife refused to give back my mother's diamond ring when we got divorced."

"Where did you live the rest of your senior year?"

"I was eighteen. That meant I was too old for the county foster care program. But I didn't care. I didn't want to live with a strange family, anyway. I had buddies, and I stayed with a few of them. Then after graduation, my best buddy and I joined the army."

"You left the army after eight years. Is that correct?"

"Yeah. One reason I went in was to use the G.I. bill to get a degree in nursing when I got out. The other reason I left was because of favoritism when it came to promotions. I was in the military police and commended for doing a great job. You know military police are tough, don't you? Military police are held to a higher standard than other army guys.

"Obviously, I didn't violate the law before or during my stint in the army. I couldn't be an MP if I had a serious record either beforehand or throughout my military career. That's why this trumped-up murder charge is so ridiculous. I didn't deliberately shoot my wife. I *loved* Olivia. I mistook her for an intruder. My Post Traumatic Stress Disorder preceded my tours of duty and got worse by what I saw firsthand in the army."

"What exactly do you mean when you say there was favoritism?"

"If you weren't married, they didn't consider you stable. Can you imagine that? Being good enough for the military police, then being judged by *marital* status? I mean, c'mon!"

"We both know you shot your wife, mistakenly or not. You sat through the trial and heard the testimony of many witnesses. Is there something you would like to say about that?"

"Yes, I would. Most of what I heard was a pack of lies. I *didn't* know it was my wife that day. I thought it was an intruder. You know they think my mother's death was due to a home invasion. Have you heard that? Well, I took that to heart and am extremely sensitive to anything that smacks of a break-in. I have PTSD and problems with flashbacks, nightmares, being able to focus and paying attention at times."

"I see," Rosie replied as Larson's voice escalated, its pace quickened.

"Other than listening to witnesses, the prosecutors, and your attorneys, did you have any other thoughts in that courtroom?"

"I had to look at Olivia's remains on that big screen. If I had known that would happen, I would have shot her to bits, so there would have been nothing to see." He blurted the statement out before he thought about its ramifications.

Almost instantly he tried to backtrack, but as far as Rosie was concerned it was too late. What he had said revealed his guilt, his narcissistic nature, and his psychopathic tendencies.

During their talking, Rosie had noticed Larson standing up and pacing the room. As their conversation had continued, he had walked around the center table, even sitting on a corner of it at one point while she sat in her chair close by the door.

Then, without warning, Larson moved quickly and propped one of his feet against the doorjamb, kneeling beside her chair. She felt his hand up and under her skirt before she realized what he was doing. Then he wrapped his free arm around her shoulders. She felt his hand high up on her inner thigh and heard him breathing heavily. She had to act fast.

"Get back in your chair where you belong!" Rosie

demanded in a harsh, loud voice.

"Aww, c'mon, now, Rosie," he said in sugary voice. "You *know* you want this. I can see it in your eyes."

"I said, BACK OFF!" Her voice was strident; eyes focused on the pen in his shirt pocket. *Why didn't he use that on my throat,* she wondered, *that's a lethal weapon.*

Shocked, she saw him respond to her voice. Reluctantly, he removed his hand from under her skirt, got up and brushed off his pant leg, then sat back down facing her, the table now between them. The pen had never left his pocket. She was relieved he hadn't placed it against her throat. Her heart was racing; she forced herself not to show fear or anxiety in her posture or her words.

"We're done here," she said, packing up her materials. She stood and yanked open the door, quickly walking out. Larson followed her into the hall. As they turned toward the booking area, he looked at her.

"What happened in there stays between us, right Dr. Klein?"

"Unfortunately, no, Mr. Larson. Just as the form reads, *all* of it will be reported to the judge, your attorney, and the prosecutors."

The corrections officer in charge of Larson, now approached the defendant to take charge of him. With her hands shaking, Rosie walked down the hall. Holding back tears, she headed for fresh air.

***

How stupid of me, she thought. *How did I not*

recognize I was being set up? Evaluating defendants on the first floor was unusual and being asked by a defendant to move to a different interview room was extremely rare.

I don't ever remember that kind of request being made by a male or female prisoner before. As she thought about the incident, her thoughts became fuzzy, her palms began sweating, and her heart began pounding in her chest. *Oh, my gosh,* she thought, *this is what PTSD feels like. How can I blame myself for something so out of my control? I didn't invite his response, he planned it. Now I'm beginning to understand how victims feel. I have to stop thinking that I did anything to bring on his actions.*

What would I say to a client who told me this kind of story? I would say, 'it had nothing to do with what you were wearing. It had nothing to do with anything you said or did. It all has to do with the evil manipulative mind of a cruel psychopath.' Oh, and it isn't about sex, it's about power.

***

Rosie entered her downtown office building more determined than ever to report Larson's abuse to the authorities. The elevator doors opened, and she felt relieved that no one else was riding up with her.

Another sign of PTSD, she thought. *The idea of being with someone, particularly of the opposite sex, in a closed space, suddenly terrifies me.*

Rosie looked both ways down the hall and unlocked the door of her office. She was alone, safe at last, and in need of a comfortable chair and a bottle of water. Something stronger would wait for later. She quickly dialed the phone number of the prosecutor, McKenna Day.

41

Bucky to the Rescue

Driving home now, the memory of Larsen's hand on her leg kept playing in her mind, his breath in her ear, his words: 'I know you want this.' She shuddered and pressed the "call" button on her phone then, "home." She waited for Bucky to pick up, but voice mail answered instead.

"Please leave a message and we'll get right back to you." She waited for the beep. "Hi Bucky? When will you be home? I'm almost there myself. I really, *really* need to talk to you." Rosie hung up. *He'll get the message soon, maybe I'll even be home by then.* She was glad she had called McKenna Day. McKenna had confirmed the incident was in no way Rosie's fault. She had been sympathetic, and madder than hell at the corrections officers and Larson.

"I'll report this immediately," McKenna told her. "After I tell his attorney, Bart Meyer, I'll contact Judge Brown. Larson should suffer the consequences."

Rosie felt gratified that her upset was being taken

seriously. Too often others made light of something that seemed slight, but that could affect someone deeply. Now, heading home, she realized she had forgotten to tip Geoff, who had brought her car around. *He'll know that isn't like me,* she thought. *I'll explain next time I see him* Jocko met Rosie at the back door with needs of his own. "Need a walk, boy? Give me a minute." She put her purse, briefcase, and jacket on the kitchen counter and clipped the leash onto his collar, then walked out to the patio where he found the bushes. Re-entering the kitchen, she gave him fresh water and headed to the bedroom to change her clothes. But when she sat on the bed, she dissolved into tears. She felt a sense of relief, of fear, and of humiliation. She curled into a ball and stayed in a fetal position until she fell asleep.

***

Sometime later, Bucky arrived at home.

"Rosie, are you here?" he called while coming through the door. It was strange that Jocko had not met him. Walking into the bedroom, he found his precious wife asleep on top of the comforter. "Rosie, are you okay?" Bucky asked softly. She opened her eyes and immediately reached for him. He sat on the bed and cradled her in his arms. She nestled her head against his chest without a word.

"What's the matter? Are you okay?"

"I'll be okay, but I'm so glad you're here," she said. "Would you please get me a glass of water? I need to tell you something." Bucky quickly returned with the water and sat beside her. She took a deep drink then told him the frightening story of the unexpected, unprovoked attack. When she stopped talking, Bucky responded.

"My God, the most important thing is that you escaped without harm, and now you are safe here with me. I can't believe he attempted to assault you right there in the county jail. What was he thinking?"

"Without *harm*? I'm afraid, not. Maybe without *direct* harm, but I'm deeply upset, Bucky," she said. "I've never told anyone about an attack that happened years ago when I was a college student. It happened near the college library. I was walking to my dorm and a guy pulled me into the bushes. I scratched his eyes and ran. They never caught him. But over the past years, I've had nightmares and occasional panic attacks because of it. I haven't told you about it because I've always preferred to put it out of my mind. If I think about it while driving and I get anxious, I just pull over, sit quietly, and breathe until I can regain my composure.

"I'm so sorry, Rosie, what can I do?" Bucky asked.

"You've already done it. You're a great listener and I know I can count on you. If I feel the same next week, I'll make an appointment to see Dr. Seifer, my favorite shrink. Along with some therapy, maybe he'll put me back on an anti-anxiety pill for a while. How convenient that he's located in my downtown office, right?"

"Would he also recommend pet therapy and back rubs?"

"Ha! Probably both. I'm lucky to have my own live-in personal masseuse at my command along with Jocko," Rosie said, feeling her mood lift a little.

"Meanwhile, I have a report to submit on Larson. I think I'll also have Ruth reschedule a couple of my clients." Rosie said. "I don't need extra stress right now."

"You probably have no appetite, but just the same, I'm going to grill some chicken and vegetables. As your second favorite shrink, I recommend that you eat some protein, hungry or not."

Rosie smiled a second time.

The phone rang. Bucky handed it to Rosie and walked into the kitchen to prepare the meal. He heard Rosie say, "Hi, Bart. I'm doing better than earlier today. Thank you for checking on me."

"We were all extremely upset that you were put through such an ordeal," Bart said. "McKenna is in the process of checking the visitor's log to see if other women professionals have seen Larson since he was transferred in from St. Stephen's. Even though we think it's highly unlikely. I'm also going to put in a call to the hospital administrator and report what happened. I'll ask him to investigate whether there were any complaints against Larson while he was there, and of course, to keep this report confidential."

"I did finish my line of questioning, "Rosie said. "You'll be amazed at what he said not only about his touching me, but about his own case. I'll be putting it in my report and hopefully, the jury will hear about his attitude and opinion of the trial."

"Do you feel up to sharing that information with me now?"

"Okay, he said if he had known he was going

to look at his wife's remains on the big screen in the courtroom, he would have blown her to bits, so he wouldn't have to see them."

"Whoa! *That* will cause an uproar. He didn't testify during his trial. Does he plan to make a statement to Judge Brown and Olivia's family?"

"He told me he was planning on it. But I don't believe a word that comes out of his mouth, at this point. You'll have to ask his attorney."

"Well, Rosie. Take care of yourself. Enjoy your evening as much as you can. We all think you're a courageous, talented woman, and we're relieved he didn't hurt you more."

"One last question, Bart: Why is Scott Larson's uniform a different color? It's green, why not orange? It also appears that he's getting preferential treatment in several ways. The uniform color being one, and the other is that he's permitted to keep a pen in his pocket. In my estimation, a pen can be used as a weapon."

"A pen in his pocket? He didn't threaten you with it, did he?" Bart asked.

"No, but I was aware of it, and he could have. The thought terrified me," Rosie said. "Instead of only putting his hand up my skirt, he could have put the pen to my throat."

"Rest assured I'll take that up with Sheriff Morris. You can believe heads will roll, Rosie. Both of your concerns have merit. As far as his uniform goes, I think the prisoner who wears that color uniform is assigned to *oversee* the pod or dorm. It's like being a 'trustee' in law enforcement terms, or a 'straw boss' to other inmates.

"He has no authority to control any inmates, but guards turn their heads and allow him to firmly remind prisoners of the rules if you know what I mean. It does prevent a bunch of stealing and fighting. Basically, a 'straw boss' helps the pod run smoother. But I have to say, Larson certainly wasn't there long enough to be considered for *that* position. They must have considered his hospital stay and his waiting for trial, as time spent. Still, it's all very peculiar, Rosie. I'll have to look into it."

"Questionable judgment, if you ask me," she responded. "On a similar note, I once approached the steps of a Jackson County jail and a guy in a leather jacket was sitting on the railing near the top. I assumed he was a detective. He, in fact, was a prisoner that they deemed low-risk and figured he was highly responsible. He also was big and muscular, whereas you and I know that Larson doesn't fit that bill."

"You must be kidding," said Bart. "Those old county jails have always operated under their own guidelines."

"Well, Bart, thank you for your concern," Rosie said. "My husband has dinner ready, and Jocko's eyes are pleading for attention. I plan to relax this evening and will finish my report in the next couple days," Rosie said.

"Take it easy. No rush," Bart said. "I'm going to call the Sheriff's deputy on duty and get that pen removed from Larson's pocket before he hurts somebody. He'll be removed from the trustee position, too. Severe disciplinary action will result from his assault on you."

***

Rosie walked into the kitchen and picked up the glass of wine Bucky had poured for her. Then she joined him on the patio. "Nothing like dark red wine for medicinal purposes," she said. She took a sip of the cool wine, then put her cheek next to his and kissed his cheek. They sat at the glass top table where Bucky had placed a plate of crackers and cheese. Jocko flopped down between them, sensing his owners needed a moment of solitude.

"Tomorrow, I have a couple of clients at my Summerhill office and will spend a few minutes with Ruth. I need to return McKenna Day's call to see what the prosecutor's office needs from me in their State of Ohio vs. Scott Larson case," Rosie said. "Oh, then I see Dr. Seifer at noon.

Bucky pulled Rosie to him and gave her a loving kiss and firm hug. Rosie's evening ended with a note of optimism and a sense of security. She had her sweet, supportive husband, her devoted dog, and was beginning to feel her self-confidence begin to return.

42

Sheriff Nelson

As Rosie walked in the door of her office, Ruth stretched across the desk to hand her a note. The telephone was balanced between one shoulder and her neck, while she was speaking to someone.

Respecting her privacy, Rosie accepted the note and walked to her inner office.

"Please call Sheriff Nelson at your earliest convenience," the note said. It was dated the day after she had reported her assault by Scott Larson.

She had pared back her schedule in the office and had accepted almost no professional calls, so she hadn't seen this note. Intending to pour a cup of coffee and call the sheriff back, she was interrupted by a buzz from her office phone.

"Sheriff Nelson on line one, Rosie." Picking up the receiver, she recognized his deep voice.

"Dr. Klein, this is Sheriff Nelson. I'm calling to tell you how sorry I am that you have experienced an attack by one of our inmates. I can guarantee that he has been severely dealt with as have the deputies who were on duty that day.

"Thank you, Sheriff," she said.

"First off, Larson should never have been wearing a green uniform as a position of trustee. Time served in a forensic unit of a psychiatric hospital does not qualify as "time served" the same goes for an inmate in county jail. Secondly, he should never have been permitted to carry a *pen* outside the pod or even out of his cell. You handled the situation in a very professional manner. I applaud you for that." The sheriff did not let Rosie get another word in edgewise. Finally, he took a breath.

"Well, sheriff, I was just about to call *you*," she said. "I just walked into my office now and received your message from the other day. Thank you for this call. I appreciate it and especially the prompt, effective attention to the matter. It's a huge relief that you corrected what could have posed a serious threat to anyone else as well. I should never have agreed to conduct the evaluation in a different interview room without requesting that a guard be positioned outside the room. That was my error, and one I won't make again."

"Don't blame yourself," Sheriff Nelson answered quickly. "The guard was way too lax and this whole matter brought it out into the open. Sometimes, guards assume inmates will naturally respect all visitors because they're doctors and lawyers assigned to their cases. But as we've learned, each inmate is a different animal, so to speak, and needs to be watched carefully at all times."

"Thank you, Sheriff for your vote of confidence."

"You're very welcome, Rosie. Oh, by the way, the coroner's report came back and low and behold, we have a motive. Olivia was four months pregnant. Larson found out about the pregnancy from a gynecologist at the hospital. Apparently, she hadn't informed the doctor that her husband wasn't aware she was pregnant yet, and she didn't want him to be told. But the good doctor let the cat out of the bag when he bumped into Larson in a hallway.

"Doc Davidson is a really good guy, but he talks too much. His friends call him 'Chunky' and he's just the nicest man; tries real hard to be friendly. He told Larson, 'Now that Olivia's spotting has stopped, there's no more danger of losing the baby.' What he didn't know is that Larson and Olivia had agreed *not* to have children and Olivia supposedly was on birth control pills. Obviously, Larson was stunned by this revelation, and furious beyond belief.

"So, he went directly home from work that morning and shot her in the abdomen. Obviously, the fetus did not survive. That answers the question of why he didn't shoot her in the head, or chest, if he believed she was an intruder, or, as he's told us, an Iraqi woman with explosives. It's a terrible tragedy."

"Unbelievable, Sheriff. Will he be retried for aggravated murder? He obviously planned to kill Olivia and the baby she was carrying?"

"Well, most likely, the grand jury *will* indict Larson on two counts of aggravated murder. In some states, what constitutes 'life' is when the fetus is at the stage of viability and can only survive outside the womb at the time the mother is killed which doesn't apply to Olivia's case. But here in Ohio, we have a new law called the Daly Law. It resulted from a case back in 1995 when a drunk driver killed a woman by the name of Suzanne Daly and her unborn child. Ohio law now provides rights to unborn babies at any stage of development."

"So, you're saying that in Ohio, taking the life of someone known to be pregnant with the end result being the loss of the baby, is considered *double* homicide?"

"That's right, Dr. Klein. Murder is now defined as the unlawful killing of a person or fetus with 'malice aforethought.' As you probably know, that means with the intent to kill. Rest assured, Dr. Klein, even though the prosecutor won't indict him on a new charge, the judge most certainly will consider it when he sentences Larson."

"I would think that means life without parole," Rosie said. "Either murder would have qualified him for the death penalty, right, Sheriff? I was on a case once where one shooter received the death penalty, and the second shooter was sentenced to life without parole. Even though both crimes were heinous enough for the death penalty."

"That's been my experience, too. Probably one shooter was younger with no priors and that's why he didn't get the death penalty. By the way, not that it's an issue, but the DNA test substantiated that *Scott* was the biological father of this fetus."

315

"I don't know how that would even have been questioned since she was viewed as a loyal wife by those who knew her well," Rosie said. "Well, once again, thank you for calling, Sheriff. Nothing in my interview suggested that Larson knew his wife was pregnant. He just clung to his version that he didn't recognize her in the dim light of morning, and that he acted impulsively. He still claims his PTSD caused him to startle easily, and that he acted defensively to save his own life.

"Well, his claim of suffering from PTSD stuff is a bunch of bull," the sheriff said. "Attacking you didn't help portray himself as a victim, now did it?" he said vehemently. "I don't call that so smart."

"Not for an instant," Rosie answers. "He is a predator who justifies all his decisions and portrays his previous actions as self-defense in nature. There is nothing about Scott Larson that suggests he has ever been a victim or ever will allow himself to be one. He holds himself above the law, thrives on an enormous sense of entitlement, views everyone else as failing to conform to *his* standards, therefore, is deserving of his wrath or a terrible fate. That's the description of a sociopath if I ever heard one."

"Well, Dr. Klein, this has been a most interesting conversation. Please feel free to contact me directly if you ever need my input or want me to intervene in other cases. And don't hesitate to call if you are ever threatened again in any way. I will e-mail you my private phone number."

"That's very kind of you. Oh, and thank you for

the storehouse of information you've just shared."

"Have a nice day, Dr. Klein. Bye for now."

Rosie took a sip of her now tepid coffee. She entered the hall to dump it out in the sink and get a fresh cup while her thoughts were going a mile a minute.

McKenna Day should call me soon, she thought. *Everything the sheriff told me is starting to make sense for this entire situation. The only question remaining is whether Olivia deliberately skipped her birth control pills to become pregnant, or if it truly was accidental.*

Was Olivia afraid to tell her husband? Probably, given their agreement not to have children. Is that why she went through the first trimester in silence? Did anyone else know? Did she figure she would tell Scott once she knew she wouldn't miscarry? The morning he killed her Dr. Davidson had just confirmed the baby would be carried to term.

"Rosie," Ruth called out to her. "Attorney Day is on the phone. Can you pick it up?"

"Yes, and if the gals arrive for the group therapy session, just have them drink coffee and chat together in the waiting area."

Rosie seated herself at her desk and picked up the phone. "Hi, McKenna? I think I know what you're about to say. Sheriff Nelson called to tell me that Olivia was pregnant, which means Scott Larson can be indicted on two aggravated murder charges, right?"

"Exactly. If the state medical examiner's report hadn't been delayed, and if we had not rushed to convict him, a jury might have fried him for both murders. Get this, Rosie. Olivia had just had an ultrasound which showed the baby was a boy. Can you imagine being raised by a father like Larson?"

"No, I can't. My diagnosis will be different given this latest information. He's not simply a narcissistic personality disorder. He has demonstrated a pervasive pattern of disregard for and violation of the rights of others. He is, in fact, a psychopath."

She ticked them off:

- He can't understand the pain he's caused others because he lacks empathy.
- He easily uses people in a self-serving manner, unfettered by guilt or remorse.
- He has an enormous sense of entitlement and an absence of attachment or bonding with anyone.
- He's manufactured a life history that is littered with a pack of lies.

"It amazes me how he can be so successful in his academic pursuits and professional career yet fail to function according to societal norms in all other areas," Rosie said. "Based on his academic performance following his stint in the army, he is highly intelligent. Even though he was not popular at the hospital, he was known to be a great nurse with a future that most likely would have resulted in him becoming a nurse practitioner. I shudder at the thought."

"The sentencing hearing is next week," McKenna Day said. "We'll have several witnesses speaking on behalf of the victim, and we have your testimony. What you just explained to me is powerful, Rosie. Expect the defense team to cross-examine you in hopes that your testimony can be watered down a bit. I'm sure you're up for that, and your diagnosis will pack a punch they don't see coming."

"It will be my pleasure to elaborate on any point they choose to pursue," Rosie said. "They need to be cautious, don't they? The fact that she was pregnant was never brought forward during the trial phase. If they push me on my diagnosis, for example, it will open the door for me to state that"

"Absolutely right," McKenna said. "Then it goes into the record and the district appeals court and/ or parole board will factor the information into their future decisions. Let's hope the defense fails to think of that, and they go forward and needle you a little. That would be stupid on their part for several reasons. For one thing, we have all read your reports in the past and listened to your testimonies. You are extremely convincing. Secondly, as I've just pointed out, it will put the second murder on record."

"Thanks for your appreciation, McKenna. I'll be prepared to respond if I need to. I take it there are no witnesses who will come forward to speak in support of Scott Larson."

"As far as I know, you're correct. He doesn't have a friend in the world. By the way, may I ask you something, Rosie?"

"Certainly."

"Did he discuss his mother's mysterious death

with you? Just curious about that," she said.

"Not really. But I understood she was an alcoholic and a smoker."

"Is there a chance she accidentally left a cigarette burning and passed out?"

"Funny, you should think of that," Rosie replied. "The fire investigator said he felt the fire was deliberately set to suggest an unintentional suicide. So, on one hand, it could have occurred the way you described, or, it could have been an act of arson."

"Did Scott say where he was the night of the fire?" McKenna asked.

"In fact, he did. He stayed at his girlfriend's house after a home football game. He would have gone home, but his mother wasn't at the game again. He remembers looking for her when he left the field and was disappointed when he didn't see her. So, instead of going home that night, he went to his girlfriend's house," Rosie said. "In the discovery materials, it said the coach told the investigator that his mother's absence was not unusual."

"Okay, maybe it happened that way," McKenna said, "or maybe he detoured to his house, set the fire, then went to the girl's house as his alibi. We should find the girl and see what time he got to her house. I think there's more to the story, don't' you?"

43

Unexpected Turn of Events

Rosie welcomed each woman in her support group with a smile and hug, then seated herself in her comfortable wingback chair. Three of the women sat cross-legged on the carpet with mugs of coffee placed on the low, square table in front of them. The other three ladies sat in the other cushy chairs as they waited for Rosie to begin the session.

Homemade chocolate chip cookies donated by one of the women reminded Rosie of Olivia's reputation for baking cookies. It made her pause for a moment, lost in thought about the deceased woman's memory. Absentmindedly, Rosie patted Jocko's head. His presence always brought joy to the group.

Then, coming back to the moment, Rosie looked around and sighed. For now, court work was behind her. It was time to concentrate on this group of women who needed her for a while. She felt pleased that her own therapy with Dr. Seifer would begin tapering off to every other week. She enjoyed engaging with these clients who met in a group to learn coping skills for stressors in their lives: Marital problems, adjusting to divorce, and raising children.

This group was unique. The three women sitting on the floor were having affairs. Two of them hadn't known their lovers were married, and one was involved with her much older boss who held her future career success in his hands. That woman was dressed in a navy pants suit with a long sleeve, white, silk blouse beneath her blazer. Her dark blue pumps and horn-rimmed glasses gave an air of professionalism.

Everyone else, including Rosie, wore casual clothes and sandals or shoes – no socks - which they could remove during the session. The three women seated in comfortable chairs were wives of husbands having affairs. One had confronted her husband and insisted he end the relationship. They were now in marriage counseling with a therapist Rosie had recommended. The others had just recently discovered their spouses' betrayals. Those two had small children and were stay-at-home moms. They both had joined the group to figure out what to do next and how to deal with what might lie ahead. They were also exploring reasons from the women who were having affairs with married men as to why their husbands might have strayed.

When the group had originally formed and the

ladies heard one another's stories, at first, they had wanted to gouge each other's eyes out. But over a few sessions, they had bonded. A few had placed the blame squarely on the shoulders of the men. Those seeing the married men, said the men blamed unloving, unresponsive wives for their desire to have their needs met elsewhere.

Today, two hours passed quickly by the time each women brought their stories up-to-date, and all had reported on the homework Rosie had previously assigned them. When Rosie dismissed the group, Jocko stood in the doorway wanting to be patted by each gal as they departed. They hugged one another and lined up at the sink to rinse out their coffee cups.

Rosie noticed a message Ruth had strategically stuck on the outside of her office door. Although it was seven o'clock, Rosie was curious and decided to return Jake Morgan's call. What in the world would prompt Scott Larson's attorney to contact her at this stage of the case?

When the last woman departed, she dialed the number. He answered on the second ring.

"Hello, Jake Morgan."

"Hello, Jake. This is Rosie Klein returning your call." She didn't see the need to apologize for calling so late. She wanted to hear him out.

"Well, Dr. Klein, thanks so much for getting back to me. You won't believe it, but Scott Larson just fired me for not agreeing to interrogate you on the stand. He wanted me to say that he denied attacking you at the county jail and to make you confess to lying about it. He also wanted me to refuse to acknowledge you as an expert witness. Since I declined all his demands, he fired me. He's planning on representing himself and has already secured a lawyer for his appeal."

"Wow," Rosie said, completely surprised by the change of events. "I'm sorry you were fired, but I appreciate your position about me," Rosie responded. "I think he's just made things harder for himself."

"Don't be too sorry. He was, without a doubt, the most difficult client I've ever been assigned to represent. You did know it was pro bono, didn't you?"

"Really?" Rosie said. "Actually, I didn't know that."

"Yeah, Judge Brown randomly assigns private attorneys to take murder cases pro bono occasionally. It only happens about every five years, but I won the lottery on this one," Hanson laughed.

"So, will the sentencing hearing continue as scheduled and will Scott Larson be permitted to represent himself? If so, will he ask that my testimony not be allowed?"

"That's correct, Rosie. But don't worry about it. I predict Larson will ask for a continuation to have time to prepare. Ha, I find that funny, as if he could. "

"Okay. Then what?"

"Judge Brown will likely allow the continuance but will not accept Larson's motion to dismiss you. You were already acceptable to the defense team and the state of Ohio. Maybe Larson will come to his senses about cross examining you once he realizes you're aware that he *knew* Olivia was pregnant when he shot her.

"As it stands now, he's only facing one murder charge. But if he brings you to the stand and your testimony goes on record regarding the murder of his unborn child, it will only assist the judge in sentencing him to the max. That will lessen the likelihood of any appeal or even parole being successful. He may not be aware of all that."

"I see," Rosie said. "That's good."

"How familiar are you with the Ohio sixth district court of appeals and its proceedings?"

"I know that transcripts of my depositions, reports, and testimonies have been submitted to the sixth district and other appeals courts in the past."

"That's true. I've seen some of your materials in the past. The petitioner is the side requesting the appeal with the hope that the verdict will be overturned. That's why he or she hires an appeals attorney like Larson just did.

"The respondent who, in this case, is the prosecutor for the state of Ohio, will argue *against* the petitioner who, in this case, is Larson. Since the courts don't re-try cases or hear new evidence, they just review all the procedures and decisions from the trial court. The appeal will make certain that all proceedings were fair, and the proper law was applied correctly by the judge. I don't see how Larsen can win."

"In your experience, have there been many cases

overturned or submitted to a higher court?"

"Only twice: One time, the sixth district court found a prosecutor had said something inadmissible in his closing remarks to the jury. It was something that the judge had sustained after the defense objected. The jury was to disregard what was said, but the prosecutor included it, again, in his closing remarks, so the case was overturned.

"In another case, the court determined that the judge gave improper instructions to the jury. So, yes, I recall at least those two cases."

"Does McKenna Day know you've been fired?"

"Yes, I called her first and told her I wanted to personally tell you the news. Speaking of breaking news, you'll probably hear the angle Larson will present on the channel thirteen report this evening at eleven o'clock. They weren't allowed to interview him, so he wrote a statement and sent it to the editor of the Toledo Blade. The editor passed it on to his cousin who happens to produce the news program. It will be breaking news tonight and make headlines tomorrow.

"He'll say I was fired for inadequate representation, or something like that. He won't mention you because he's afraid, they'll interview you and he realizes how believable you'll come off. Instead, he's going back to the Pendleton report that caused his PTSD defense to be tossed. He'll blame everything that didn't go his way on me as his 'incompetent' attorney Jake Morgan

"Jake, I really appreciate your call. I think Larson isn't going to get what he wants, and I think you're a very competent, ethical attorney. Thanks so much for calling and have a good evening."

"Thanks, Rosie. I appreciate your compliment," he said. "Have a good evening yourself. I'm sure I'll see you on another case soon."

44

Intimidation Begins

Rosie put Jocko on his leash as he patiently waited inside the door of her office. She turned off the lights and they stepped outside as she locked the door. Within minutes, they were at the parking lot where she unlocked her car, all the while thinking about her recent conversation with attorney Jake Hanson. Jocko hopped inside the back seat as Rosie tossed her briefcase onto the passenger side. On the drive home, she listened to Southern gospel music which set her in a pleasant mood for an enjoyable evening at home with Bucky.

He greeted them both with a smile and hug for Rosie. He bent down and cupped Jocko's head between his hands. "How are you doing, boy?" he said, rubbing both sides of Jocko's ears. "I've got fresh water for you and maybe a greenie treat." Jocko considered the nugget a delicious wonder, but it secretly cleaned his teeth and freshened his breath.

Bucky handed Rosie a glass of Shiraz, her favorite

dark red wine. Then, he slid open the patio door and they stepped outside, looking over the rail. The familiar sound of the fountain in the pond and croaking frogs made Rosie feel a sense of serenity. For a moment, she was able to forget about the Larson case, so riddled with turbulence, confusion, and disorder. Recently, it had taken its toll on her usually upbeat mood.

"What's that delicious smell?" she asked. The aroma of roast beef wafted out from the kitchen. It had been in the slow cooker all day simmering with potatoes and carrots. Bucky had added just a bit more beef broth along with peas and mushrooms. He loved creating his own recipes, and Rosie appreciated his passion for cooking.

The abrasive sound of the phone startled her and for a moment, she considered not answering. Then, she thought better of the idea and excused herself.

"Hello. Dr. Klein? This is Sharon, from today's group." The sound of her voice alarmed Rosie.

"What's the matter, Sharon? You sound upset." Sharon had been through a lot lately with her husband and Rosie assumed that was the nature of her call.

"When I left your office this afternoon, I was followed. I think the guy was waiting for me in the little meat market across the street. I noticed his yellowish headlights following me when I turned into McDonald's to go through the drive-through. But the driver just pulled into a parking spot and didn't leave his car. Then, as I left and merged onto I-475, I noticed those same headlights behind me. That's when I realized

I was being followed. From the rear-view mirror, I couldn't see his face because his windows were tinted.

"Dr. Rosie, I'm terrified! He didn't tailgate me or anything. He stayed a distance back, but when I changed lanes, he followed me. I deliberately turned off the ramp early instead of driving directly to my house. And, again, he followed. That's when I knew I needed help, so I drove to the closest fire station. That's when he picked up speed and drove on by.

"I ran inside and told the fire chief what just happened. One firefighter sitting in a chair outside, witnessed me pulling into their driveway and watched the car behind me drive by. He got more of a description of the vehicle than I did."

"Oh, my Lord, Sharon. That's horrible!" Rosie said, realizing her terror. "What color was the car?"

"Black. It looked like a four-door, late model. I'm not sure. I just know that the headlights were yellowish. The Sylvania police are on their way here now, but I just had to tell you. I'm scared, Dr. Klein."

"I understand, and I'm glad you called, Sharon. This might not be an isolated incident. Have you thought about where you want to stay tonight? Will you go home or stay with a friend?"

"I am heading to my mother's. She lives in a secure high rise and is expecting me. I know her code for the parking garage, so I'll be okay going in there," Sharon said.

"I want you to stay in touch," Rosie said.

"I will. Thanks for picking up. I feel a little better

now," Sharon said, still sounding breathless. "The police said they'll want to talk to you, too. I hope you don't mind."

"Of course, I don't mind. We'll get to the bottom of this. Try to stay calm, okay? We'll talk soon."

Bucky joined Rosie at the kitchen counter, seeing her obvious distress as she hung up the phone.

"A client of mine was followed this evening. Did you overhear my conversation with her?"

"I only heard your end of it. Come, sit down; you're shaking. Tell me what's happened." Bucky put his arms around Rosie and led her to the loveseat. She sat and repeated everything Sharon had told her.

Then Rosie began to wonder: This evening, she had been dressed casually in jeans for the group session. Sharon, on the other hand, had been dressed professionally. Was Sharon the person being followed, or could Rosie have been the target, and Sharon followed by mistake since she was more professionally dressed? On the other hand, Sharon had revealed in group talk recently that her husband had found out about an affair she was having. His angry personality had driven her to the affair, so Rosie knew he might be violent. Could he be the one following her?

The doorbell rang and Jocko barked loudly. Bucky left Rosie sitting in the family room to answer the door. He greeted an officer and brought him into see Rosie.

"Good evening, ma'am. I'm officer Gray. I'm here about an investigation."

"Hello officer. I'm Rosie Klein. Are you here about Sharon Leonard?"

"Yes, ma'am. How do you know her?"

"I have a psychology practice here in Summerhill. I see her in a group session with several other women. She called me before you came over and told me that today, when she left the office after our group session, that she was followed. She thinks the car was parked across the street in front of Johnson's Meats. All she remembers is a black, late-model car with yellowish headlights. When she realized she was being followed, it frightened her enough that she drove into a fire station in Sylvania and reported it, then called me. I have reason to believe the situation could become violent as she is dealing with an angry, abusive husband."

"How long have you known her?" Gray asked.

"For several months now."

"All right. I'll check with the owner of Johnson Meats in the morning and see if their surveillance cameras picked up anybody tailing her. Do you know any reason that your client would be followed?"

"As a matter of fact, I do have a theory. She was dressed professionally today, while I was dressed casually, in jeans, not my normal attire. It may have been a case of mistaken identity. I'm currently involved in a murder case in Toledo serving as an expert witness for the prosecutor's office. Circumstances changed today and could have prompted someone being directed to follow me. The intent is to silence me and prevent my testimony at the sentencing trial. These people don't wish me well, to say the least. Perhaps, whoever followed her, was supposed to be following me. At the very least, it was an attempt to intimidate one of us," Rosie said.

"In that case, we'll put a couple of plainclothes officers near your home and in front of your office right away. It's not unusual in cases like this for them to ransack your office. It's another way to get their message across and make you feel unsafe and violated," Gray said.

"Thank you, officer. I appreciate it. I have a second office downtown in the LaSalle Building, and I teach at the University of Toledo. Do I need to be concerned?"

"When do you go to either of those places?"

"Usually, I'm at the LaSalle office downtown on Fridays. I lease space from Dr. Seifer, a psychiatrist colleague of mine."

"Did you say, Dr. Seifer?" Gray was suddenly alert. "Dr. *Robert* Seifer?"

"Yes, do you know him?"

"He was shot about an hour ago. Apparently, the doctor stepped into the hallway outside his office suite when an assailant walked up and asked if he was Dr. Seifer. When the doctor answered 'yes,' he was shot three times with a twenty-two. Fortunately, the cleaning crew heard the shots, saw the guy run toward the stairwell, found the doctor, and called the rescue squad. He's in surgery now but expected to survive."

"I can't believe what's happening," Rosie said in distress. "Where was he shot?"

"Hit in the right elbow, right knee, and abdomen. No vital organs, luckily. He stayed conscious and gave a pretty good description to the detective at the emergency room."

"I can't help but think this is all my fault. Poor Dr. Seifer," Rosie said, tears welling in her eyes.

"How's that, ma'am? The perp asked the victim if he was 'Dr. Seifer,' not 'Dr. Klein.' There is no mistaken identity there."

"The officer is correct, Rosie," Bucky said. "You can't take this all on yourself. The authorities will get to the bottom of it." He looked at the man. "Thank you, Officer Gray, for coming over. How will we recognize any undercover policemen?"

"You won't. That's the idea for now. They'll introduce themselves when, or if they think it's time to do so. Meanwhile, I'll get together with the Lucas County Sheriff's Department and see who is investigating Dr. Seifer's shooting. We'll exchange information with them and with the Sylvania police. That's all for now, Dr. Klein. Take care and hope you can relax a little for the rest of this evening."

Gray handed his business card to Bucky, nodded at Rosie, and walked out the door. She remained seated on the loveseat, clutching a tissue in one hand, and shaking her head in disbelief.

"Is there anything I can get you?" Bucky asked.

"Not really. Maybe a glass of water. In the morning, I'll need to call McKenna Day and Jake Hanson to give them this information. I wouldn't put it past Scott

Larson to have arranged these treacherous acts while sitting in a prison cell. The man is devious."

"Money talks, Rosie. Now that he's representing himself, he's likely also being allowed unmonitored phone calls. He, or his appeals lawyer, have some nasty connections, it seems." Bucky handed her the water.

"Do you think we should go to the hospital to support Dr. Seifer's wife?"

"No," Bucky said. "For your safety, you need to hunker down here, Rosie. She knows how much you care about them. I'll call the surgery waiting room and see if we can speak to her. How does that sound?"

"That's good. Thank God no vital organs were struck."

Bucky dialed the hospital and asked for the surgery waiting room. A volunteer attendant answered, and Bucky asked to speak with Dr. Siefer's wife.

"Hello?" Nancy Seifer said in a soft voice when she came on the phone.

Bucky handed the phone to Rosie. "Oh, Nancy I'm so sorry to hear Robert was shot. How are you doing? What can we do for you?"

"I'm holding up. The doctors are optimistic about his recovery. Surgery may take a while. Just pray, Rosie," Nancy said.

"We're doing that, Nancy. Will you call when he's out of surgery? Do you need anything, a ride home?"

"I don't plan to go home. I'll sleep in the surgeon's lounge on a sofa. The nurses who work here with him just love Robert. They want to make me as comfortable as possible. But thank you. And thanks for being such a caring friend."

"You're welcome. Call if you need anything at all." Rosie hung up and said to Bucky, "One way or another, let's go to the hospital tomorrow. They both need our support."

"Okay, Rosie, but for the time being, there's nothing more for you to do. Use your thought-stopping technique to distract yourself. What can I get you?"

"Nothing. You're right. I need to practice what I preach to my clients. I'm going to focus on gratitude: Sharon wasn't hurt by the stalker, Dr. Seifer will survive his injuries, and I avoided a possible rape." Rosie took Bucky's hand and rested her head on his shoulder.

"Best of all, I have you."

45

The Phone Call

The telephone startled Rosie awake. She had dozed off on the loveseat and Bucky had covered her with a soft lap blanket. Now, she heard Bucky speaking to someone. *Oh, I hope it's not Nancy Seifer. If it is, that could be a bad sign*, she thought. *Robert's surgery shouldn't be over this soon.* The clock showed close to 10 p.m.

"Honey," Bucky called to her. "It's officer Gray. They've picked up a guy they think may be involved in the shooting and stalking earlier tonight. He wants to talk to you."

Rosie sat up and Bucky handed her the phone."

"Hello?"

"Dr. Klein? Officer Gray. We've arrested a man whose car was seen on the meat market's security camera at seven p.m.," Gray said. "At the end of the block, the traffic light camera also picked him up behind Sharon Leonard's car. Now, get this: Video surveillance also picked him up at the traffic light by the LaSalle Building at five forty-five p.m. and again at six-fifteen. He's been plenty busy. We figure he must have waited for Dr. Seifer to come out of his office building at six which then gave him plenty of time to get to your Summerhill office by seven."

"I hope you're right, officer. Was he pulled over? Did he resist arrest?"

"He was pulled over near the hospital. His yellow headlights alerted the deputies who stopped him, and he did not resist. A gun was found in the glove compartment with a note showing both your address and Dr. Seifer's. Sharon's name wasn't listed.

"We're thinking the bullets in his gun will match those being removed from Dr. Seifer. The doctors have been instructed to turn them over as evidence when they finish his surgery."

"So, what's next, Mel?" Rosie asked.

"I'm not sure, but McGuire and Spicer are on their way over to county jail to interview Larson. Maybe that'll help them sort out the truth, although undoubtedly Larson will deny any involvement. Meanwhile, the man we've apprehended will be booked on attempted murder and a public defender will be appointed. It doesn't look like he had an accomplice, so we'll go from there," Gray said.

"Good news, Officer, the best I've had in a long time. Does that mean you'll remove my bodyguards?" Rosie mustered a laugh. "I kind of like knowing they're here."

"No, not remove them. We're going to maintain

your protection for now in the event the perp didn't act alone. But it's not likely anyone else is involved."

"Okay and thank you for the information. I'll call my office manager and bring her up to date," Rosie said. "I don't think she's aware of the stalking or the shooting yet since we haven't spoken this evening. But if she sees your men in a vehicle tomorrow morning, she'll be concerned."

"Sounds like a good idea, Dr. Klein. I'll keep you posted. Rest assured, we'll get to the bottom of this, and the assailant or assailants will be prosecuted to the fullest. Have a good rest of your evening."

Rosie dialed Ruth's number and was relieved when she answered on the second ring. "Ruth, you won't believe what's been happening."

"What is it, boss? You sound rattled," Ruth said. Rosie spent the next fifteen minutes telling Ruth about all details of Dr. Seifer's shooting and the intimidation.

"Oh, my gosh. Why in the world would anyone want to hurt you guys?" Ruth asked.

"It could be linked to the Scott Larson case. Someone is intentionally attempting to intimidate me and, Ruth, I've just learned some important information that maybe somebody thinks I've shared with Dr. Seifer. He also works at the same hospital as Scott Larson and his wife, Olivia. Since he has access to patients' records, they might think he knows more than he really does. Other than that, I'm not sure *why* he was a target, but *somebody* does."

"Thank goodness, you're okay, Rosie. Is there

anything you want me to do?"

"No, Ruth. But there will be plainclothes men near the office tomorrow. I wanted you to know in case you noticed them and wondered what was going on," Rosie explained.

"Well, let me know if I can help in any way. Are you coming in tomorrow?"

"Of course. See you bright and early. Don't pick up donuts. My waistline doesn't need any more expansion."

"Coffee will be hot and fresh, boss. See you tomorrow."

After hanging up, Rosie looked at Bucky. "Now, that's what I call one full day," she said, wondering how so much could happen so quickly. "Not sure we can ever top this one."

46

A Suspect Squeals

O fficer Mel Gray led two detectives down the hall to the interrogation room. A shooting suspect had just been picked up for the attempted murder of Dr. Seifer in the Scott Larson case. Detective Cot McGuire, and his partner, Detective Beth Spicer, were coming in to see what he knew. Gray respected McGuire from previous cases and liked the way he worked. Now, he would observe McGuire and Spicer through a one-way window as they talked to the man.

"I don't think Joe Bench has any prior charges," Gray said as they walked. "It's a bit of a mystery why he'd resort to shooting a prominent psychiatrist like Dr. Seifer." Gray scratched the back of his head as he turned and looked at them intently.

"The theory you mentioned on the phone about being put up to it by Larson may hold true. The question becomes: Why would he agree to do something as serious as that if he has no prior offenses?" McGuire answered.

"There's obviously a strong connection between the two men. It'll come out along with motives, I'm sure," Spicer said as she glanced through the window at the defendant.

"He looks nervous; look how he's cracking his knuckles and looking up at the ceiling," Gray said.

"Maybe he's praying or thinking how to manufacture a story to lessen his responsibility for shooting Doc Seifer without incriminating Larson," Spicer said.

"You two may be in for a long night. I'll make a fresh pot of coffee," Gray said as he retreated down the hall.

"So, who's gonna be the good guy? You or me?" McGuire asked.

"You must be kidding, partner," Spicer laughed. "Your scruffy, unshaven face doesn't compare to my smile and sparkling eyes." She batted her lashes once at him. He grunted. They entered the musty-smelling room and sat across from Joe Bench who stared at them with glassy eyes.

McGuire introduced himself, opened his legal pad, and took out a pen. "Do you understand that you don't have to talk to us and if you did, nothing will be held as confidential?"

"I know that Miranda stuff," Bench said. "And I *will* talk without a lawyer, but I guess one will be assigned to me anyway, right? I just want to tell the truth and hope the doc survived. I'm really . . . sorry."

"Really," Spicer said, not sure she believed him.

Still, it was an odd thing to say right off the bat. She introduced herself and asked if he needed water or a cup of coffee. He looked back at her.

"Coffee . . . thanks. I don't know what time it is, but it feels late. I work from six a.m. to two p.m. at the Greyhound Bus Depot," Bench offered. He looked nervous and began biting his dirty nails. "My wife works from two to ten there. We take turns watching the kids,"

"Doesn't look like you'll be returning to the bus station very soon, does it?" McGuire said.

"I can't believe this is happening. It's like a nightmare. How could I have gotten myself into such a mess? I ain't never hurt nobody in my life. I was the one who was teased and bullied as a kid," Bench's voice wavered.

"Where did you grow up?"

"Can't rightly say, we moved around a lot. My dad left us when I was four. I had two little sisters and my mom worked as a waitress at a diner downtown. Not downtown Toledo . . . downtown Sylvania. People think Sylvania is just for rich folks, but we lived in a trailer behind a used car lot. Before my dad left, he worked there cleaning cars up before they was sold. He stashed liquor in the glove compartments of cars he knew would be there at least a week. Called them his 'cupboards.'"

"How long did you live there?" Just then, Spicer walked into the room balancing three cups of coffee. She placed one in front of Bench.

343

"Thanks," he said.

"We were just talking about Joe's childhood. Go on, tell me how long you lived in Sylvania with your mother and little sisters."

"When I was six, we moved behind a church in East Toledo. My mom got room and board and a little pay for doing janitorial and yard work. I got to go to the Catholic school. The kids didn't bully me there. We wore uniforms so I didn't look poor. But she got caught stealing money from the offering plate. Instead of her being arrested, we left in the middle of the night."

"Did you graduate from high school?" Spicer asked.

"No. We moved so much that my records never caught up with me. I gave up after repeating the eighth grade at Lincoln School in Monroe, Michigan. I did get a GED though after I met my wife. She said it would help me get a better paying job."

"Your current address is 648 Scottwood Avenue. Is that correct? Spicer asked.

"Yeah. We live in a second-floor, two-bedroom apartment. Been there four years. Had a lot of medical bills that kept us from buyin' a place," Bench said. "This is gonna just kill my wife. She's what the doctors sometimes call, 'in remission' for breast cancer. She don't deserve this. If I go up, she'll be in the same spot my mom was, but worse, with serious health issues. We have two small kids. My God, what have I done?"

"Tell us why you did it, Bench. Why *did* you follow Sharon Leonard and shoot Doc Seifer," McGuire asked.

"Maybe, if you confess, your sentence won't be so long." *Could be nobody needs to play bad cop, after all,* he thought. *So far, Bench seems cooperative. But will he tell the truth?*

Bench took a deep breath, a swallow of coffee, cracked his knuckles, and began: "I owed Scott Larson a favor. He saved my wife, Lilly, in the ER about two years ago. Her heart stopped while she was waiting to be seen for a terrible cough and fever. He didn't ask me to kill anybody. But he said I owed it to him just to scare Dr. Klein and Doc. Seifer . . . he even offered me two thousand for it. I think he just wanted to keep them from talking against him in court. I heard on the news that he shot his wife. But I can't imagine a fine nurse who saves lives doing that. Can you?"

"Go on, Joe. What exactly did he ask you to do?" said Spicer in a soft, caring voice.

"He told me to wait until Seifer came into the hall from his office, then shoot *toward* him, but not hit him. He said when the doc jumped back into his office I should run down the stairs at the end of the hall. He said when I got down three floors to take the elevator to the parking garage. My car was on the street near the exit."

Bench teared up and nervously wiped his eyes with the back of his hands. To Spicer, he didn't resemble any killer she and McGuire had ever interviewed. She looked at McGuire and could tell he didn't think Bench was an ugly, determined assailant either.

"So, why did you shoot him, if you were instructed

PHYLLIS K. WALTERS

to simply scare him?" McGuire asked.

"It was an accident. I got jumpy. The gun belongs to Lilly for her protection coming home at night. Scottwood is safe until the sun goes down. I thought I was pointing it at the wall above the drinking fountain outside his door, then suddenly, it goes off about three times. He fell to the floor gripping his arm, and I ran like hell, just like Larson told me to."

"What happened next, Joe?" McGuire asked.

"I was shakin', but drove to Summerhill real careful. Didn't want to get pulled over for runnin' a light or speeding. I sat across the street from Klein's office. There was a blacktop parking lot that belongs to a meat market. I waited for somebody to come out. When they did, I could see from the light in front of the door that the last two ladies weren't dressed alike. One had a pantsuit on and the other, a taller one, was wearing jeans. I figured the one in the pantsuit was the doctor. So, I followed her, but not too close. Scott told me it's not against the law to follow somebody, if you don't tailgate 'em or act aggressive. She pulled into a fire station. I drove away, but maybe somebody could of seen my license plate." Bench looked like he was thinking about something.

"Oh, and Scott said I could use his wife's car because she didn't need it anymore. I went to his house before work when it was still dark and got the car from out front. If anybody ran the plate and saw it was hers, they wouldn't blame Scott because he couldn't have been driving the car because he's in jail. They would

346

think it was stolen."

"Your lawyer will get any charges related to that incident thrown out and focus on the attempted murder charges," Spicer said. "And if you're willing to testify at Scott Larson's trial, your charges will likely be greatly reduced. We're not lawyers. Only your lawyer and the prosecutor can come to a plea deal. You understand, right? We aren't making promises, Joe."

"I know. But will you believe me over Scott Larson? He's smart and will try to make it out like he doesn't know anything about the scheme . . . that I made all this up to save myself," Bench said. "But I didn't. Do you believe me?"

McGuire and Spicer assured him they believe his version of the events to be true and accurate.

"Oh. Guess what? I accepted a collect call from him. I can prove he contacted me yesterday. He said the money would be in an unlocked shed behind his house," Bench said as his demeanor perked up a bit.

"You never retrieved it, right?" Spicer asked.

"No. I was supposed to climb through a side window and the money would be in a brown backpack beneath a desk."

"Okay, we'll send someone over to retrieve it, Joe. Does your wife know you have been arrested?" Spicer asked.

"Officer Gray said he would personally go over and tell her. He should have been there by now. The guards will let me make my one phone call when you leave. I've gotta call her, but I dread it."

The detectives walked out of the interview room and acknowledged the two correction officers, waiting to allow Bench to make his call before taking him back to his holding cell. In the morning after his public defender's visit, he would be taken to his cell until arraignment.

"Okay partner," McGuire said. "Now to interview the tough, smart guy, Larson. He'll be surprised to see us at this time of night."

"Yeah, well, I won't be offering him any coffee," Spicer said as she dumped their used cups in the trash.

47

The Aftermath

Two days later, Rosie and Bucky were just finishing dinner when the phone rang. The caller ID showed it was from the Toledo Blade. She declined to answer. Bucky handed her a glass of wine and she took a sip. The phone rang again. This time it was Jake Morgan.

"Hi, Rosie. It's Jake. I'm calling to give you some breaking news.

"Okay, I'm ready, Jake."

"Well, while representing himself today, Larson confessed to the aggravated murder of his wife. He didn't want to be charged with knowingly killing his unborn son, and when he heard that the guy he hired to intimidate you, spilled the beans, he rolled over to avoid further charges. Since he wasn't calling any witnesses, now he'll be sentenced without a hearing."

"That's great news!" Rosie said. "What happens next?"

"The hired guy, Bench, will be charged with attempted murder of Dr. Seifer and is expected to incriminate Larson in order to get a reduced sentence himself. His intimidation of your client will be dropped, in exchange for his willingness to testify against Larson, if needed. Obviously, that won't be necessary."

"Why do you think Larson is giving up this easily?" Rosie asked.

"He's conniving, I'm sure of that. He'll be looking ahead to a strategy for an appeal. Either he'll say Dr. Pendleton misdiagnosed him and will contend that his PTSD rendered him Not-Guilty-by-Reason-of-Insanity. Or he'll say he was inadequately represented by me and, without legal counsel, was coerced into making a false confession. He'll contend he was not competent to render a confession at all. But don't worry; none of it will succeed."

"That's even better news, Jake. I can't thank you enough for calling."

"You're welcome, Rosie. Now, you can relax. I hope Dr. Seifer will heal one hundred percent," Jake said.

Rosie hung up and smiled at Bucky sitting beside her.

"What if we take Jocko out for a walk in the moonlight? Are you up for that?" Bucky asked as he stroked her cheek.

"That's a magnificent idea. How did I ever marry such a brilliant man?"

One month later . . .

"Who could have predicted back when we were freshmen in college, that we'd be sitting here on this beautiful beach with great husbands, sipping piña coladas, and watching dolphins play in the surf?" Rosie asked, looking over at her friend, Stella.

"Not me," Stella said. "I put it squarely on God's plan."

"How nice of Roger and Grace to rent us their Hilton Head house now that they're living in Ohio and caring for Roger's nephews."

"I feel the same. Did you tell me they might buy a little breakfast restaurant?"

"That's what his grandma Noni told me when I picked up the keys to the house," Rosie said.

"I'm glad they didn't have to abandon their dream of owning a restaurant. Do you think they'll be disappointed that it won't be in a tourist site?" Stella asked.

"Not really. They value family and want to be sure little Todd and Eric have love and stability. Besides, they'll be close to Noni and his sister, Susie. Noni, being a widow and living alone, can use their support as much as Susie will. She's trying to find her own path in life with no direction from her mother," Rosie explained.

Stella saw her husband and Bucky coming up the beach. "Here come our guys. I think their two-mile walk ended prematurely. I didn't expect them back this soon, did you, Rosie?"

"No. I'd say they were both a bit ambitious thinking they could manage two miles without building up to it." The girlfriends laughed. Travis and Bucky plunked down on two low beach chairs.

"Hey, girls, what's happening?" Travis asked.

"Just counting our blessings and glad to be here," Stella said. "Now, if we can get Devon and Brenda's twins born, we can get back to feeding and diapering babies. Won't that be fun," Stella said, anticipating her new role as grandmother.

"Let's hope it doesn't happen for a week or so. This lifestyle has captured my heart," Travis said.

"When is she due?" Rosie asked.

"Soon," Travis said. "The last we heard, the babies are 'breach,' so if they don't turn, they'll need to be born by cesarean section."

"Well, let's pray for healthy babies. You said they're girls, right?" Bucky asked.

"Yes," Stella said. "They've picked names that rhyme, instead of beginning with the same letter. I think they're thinking of Kay and May."

Rosie looked at her two friends and a husband she loved. Feeling the warm sun and looking out over the calm water lapping at the shore, she felt grateful for this moment of solitude. *There will be more challenges ahead,* she thought, *there always are. But for this moment in time, I am grateful.*

Silently, she prayed: *Thank you, Lord, for your protection, mercy, and grace. Without your guidance and love, I would be lost. I am grateful you have placed me here, for such a time as this. Please help me finish the race on the path you have set forth for me. Amen.*

DISCUSSION QUESTIONS

1. If Rosie had stayed connected with Randy Evans, or visited, while he was in juvenile detention, do you think his abuse would have been disclosed?

2. Could the death of Randy's father have been avoided? If so, who should have recognized the abuse of his mother, Jackie Evans, as well as his brother and himself? What could have resulted from that knowledge?

3. Who is the person with whom Randy is the angriest? His father? His abusers in juvenile detention? His mother? Himself? What coping skills does he possess?

4. How could the death of Joanie Evans have been prevented? Explain, please.

5. Do you think Olivia Larson became pregnant deliberately? Was she afraid to tell Scott?

6. What is your opinion of Scott Larson's first wife, Dr. Alexis Jackson?

7. Have you experienced being used by someone for their own personal gain? How did it make you feel once you recognized it? What did you do?

8. What is your opinion of Rosie and Bucky's relationship? Does it add to the reader's enjoyment or detract from the storyline?

Phyllis Kuehnl-Walters Ph. D.

Dr. Phyllis K. Walters has retired from a forty-year career as a psychologist in private practice and an adjunct professor at The University of Dayton. She specialized in forensic psychology and was appointed by nine surrounding court jurisdictions to determine the mindset of defendants charged with heinous crimes. She is "re-fired" as an author of three novels, inspired by these cases and by the innocence of some of the men and women she has evaluated.

More Books by Phyllis K. Walters

THE CHRISTMAS SLAYINGS

One Week .Six Murders. Based on a True Story. On her 21st birthday, Angel Morgan steps out of Juvenile Detention after serving five years for grand theft auto. The next 12 hours will change the course of her life forever. About to purchase a bus ticket to live on the beaches of Florida, she meets Sam and April. Never having any real friends before, these two offer Angel comfort such as she's never known. Little does she suspect their dark path will turn her world upside down. Soon, Angel is sitting in prison awaiting sentencing for six murders committed by her new "friends" in the week before Christmas.

Then, Dr. Rosie Klein, enters Angel's life. A court-appointed forensic psychologist, Dr. Klein looks at all the mitigating factors of Angel's childhood that could influence the Judge in sentencing this young woman, including abuse suffered at the hands of her mother and the men who used her. Angel takes Dr. Klein on a journey depicting the slayings of six innocent people the week before Christmas and to which Angel becomes guilty by association.

In her 35-year career as a forensic psychologist, Dr. Phyllis Kuehnl-Walters has written this book inspired by this one case she will never forget.

The Christmas Slayings

Available now on amazon.com and

www.thewritersmall.com

More Books by Phyllis K. Walters

WIVES WHO KILL

Sophie and Hannah: Two women with different backgrounds, different circumstances, and different mindsets. Yet, both are wanted for murder.

What made them do it?

Court-appointed forensic psychologist, Dr, Rosie Klein untangles the web of circumstances surrounding each act of violence, and so much more. At the recommendation of judges and attorneys who appoint her to the cases, Dr. Klein first evaluates Sophie's case, then Hannah's state of mind at the time the women committed their separate crimes. Her search for mitigating factors and her recommendations will assist the Court during the sentencing phase of each woman's trial. Or should their charges be commuted .. . based on what Dr. Rosie Klein finds?

You be the judge . . . after you read the reasons why they committed murder in ***Wives Who Kill***.

Wives Who Kill

Available now on amazon.com and

www.thewritersmall.com

More Books by Phyllis K. Walters

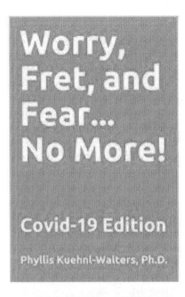

Worry, Fret, and Fear... No More!
Covid-19 Edition

This is a six-week challenge for you to stop worrying and build faith and confidence.

learn to face your fears while moving forward toward a life filled with hope and a sense of purpose. Read, write, pray, and plan your next six weeks to be followed by the rest of your life!

Completing this challenge will put your concerns in perspective. It will foster confidence as you will remember who you are; a child of a merciful, loving God. Know that He loves you and that with the direction of the Holy Spirit all things will work out for your own good.

ALSO AVAILABLE!

A companion workbook to Worry, Fret, and Fear... No More!

This workbook helps you write out your thoughts and feelings as you go through your six-week challenge as suggested in the primary book.

AVAILABLE ON AMAZON.COM AND THROUGH
HTTPS://WWW.THEWRITERSMALL.COM

Become a Beacon of Light

Develop the Fruit of the Spirit
and Reflect God's Love

Phyllis Kuehnl-Walters, Ph.D.

Creating Balance & Purpose in Life

Finding Meaning in All Seasons &
Stages of Life

Phyllis Kuehnl-Walters, Ph.D.

Become a Beacon of Light:
Develop the Fruit of the Spirit and Reflect God's Love

Dr. Phyllis Kuehnl-Walters guides the reader in becoming more like Jesus by developing the gifts of the Fruit of the Spirit. Her personal story, scripture and other supportive information provides a sound, enlightening and thought provoking read. Action plans and Group Discussion Questions promote personal growth and/or group study.

Creating Balance & Purpose in Life

In Creating Balance & Purpose in Life, the reader will be led to create balance in this season of life: physical, mental, emotional, social, and spiritual. The emphasis will be on learning to deal effectively with life transitions and unforeseen challenges. The reader will develop strategies for planning and implementing purposeful goals to experience joy, peace, dignity.

Available on Amazon.com and at

www.TheWritersMall.com

Made in the USA
Columbia, SC
23 December 2022

73973941R00200